James Newton Howard's *Signs*

Film Score Guides
Series Editor: Kate Daubney

James Newton Howard's
Signs

A Film Score Guide

Erik Heine

ROWMAN & LITTLEFIELD
Lanham • Boulder • New York • London

Published by Rowman & Littlefield
A wholly owned subsidary of The Rowman & Littlefield Publishing Group,
Inc.
4501 Forbes Boulevard, Suite 200, Lanham, Maryland 20706
www.rowman.com

Unit A, Whitacre Mews, 26-34 Stannary Street, London SE11 4AB

British Library Cataloguing in Publication Information Available

Library of Congress Cataloging-in-Publication Data

Names: Heine, Erik, 1976-
Title: James Newton Howard's Signs : a film score guide / Erik Heine.
Description: Lanham, Maryland : Rowman & Littlefield, [2016] | Series: Film
    score guides ; 17 | Includes bibliographical references and index.
Identifiers: LCCN 2015040273| ISBN 9781442256033 (pbk. : alk. paper) |
ISBN
    9781442256040 (ebook)
Subjects: LCSH: Howard, James Newton. Signs.
Classification: LCC ML410.N57144 H45 2016 | DDC 781.5/42--dc23 LC
record available at http://lccn.loc.gov/2015040273

Contents

Examples

All examples come from *Signs* unless otherwise indicated

Tables

Editor's Foreword

In an era of the cult of personality and ever-increasing emphasis on celebrity, James Newton Howard exemplifies the prioritization of the art form over the artist. Despite his prolific authorship, the stylistic breadth of his work over such a wide range of film genres, and the diversity and sheer number of his director collaborations, the service of the score to the film is still his main priority. That said, his collaboration with M. Night Shyamalan presents an opportunity to examine a very particular kind of service of score to film, in the context of Shyamalan's own striking and original authorial voice.

Howard's approach to scoring science fiction is also fascinating, for it challenges some of the standard approaches to embodying the genre musically, from the massive orchestral timbres of some of the blockbuster sci-fi movies of recent years to the unsettling qualities of some of the more innovative electronic scoring to feature in the genre. Indeed with respect to the latter, Erik Heine will demonstrate that Howard understands how to use the way music makes us feel to pinpoint the questions that Shyamalan is asking us to consider when we watch his films.

As a Steiner scholar, I am particularly struck by a sense of circularity in film music composition demonstrated by this score. For while Dr. Heine will make a compelling case for the influence of one of the most significant pieces of twentieth-century concert hall music over this score, Howard's music can also–it seems to me–be seen through the lens of the history of Hollywood film scoring. Howard's claustrophobic use of the three-note motive echoes very directly the motivic manipulation that Max Steiner used in many of his scores over seventy years ago, not least in the way he structures Charlotte Vale's emotional insecurity throughout the score for *Now, Voyager*. While the two composers have absorbed quite different points of reference in executing essentially the same approach, what Howard's score shows is the far greater capacity in contemporary scoring for music to deliver complexity. Perhaps audiences have higher expectations, but composers certainly do, bringing to fruition the sort of compositional precision that once separated concert hall music from that of the cinema.

The Series of Film Score Guides was established to promote score-focused scholarship, but that simple aim has long since been out-stripped by the achievements of the Series' authors in divulging great variety in what the analysis and scrutiny of content and production of film music reveals. Dr. Heine's use of some quite complex analytical tools to create a very readable interpretation of Howard's score continues that tradition. The Series has given us revisions of our understanding of some of the figureheads of film score composition and revelations of the logistics of their compositional practice. Some canonic score sounds that have permanently permeated the public consciousness have been deconstructed, and bewitching and byzantine aural textures have been explored in critical and theoretical ways that push the boundaries of music out into the wider soundscape of film. Certainly, Shyamalan's films are meant to be experienced in the fullest sense, and Howard's scores are critical in that respect. Indeed, what binds this latest volume together with all its predecessors is an essential engagement in our experience of music in film, and a fascination for the means by which we are drawn in. That original principle behind the establishment of the Series has remained largely unchanged, even if the disciplinary environment in which the work is undertaken has evolved as a consequence of the work itself.

Dr. Kate Daubney
Series Editor

Acknowledgments

Excerpts from *Signs*
By James Newton Howard
© 2002 Touchstone Pictures Music & Songs
This arrangement © 2015 Touchstone Pictures Music & Songs
All Rights Reserved Used by Permission
Reprinted by Permission of Hal Leonard Corporation

Excerpts from *The Sixth Sense*
By James Newton Howard
Copyright © 1999 TRD Music Publishing LLC
This arrangement Copyright © 2015 TRD Music Publishing LLC
All Rights Administered by Sony/ATV Music Publishing LLC,
    424 Church Street, Suite 1200, Nashville, TN 37219
All Rights Reserved Used by Permission
Reprinted by Permission of Hal Leonard Corporation

Excerpts from *Unbreakable*
Music by James Newton Howard
© 2000 Walt Disney Music Company
This arrangement © 2015 Walt Disney Music Company
All Rights Reserved Used by Permission
Reprinted by Permission of Hal Leonard Corporation

In creating a film score, a large number of people contribute throughout the process, but the name of the composer is the most prominent one that appears on the final product. The same concept applies to this book. Although my name is the one on the cover, a large number of people helped and contributed to the creative process. I need to first thank my colleagues, students, former students, and administrators at Oklahoma City University. I was awarded a one-semester sabbatical in Fall 2014. Without this time away from the classroom, I would not have been able to complete this project. My colleagues, both at OCU and around the world, and former students, specifically Michael Baker, Karen Bottge, Marc DiPaolo, Dave Easley, Beth Fleming, Kevin Holm-Hudson, Kayla Masnek, Ian Sapiro, and Sarah Sarver, provided assistance and valuable feedback. Many friends provided encouragement and thoughtful words during the research and writing process.

Eric Swanson at JoAnn Kane Music was able to provide orchestral breakdown and cue information for the Shyamalan films. John Brockman and Dace Taube at the USC Special Collections Library were extremely helpful in allowing access to Howard's MIDI sketches and the full score for *Signs*, through the James Newton Howard Collection. Without their thoughtfulness and guidance, I would not have been able to study the score in much detail. Pete Anthony, Howard's lead orchestrator and conductor, was exceedingly generous with his time and thoughts, and explained specific composition and orchestration choices.

My in-laws, John and Janet Schmitz, read through chapters multiple times, helping me focus my attention and detail on what needed to be said. As nonmusicians, but lovers of music, they served as an excellent focus group, making sure that the analytical content never became too heady and still conveyed my points.

Kate Daubney, the series editor, was a constant source of support and encouragement. Her comments were never negative, even when they could have been. It was an absolute pleasure to work with someone who was so positive and helpful, an ideal model for how all commenters and reviewers should be. Stephen Ryan and Megan Delancey at Scarecrow Press also provided great guidance and aid.

My final acknowledgments are to my wife and my son, Patty and Stephen. This project has taken a bit of time away from them, but they have been unwavering in allowing me to finish the book. I could not have completed it without knowing that they wanted me to do so. Patty watched most of the films discussed in this book with me, never once complaining. For that, I am truly grateful.

Introduction

> When I finished composing *The Rite of Spring*, I played it for Diaghi-
> lev. And I started to play him this chord, fifty-nine times this same
> chord. Diaghilev was a little bit surprised. He didn't want to offend
> me. He asked me only one thing, which was very offending. He
> asked me, "Will it last a very long time, this way?" And I said, "Till
> the end, my dear." And he was silent, because he understood that the
> answer was serious.[1]

Director M. Night Shymalan's *Signs* was his third film on which he
collaborated with composer James Newton Howard. Their first film,
The Sixth Sense, was a surprise blockbuster. Their next film, *Unbreakable*, was not nearly as critically or commercially successful. *Signs*
regained the magic of *The Sixth Sense*, and was more overtly based in
the science fiction genre than either of their first two films. The film
depicts a global alien invasion, and the reason for their presence is initially unclear. Rather than showing how the invasion affected multiple
people, Shyamalan's film focuses solely on one family, their farmhouse, far away from others, and the sort of claustrophobia that was so
effective in films such as *The Birds* and *Night of the Living Dead*. In
Signs, Howard's music is derived from a single three-note gesture that
is rhythmically consistent throughout the film. Like the family, who
ultimately become trapped in their house, the audience is trapped, seeing no way out, and the music is trapped within the three-note gesture,
rarely able to break out of the repeating rhythm.

This volume of Scarecrow's Film Score Guide Series looks at
James Newton Howard's score for M. Night Shyamalan's 2002 film
Signs. Over the course of the book, various issues, such as use of Leitmotiv, collaborations with directors and with a small group of orchestrators and conductors, and Howard's compositional style and
technique will be examined. He may currently be best known for col-
laborating with Hans Zimmer on the scores for the first two of Christopher Nolan's "Batman Trilogy" films, *Batman Begins* and *The Dark
Knight*, as well as his work on Peter Jackson's *King Kong*, but Howard
was well respected and highly successful long before he became involved with Batman.

The opening two chapters present Howard's music background, describe his musical style and influences, and present a detailed summary of his film music leading up to the composition of the music for *Signs*. These chapters show a trajectory of Howard's rise from session keyboard player to arranger to film composer to a highly regarded film composer. The chapters also present significant musical details about some of his most important films of the 1990s, including his repeated work with the same director, in order to better understand his more mature music and style. Chapters 3 and 4 present a history of alien invasion films, a subgenre of science fiction, and how music in those films both operates and sounds, in order to situate *Signs* within that canon. Chapter 3 presents a great deal of critical analysis of the film, and shows how the film is viewed both by film critics and religious scholars. In addition to describing the sound world of alien invasion films, Chapter 4 situates the *Signs* soundtrack as a stand-alone entity. The final two chapters deal with the notes: the sketches that Howard made and the final orchestral cues that were used in the film. In some cases, multiple versions of sketches and cues were available, which provides even greater insight into how the music evolved, and which ideas were kept and which were discarded.

James Newton Howard's music for *Signs*, like many of his scores, takes a new approach for a film. The idea of basing the music on a single gesture is an approach similar to that of the early twentieth-century composer Arnold Schoenberg, but the largest influence on the score comes from Igor Stravinsky, specifically his music for the 1913 ballet *The Rite of Spring*. This addition to the Film Score Guide Series demonstrates Howard's approach to this film, an outlier when compared with the rest of his career. In doing so, his music for *Signs* will be recognized, not only within his work with Shyamalan, but as one of his most significant and best film scores.

1

Howard's Musical Background

James Newton Howard (b. 1951) has been scoring Hollywood films since the mid-1980s, and rose to prominence in the early 1990s, scoring films such as *Pretty Woman*, *The Prince of Tides*, and *The Fugitive*. He has received six Academy Award nominations for Best Original Score and two Academy Award nominations for Best Original Song. Howard has written some of the most memorable film music of the past twenty years, and his consistent quality has made him one of the most in-demand composers in Hollywood, as well as one of the most respected.

While Howard began studying piano at an early age, and did have advanced training in music, he dropped out of college after just six weeks, preferring to work professionally as a studio musician, and then as a touring performer and arranger in Los Angeles in the 1970s and into the 1980s. Despite his professional rock background, he was familiar with the typical giants of Western classical music, which allowed him to begin to merge his rock performing with his string arranging on rock albums.

Howard's deep understanding of both popular and classical music makes him a highly effective composer, particularly because of the variety of genres in which Howard has scored films. Howard spent nearly fifteen years working in popular music as a performer, songwriter, and arranger. His performance chops led to gigs as a studio musician, a touring musician, and eventually a film session musician. Howard worked with several popular musicians in the 1970s and 1980s, and often received new jobs through word-of-mouth recommendations. He was well known in the industry as a synthesizer performer, and had an endorsement from Yamaha. As an arranger, Howard began to work with other musicians' material, helping them have their respective musical ideas fulfilled. This process was similar to what he would do for film directors.

When Howard started scoring films, many of his early scores were composed and performed largely on the synthesizer. As he grew into his new role as composer, he was the one to realize the musical ideas of the director, and because of his previous experience in that role as arranger, his ego did not interfere with the process.

Howard's early orchestrations largely involved strings, piano, and melodic woodwinds. These orchestrations came from his arranging days with Elton John's band, as Howard was orchestrating what he knew. But, when given a chance to musically experiment, he began to incorporate brass and percussion, as well as choir, to have a full orchestra at his disposal. In the film world, Howard once again earned new jobs through word-of-mouth recommendations, and moved freely through genres, a task that few composers can do well. A number of directors prefer to work nearly exclusively with Howard, such as Lawrence Kasdan, and M. Night Shyamalan. Regardless of a film's themes, genre, or director, James Newton Howard is able to take the musical ideas of the director and realize them to help elevate a film and give it musical substance.

Early Years and Education

James Newton Howard was always around music. He started playing piano at the age of four on a piano owned by his grandmother, who played violin with the Pittsburgh Symphony in the 1930s and 1940s during the Fritz Reiner era.[1] Because his grandmother was a professional violinist, the dominant style of music as he was growing up was classical. Howard recalls,

> I think without question the private study that I did with the piano, from the time I was four until I went to college when I was eighteen, was the most influential musical period of my life. Because it wasn't just that I studied piano and was exposed to a good deal of the piano repertoire, I was also going to a lot of symphony concerts and listening to a lot of classical music. So I had the benefit of fourteen years of constant exposure to classical music, so I think that is responsible certainly for my composition influence and probably more for my composition development.[2]

Naturally, Howard gravitated toward some composers more than others. When asked about his favorite classical musician, like so many other people, he said, "Probably my single most favorite composer is Beethoven. For me there is a nobility and at the same time this incredible yearning and tenderness and a strength in the music that I found absolutely irresistible as a child."[3] Howard also cites composers such as Tchaikovsky for being a strong melodic influence, and that he takes his orchestration cues from French composers Debussy and Ravel.[4]

At the age of eighteen, he was accepted to the Music Academy of the West in Santa Barbara, California, where he continued his piano studies with renowned artist-teachers Leon Fleischer and Reginald Stewart. Fleischer's principal teacher was Artur Schnabel, whose teaching lineage could be directly traced back to Beethoven. Following his studies at MAW, Howard enrolled at the University of Southern California, in the studio of Joanna Growden. However, Howard left USC after just six weeks, "because, he recalls, 'I'd been doing it for about 14 years at that point, and I was kind of tired of practicing other people's music. I just knew it wasn't in me to keep doing that for the rest of my life.'"[5]

Popular Music and Performance

Throughout his childhood and teenage years, Howard grew more interested in popular music and less interested in classical music. Howard has stated that his interest in popular music stems from hearing The Beatles. He said,

> Without question the biggest influence for me were The Beatles. I heard the Beatles in the mid-Sixties, I just thought that they were absolutely extraordinary. I really fell in love with the music and, you know, they really described where I was at as an adolescent . . . but it also really intrigued me musically and I found the melodies absolutely irresistible and the songwriting superb. Not that I was really thinking about it in those terms, but the Beatles were a very big influence on me, they really – sort of – gave a real legitimacy to popular music for me. From then on I went on and listened to Jimi Hendrix, The Doors, Led Zeppelin and lots of people. But the Beatles were really the first big one for me.[6]

The one song that piqued his interest in rock music was The Doors' "Light My Fire," due to its elaborate keyboard part.[7] It wasn't just the idea of rock music that interested him, it was the inclusion of the keyboard in rock music, something that was still relatively novel in the mid- to late-1960s, and something to which Howard could relate.

After Howard left USC, he looked for work as a keyboard player, and joined Mama Lion, a rock band in Los Angeles. Howard played keyboard on two of Mama Lion's albums in 1972–73, and while the band did not receive a large level of recognition, it afforded him the access to various keyboards, which enabled him to record an album of his own music. In 1974, he released a self-titled album of keyboard solos. Howard recalls: "I had to do an incredible amount of overdubs. I'd lay down the bass with just the piano, then go out and pile everything else on. I did it all in two weeks. I was young, the record was experimental, and the whole thing was fun."[8]

Because of the scarcity of the record, a brief summary of the album is necessary. The album consists of five songs, with three on Side A and two on Side B. One tune, "Bovere," uses meter changes in a two-measure pattern, alternating measures of $\frac{6}{8}$ and $\frac{4}{4}$, before returning to the more standard $\frac{4}{4}$. The use of asymmetrical meter is a technique that Howard uses in his film scores, particularly in the 1990s in films such as *Wyatt Earp* and *Outbreak*. Side A's last work, "Newton's Ego," is over eight minutes long, and contains three distinct sections, two of which contain ostinatos, another technique used by Howard in his film scores. The final work on the album, "Ducks," is based on a standard rock groove, but modulates up a third in the first "verse," a technique common to the piano music of Romantic composers Chopin and Schumann. Despite the affinity for nineteenth-century harmonic gestures, the piece contains a great deal of rock syncopation; syncopation would become one of Howard's compositional hallmarks in his film music. Howard referred to the album as "experimental," but the styles are familiar. The forms of the pieces do not exactly correspond to classical or popular music, but bear early style features of Howard's music. The experimentation came from the various uses of synthesizers, in an attempt to find out what sounds could be produced.

Once Howard's name and abilities were a known commodity, he became a session musician in Los Angeles, playing keyboards on albums for performers such as Ringo Starr, Carly Simon, and The Pointer Sisters, among others. He did additional work as an orchestrator and arranger, particularly of string accompaniments, for singers such as Olivia Newton-John and Barbara Streisand. Then, in 1975, Howard was contacted by Elton John for a gig. Howard recalls, "I didn't play a note for Elton. I just went up to his house, and we sat on the couch together. We couldn't talk—we were both very nervous—so instead he played me *Captain Fantastic*, and after it was over he just said I had the gig if I wanted it. He just went on his gut feelings."[9] On the basis of the "meeting," Howard got the job, performing with John from the mid-1970s through the early 1980s. Howard was the touring keyboard player, and wrote string arrangements for various songs, such as "Sorry Seems to Be the Hardest Word" and "Don't Go Breaking My Heart." Howard speaks fondly of his early days of arranging for Elton John, recalling, "I was really interested in doing that [arranging strings on rock songs], so when I joined Elton's band he gave me the chance to do it and I did a whole lot whenever I could."[10] He also played on John's albums during this time period: *Rock of the Westies*, *Blue Moves*, *21 at 33*, and *The Fox*, earning co-writing credits for songs on *Blue Moves* and *The Fox*. The song "Don't Go Breaking My Heart," the Number One song on Billboard's pop charts for six weeks in 1976, featured a string arrangement from Howard. He said,

> I didn't study orchestration in school, I kind of just learned by myself. I was a classical piano student, so I knew how to read and write music. And I just sort of knew that I would be able to arrange for strings. That song was one of the first things I'd ever done. It definitely had a lot to do with the tradition of Motown strings and things like "My Girl." The one thing I remember Elton saying is, "You should do a string solo." The solo in the middle is full orchestra. So that was kind of fun.[11]

In addition to performing, arranging, and touring with Elton John, Howard was also an in-demand session player, performing on numerous albums throughout the late 1970s and early 1980s. During that time he also began writing songs. Howard formed a band in the late 1970s called China, which only released one album, but Howard was listed as the co-writer of every song on that album.

Even in the early 1980s, Howard had his eye on other things than just performing rock music. In a biographical piece for *Contemporary Keyboard* in 1981, Bob Doerschuk wrote "James' plans for the future include studies in orchestration with David [Paich of Toto]'s father, the well-known Hollywood arranger Marty Paich."[12] By studying and beginning to master orchestration, Howard could compose at the piano, and then begin to orchestrate for an ensemble larger than just strings. Through his relationship with the Paiches, Howard conducted and wrote orchestral arrangements for Toto on their most successful album, *Toto IV* (1982), which featured the songs "Rosanna" and "Africa," and earned six Grammy Awards, including Album of the Year, in 1983.

In 1984, Howard released a second album, *James Newton Howard and Friends*, an album that featured members of the band Toto. The project was created as a vehicle to promote Yamaha's synthesizers, as only synthesizers (the Yamaha DX7, DX9, and GS1), grand piano, drums, and percussion were used on the album.[13] Howard is listed as a composer or co-composer on four of the album's nine works, all of which are instrumental, and range in length from less than a minute to approximately five minutes. Howard is given the first musical credit, and performs on synthesizers, followed by the "friends." The pieces range in style from funk and blues to mid-tempo rock to ballad, and an example of world (i.e., Indian) music. Many of the compositions feature extended solo passages over a repeated bass pattern, largely to demonstrate the different sounds and timbres available to performers with the Yamaha keyboards. The final work on the album, "Amuseum," sounds like a wordless song, while another work, "Slippin' Away," foreshadows Howard's work on the film *Major League.* In general, the album *James Newton Howard and Friends* provides something of a template for Howard's early synthesizer-based film scores. Howard used timbres and styles, sounds and rhythms that would be used throughout his career.

Performing on Film Scores

Howard did not leap from performing and arranging popular music into composing film scores. The biggest crossover point was when he had the opportunity to perform on the score for *Twilight Zone: The Movie* in 1983, performing Jerry Goldsmith's music. Reflecting on this experience, Howard said,

> Jerry Goldsmith asked me to play keyboards. For a while I was sponsored by Yamaha Keyboards in the early Eighties. He asked me to play this Yamaha synthesizer called a GS-1, which had this touch-sensitive capability so if you pressed a note and the harder you pressed it, the more a filter would open up or the more the amplitude would increase or some dynamic would change, and he wrote for that instrument where he would indicate how much pressure to put on a keyboard, and that was for the *Twilight Zone* movie. It was a very difficult piano part and Jerry is an incredible writer. He writes very difficult keyboard parts and I had never scored a movie. At that point I was absolutely in awe of him and I still am. But that influenced me; I mean, I had worked with orchestras many, many times before that, so that wasn't my first orchestral experience but it had some influence. I later went on to produce the single for that movie ["Nights Are Forever," performed by Jennifer Warnes].[14]

Through the experience of performing on a film score, Howard was able to learn some of what went into composing one, and how to get certain sounds and moods out of the instruments, not just the synthesizer. Howard also co-wrote a song, "Prove Me Wrong," for the film *White Nights* in 1985. The challenge of the song was to synchronize the music to the film's dancing, and Howard was up to the task. The director of *White Nights*, Taylor Hackford, would eventually work with Howard again on 1988's *Everybody's All-American* and 1997's *The Devil's Advocate*.

Composing Film Scores

Howard's first film score was for a small comedic film titled *Head Office* (1985, dir. Ken Finkleman).[15] The film's protagonist, a newly graduated business school alum, begins climbing the corporate ladder, and is exposed to the dirty decisions and people within the company. The opportunity to move into film scoring was presented to him by his business manager at the time. Howard was asked, in a 2000 interview, what drew him to film score composition. He replied,

> Film scores were a natural evolution for me. I was an instrumentalist who was working in the record business. I was frustrated by not having the opportunity to work on records that I found musically interesting. I wasn't interested in working with a lot of artists. Those I wanted to work with were already working with other people and weren't particularly interested in working with me. Film scoring is an amazing, unparalleled opportunity for an instrumentalist. Each film score is a solo record of some sort. It was something I immediately loved doing.[16]

Howard's quote indicates a certain level of frustration, even when working with Elton John and others. He does not define what was "musically interesting" or who, at the time, was making "musically interesting" records. Howard does mention the idea of new composition rather than playing someone else's music, one of the reasons he cited for leaving USC. Having released *James Newton Howard and Friends* in 1984, the idea of composing more music would surely have been on his mind. In a different interview, Howard confessed to being a bit more frightened. He said,

> I was really terrified because I really didn't know whether I could write on command like that. And I was afraid of the technology. How do you lock up the music to the picture and all that stuff. So I – sort of – very tentatively said yes and I remember I had six or seven weeks to do that and I immediately just fell in love with that. And I

guess I did a decent job. I got offered a couple more and I have just been doing it ever since. For some reason, I couldn't go back to the pop world once I began scoring film and television. It felt like what I was supposed to be doing, so, right or wrong, away I went.[17]

While the prospect of writing film music was clearly exciting, the process of putting together sound and image was what was most difficult for him. However, his first score earned him several more opportunities to write and work with the technology to learn and improve. The score is similar to the album *James Newton Howard & Friends* in that the score deals largely in timbres and recognizable styles rather than memorable melodies.

From 1986 through 1988, Howard continued scoring films, working on twelve films in those three years. None of the films were highly popular or successful. Perhaps the most well known of that group is *Everybody's All-American* (1988, dir. Taylor Hackford), based on the novel of the same name by renowned sportswriter Frank Deford. While the film itself was not very successful, commercially or critically, the cast was full of stars: Dennis Quaid, Jessica Lange, Timothy Hutton, and John Goodman. The film follows an outstanding college football player who has some level of success in the NFL, his wife and family, and the aftermath of his retirement from football.

In 1989, Howard scored three films, all of them completely different. *Tap* (dir. Nick Castle) starred Gregory Hines, Sammy Davis Jr., and Savion Glover. Hines stars as a recently released convict, torn between returning to the life of crime and trying to make it as a successful dancer. *The Package* (dir. Andrew Davis) is an espionage thriller starring Gene Hackman and Tommy Lee Jones. Hackman's character must thwart Jones's character from assassinating the Soviet Premier. Finally, *Major League* (dir. David S. Ward), which starred Charlie Sheen, Tom Berenger, and Corbin Bernsen, was about the Cleveland Indians, the worst team in baseball, that somehow wins the American League East.

These three completely disparate types of film were scored in ways suited to their genres. Howard even served as co-writer of two songs used in *Major League*, a compositional path that he would continue to follow. These early scores show how Howard used the synthesizer in his scores, an instrument he had mastered, and how the types of syncopated rhythms from his two albums found their way into his synthesizer and orchestral film music.

Howard's Films in the 1990s

As Howard started to become established in Hollywood in the 1990s, he began to form partnerships with multiple directors. In some cases, those collaborations were on films in the same genres, which enabled the directors to have a stronger set of expectations regarding Howard's music. In other cases, Howard and the respective directors worked in several film styles, but previous experiences gave the directors trust and faith in Howard's abilities to compose the right music for their next film. Taken to an extreme, director Garry Marshall, in an attempt to recapture the magic from *Pretty Woman*, took his stars, Julia Roberts and Richard Gere, and cast them again in *Runaway Bride*, with Howard scoring both films. Howard's ability to fulfill each director's vision turned him into one of the most highly sought Hollywood composers of the decade.

James Newton Howard's "breakout" years were 1990 and 1991. In those two years, he scored twelve Hollywood films and two additional films made for television, which is an amazing work rate. Of these films, the most popular are *Pretty Woman* in 1990 and *The Prince of Tides* in 1991. Other films from these two years include *Flatliners*, *Dying Young*, *The Man in the Moon*, *My Girl*, and *Grand Canyon*. His score for *The Prince of Tides* earned him his first Academy Award nomination for Best Original Score.

In 1992 Howard earned more recognition in Hollywood, scoring two major films: *Glengarry Glen Ross* and *Diggstown*. While neither of those films can be considered a blockbuster, they both featured A-list casts and continued to give Howard further exposure and allowed him to demonstrate his range as a composer.[18] *Glengarry Glen Ross* has a jazz score, emphasizing both seduction and chaos in the film, while *Diggstown*'s score is largely rock and blues to reflect the urban location of the titular city.

The years 1993 and 1994 were two of his most successful, as he earned Academy Award nominations for Best Original Score for *The Fugitive* and Best Original Song for "Look What Love Has Done" from *Junior*, as well as an Emmy nomination for Outstanding Individual Achievement in Main Title Theme Music for *E.R.* Howard also scored the films *Alive*, *Falling Down*, *Dave*, *Intersection*, and *Wyatt Earp* during these two years. By this point, Howard had forged a number of professional partnerships that earned him repeated work. Howard was now writing effective music for any genre: comedy, romance, action-adventure, thriller, sports, and drama. Howard even did a period film, *Restoration* (dir. Michael Hoffman) in 1995. By the mid-1990s, about the only film types that he had not yet composed in were science fiction, horror, and animation.

From 1995 through 1998, Howard kept working at a frenetic pace, scoring seventeen Hollywood films during that four-year span. His scores from these four years include *Outbreak*, *French Kiss*, *Water-*

world, *Primal Fear*, *Space Jam*, *The Devil's Advocate*, and *The Post-man*. *My Best Friend's Wedding*, from 1997, earned Howard his third Academy Award nomination for Best Original Score. Once again, previously established relationships played a role in Howard's film choices. Kevin Costner, who starred in *Wyatt Earp*, starred in and produced *Waterworld* and produced and directed *The Postman*. Michael Hoffman directed both *Restoration* and *One Fine Day*, which contains the song "For the First Time," co-written by Howard, and which earned an Academy Award nomination for Best Original Song.

Howard formed two new collaborations in 1999 and 2000, one with the director M. Night Shyamalan, which will be discussed at length later, and the second with Disney studios. Howard won an Emmy for composing the theme for the television series *Gideon's Crossing*. Howard composed two scores in 1999 in the genre missing from his output, science fiction/horror, scoring both *Stir of Echoes* and *The Sixth Sense*. Having scored *Space Jam* in 1996, a hybrid live-action/animated feature, Howard began a new partnership with Disney, scoring three full-length animated feature films in three years: *Dinosaur* (2000), *Atlantis: The Lost Empire* (2001), and *Treasure Planet* (2002). Howard also embarked on his collaborations with director M. Night Shyamalan on *The Sixth Sense* and 2000's *Unbreakable*.

The 2000s

Howard maintained his tremendous work rate, scoring nearly forty films in the ten years from 2000 to 2009, including 2002's *Signs*. This decade is when Howard had his greatest level of commercial success, also scoring films such as *The Village* (which earned another Academy Award nomination for Best Original Score), *Collateral*, *King Kong*, *Blood Diamond*, *I Am Legend*, *Michael Clayton*, and *Defiance* (both nominated for Academy Awards for Best Original Score). His collaboration with Hans Zimmer on the scores for *Batman Begins* and its sequel *The Dark Knight* was groundbreaking, both for its music and for the partnership between two highly successful composers. Howard continued to work with directors he previously knew as well as forming new relationships. Through Howard's collaborations with Shyamalan, and other films like *I Am Legend*, Howard had newly mastered scores in the science fiction and horror genres, along with superhero films.

2010-present

Howard has continued scoring films across all styles and still works relentlessly, scoring, on average, four to five films a year. Howard has maintained his relationship with Shyamalan, scoring *The Last Airbender*, based on the animated series, and *After Earth*. A list of films scored by Howard in this five-year period include *Salt*, *Larry Crowne*, *The Green Hornet*, *Green Lantern*, *The Hunger Games*, *Snow White and the Huntsman*, *The Bourne Legacy*, *The Hunger Games: Catching Fire*, *Maleficent*, and he is scheduled to score both parts of the upcoming *The Hunger Games: Mockingjay* films.

Summary

While it took some time for Howard to grow in stature, he learned on the job, working his way up from scoring relatively small films to Hollywood blockbusters. He eventually earned the opportunity to score films in all styles, after making a name for himself scoring comedies and romantic comedies. In a 2006 profile on Howard, Jon Burlingame wrote, "He [Howard] has also managed to avoid that bane of most composers' existence: typecasting. His resume runs the gamut from the romantic sweep of *The Prince of Tides* to the edgy jazz of *Glengarry Glen Ross*, from the lighthearted comedy of *Pretty Woman* to the melancholy string passages of *The Sixth Sense*."[19] Burlingame's comments about Howard resisting typecasting are significant. Early in Howard's career he was typecast as a composer of romantic and/or comedic films. Through working with familiar directors who did not operate in a single style, and through recommendations, Howard was given the opportunity to move beyond the romantic and comedic films, and turned those opportunities into early successes in film with scores as diverse as *Flatliners*, *Grand Canyon*, *Glengarry Glen Ross*, and *The Fugitive*. Howard has demonstrated the ability to compose successful music in all Hollywood genres, which speaks to an ability to remain consistently recognizable, yet fresh with every score. James Newton Howard has shown, over a nearly thirty-year career in Hollywood that he can compose music for any film that is not just effective, but that is powerful, emotional, and memorable.

Howard and His Collaborators

Director-composer collaborations, or "duets," have existed since the advent of sound film. Some of the more famous duets are Alfred Hitchcock-Bernard Herrmann, Steven Spielberg-John Williams, Tim Burton-Danny Elfman, and Carter Burwell-Joel and Ethan Coen. Similar duets exist in world cinema as well, with duets such as Federico Fellini-Nino Rota, Sergio Leone-Ennio Morricone, Sergei Eisenstein-Sergei Prokofiev, and Grigori Kozintsev-Dmitri Shostakovich. Howard's most well known collaborative work is with M. Night Shyamalan, as they have worked on eight films together, and will probably continue working together in the future. Howard also has existing relationships with several directors, having scored at least two films with twenty different directors, and at least three films with eleven directors. This section will examine the most prolific associations that Howard has with various directors, to see if each operates in a particular genre, or holds a particular place in Howard's career. Because of his extensive popular and classical music backgrounds, and through his work with various directors, Howard has proven himself to be one of the most versatile composers in Hollywood. He is able to combine the rhythms of popular music with the instrumentation of a full orchestra to create a sound that is equally as effective in comedy as it is in drama and action films.

Howard and Andrew Davis

One of Howard's first film scores for a major film was for Andrew Davis's *The Package* (1989). Howard also scored Davis's *The Fugitive* (1993), which earned him an Academy Award nomination for Best Score, and *A Perfect Murder* (1998). All three films are intensely dramatic. An assassination must be prevented in *The Package*; Richard Kimball escapes from prison, attempts to prove his innocence, and must dodge authorities at every turn in *The Fugitive*; and a murder-for-hire scheme gets out of control in *A Perfect Murder*. These films had star power, featuring actors such as Gene Hackman, Tommy Lee Jones, Harrison Ford, Michael Douglas, Gwyneth Paltrow, and Viggo Mortensen, granting Howard's music a high level of exposure.

Of the three films, *The Fugitive* was both the most commercially successful and the best critically reviewed film. Since the score was nominated, it is also Howard's most well known score of the trio of films. In 2009, *The Fugitive*'s music was issued as an expanded release from La-La Land Records, and included alternate takes and several cues that did not appear on the originally issued soundtrack. In an article from 2006, Sharon Knolle asked directors who had worked with Howard what was special about him and his music. Davis was impressed with Howard's mock-up scores, commenting that they sound like finished products, a trait that few composers have.[20] Davis also commented on the music from *The Package*, stating, "He [Howard] was eager to have an opportunity to show new colors. I wanted Aaron Copland with Howard's hip rhythms. James nailed it."[21] The "new colors" to which Davis refers are the inclusion of brass, rather than the orchestration of piano, strings, and woodwinds, which is what Howard was known for early in his career. Howard's "hip rhythms" are a result of his previous work in the pop/rock world, with rhythmic figures that are syncopated within the typical ¼ meter. Howard's work with Davis largely stays within the genre of action/thriller. Howard seized the opportunity to expand beyond his early material, both in terms of genre and style and in terms of orchestral palette, and parlayed it into an Oscar nomination and a mastery of action/thriller music, resulting in a successful collaborative relationship.

Howard and Joel Schumacher

Howard's work with Joel Schumacher occurred over a short period of time. In less than five years, they worked together on three films: *Flatliners* (1990), *Dying Young* (1991), and *Falling Down* (1993). *Flatliners* and *Falling Down* are both dramatic thrillers, while *Dying Young* is a romantic drama. The common thread in all three is the concept of death. In *Flatliners*, med students induce death in an attempt to have near-death experiences. The male protagonist's health in *Dying Young* is failing due to leukemia. *Falling Down* features a man who, over the course of a day, loses touch with civility to the point where the only way that his day will end is with his death. Howard was pleased with his work on Schumacher's two dramas. He even gives *Flatliners* the credit as being one of the first films to pull him away from the romance and comedy genres into action and drama.

In Michael Schelle's *The Score*, Howard stated, "*Flatliners* was a big one for me, and an unusual opportunity—a canvas where I was given license to do anything I wanted. It was the first time I'd worked with a choir, the first time I'd worked with a large orchestra, the first time I'd blended a lot of synth and percussive elements with orchestra and choir."[22] Until 1990, Howard's film scores had been largely synthesized, but when given the opportunity to work with both a large orchestra and choir, Howard moved into the next phase of his career. Howard also spends time in the interview discussing *Falling Down*, saying that he tried to keep the score mostly restrained, in a effort to parallel the simmering rage of the film's protagonist, but with specifically placed musical explosions, again, mirroring the protagonist's outbursts.[23] Howard's score for *Dying Young* is what he refers to as a "piano-sounding" score, meaning that much of the film's music sounds like solo piano, or a string arrangement derived from a piano score.[24] This score aligns with his early style for romantic films, and largely derives from his arranging work with Elton John. When Daniel Schweiger interviewed Howard in 1994, he asked Howard about his relationship with Schumacher. Howard said, "Joel has afforded me some of the best scores of my career. *Flatliners* was an amazing musi-cal shot. Joel let me do anything I wanted, which has always been the case with him. *Falling Down* allowed me to compose one of my strangest scores."[25] With Schumacher's encouragement to experiment, Howard was able to take successful chances and moved his career to a level where he was scoring only A-list films. Howard's work with Schumacher came at a crucial time in his development as a film com-poser, and through having the opportunity to musically experiment on *Flatliners* and *Falling Down*, Howard was able to find a musical voice outside of the familiarity of romantic and comedic films.

Howard and Michael Hoffman

Howard and Hoffman have worked together on five films: *Promised Land* (1988), *Some Girls* (1988), *Restoration* (1995), *One Fine Day* (1996), and *The Emperor's Club* (2002). *Promised Land*, the first film commissioned by the Sundance Film Festival, is a drama about the shattered American Dream, while *Some Girls* is a dramedy about a young couple's relationship and her eccentric family. Neither film was commercially large, failing to make $500,000 at the box office. *Resto-ration* is a period film, set in seventeenth-century England, with much of the music in the film deriving from, or actually using, the music of English composer Henry Purcell. *One Fine Day*, a romantic comedy, earned Howard an Academy Award nomination for Best Original song, "For the First Time;" Howard was one of the song's three co-writers. *The Emperor's Club* was seen as a knock-off of *Dead Poet's Society* (1989), and was not particularly successful. *One Fine Day* was the most commercially successful of the five films, earning nearly $100 million, while *Restoration* earned two Academy Awards in 1996 for Art Deco-ration and Costume Design.

Hoffman has great admiration for Howard's work, and after hear-ing a demo tape and hiring Howard for *Some Girls*, said, "I decided I never wanted to work with another composer," and also spoke of How-ard's generosity.[26] Speaking about *Restoration*, Hoffman said, "We always find interesting starting points. I was very interested in 17th-century English music on 'Restoration,' so he got intrigued with Pur-cell and the kind of eccentric harmonies he uses. . . . He listens to my bad musical ideas and ends up coming up with something better."[27] Hoffman's admiration and desire to use only Howard as a composer speaks volumes to the importance of Howard's music in Hoffman's films. Hoffman was clearly a champion of Howard's from his start in film music, and their working partnership has spanned three decades.

Howard and P. J. Hogan

Howard and Hogan have made four films together in a relationship spanning more than a decade: *My Best Friend's Wedding* (1997), *Unconditional Love* (2002), *Peter Pan* (2003), and *Confessions of a Shopaholic* (2009). Hogan has only directed six films (through 2014), with the first and last as the only ones not scored by Howard. Aside from *Peter Pan*, the other three films are (romantic) comedies; *Peter Pan* is a live-action adaptation of J. M. Barrie's play *Peter and Wendy*. *Wedding* and *Pan* were both received well by audiences and critics, but *Shopaholic* was largely panned, and *Unconditional Love* never received a proper theatrical release.

Howard's music for *My Best Friend's Wedding* earned him another Academy Award nomination for Best Original Score, even though most of the film's music consists of songs rather than score. This approach was common earlier in Howard's career, and is extremely similar to how music was used in films such as *Pretty Woman* (1990). Hogan has a great affinity for Howard's musical work and sense. In Knolle's interview, Hogan states, "He's brilliant. What I like most about James is his passion. When he gets involved in something, he gives it his all. . . . He takes the mystery out of it [adding music]. He doesn't make you feel like an idiot if you don't know who Debussy is."[28] Howard's score for *Wedding* is reminiscent of his earlier work on films such as *Pretty Woman* and *Dave*, largely because of the genre and Howard's orchestration. However, Howard's music in *Wedding* is a much more mature and fully realized version of his earlier style. While the music doesn't completely Mickey-mouse the emotions and motives of Julia Roberts's character, Howard's music does provide insight into her motivations. Even though Hogan's films have not always been successful, Howard clearly enjoys working with him, despite the fact that the two of them argue about the music in the film,[29] and Howard clearly benefitted earning an Academy Award nomination in the process.

Howard and Lawrence Kasdan

Howard and Kasdan have collaborated on six films, in multiple genres, over twenty years: *Grand Canyon* (1991), *Wyatt Earp* (1994), *French Kiss* (1995), *Mumford* (1999), *Dreamcatcher* (2003), and *Darling Companion* (2011). Once Kasdan began working with Howard in 1991, Howard has scored Kasdan's films. Their collaborations have been across all genres.

In his 1994 interview, Schweiger asked Howard how he met Kasdan. Howard replied, "I first met Larry on the set of *Silverado*

(1985), when I came to visit my former wife Rosanna Arquette. Then Larry told my agents he wanted a different musical sound for his next picture, *Grand Canyon*. I was submitted along with Michael Kamen, and Larry ended up going with me because I lived in L.A. instead of London."[30] In the same interview, Howard referred to his creative process with Kasdan as "probably the best collaboration I've ever had with a director," and by working together to find musical solutions to the film's issues made his experience on *Wyatt Earp* particularly extraordinary.[31] When asked about Kasdan in a different interview from the same year, Howard said, "It's just a great collaboration. That's the thing that makes it work. I mean, it's not a solo gig here for me. . . . I like understanding a complex and rich vision from somebody and helping them enhance it. With Larry we have a really good conversation about all that stuff."[32] Due to the film's length, Kasdan gave Howard approximately six months to compose the score for *Wyatt Earp*, about twice the amount of time as is typical for Hollywood composers, and Howard used the time to revise his cues to where he and Kasdan were satisfied with the music. In Knolle's interview, Kasdan says, "He [Howard] can bring an enormous open mind and prodigious skills and history and talent. . . . So many composers can do a great job. What you look for is someone who feels resonance with the material. You work with him once, you're sold."[33]

Howard's work with Kasdan spans many filmic and musical styles. Their first collaboration, *Grand Canyon*, contains several musical styles including rock, jazz, and romantic, all styles with which Howard was fluent from his arranging days. Howard's statement about understanding and enhancing a director's vision is extremely important. What this says about Howard's relationship with Kasdan is that Howard is there to ensure that the film fully realizes the vision of the director. He is willing to receive input and make changes, and is willing to try musical directions that he might not feel are great, but if Kasdan wants that music, Howard will compose it.

Howard and Ivan Reitman

Howard and Reitman worked on three comedies together in the span of five years in the 1990s: *Dave* (1993), *Junior* (1994), and *Fathers' Day* (1997). Reitman was also a producer on *Space Jam* (1996), another film scored by Howard. All of these films are relatively light comedies: *Dave* is about a man hired to play the president's double for a night, who ultimately replaces the president. *Junior* features Arnold Schwarzenegger as a pregnant man. In *Fathers' Day*, Billy Crystal and Robin Williams are possible fathers of a teenager who ran away from home. Only *Dave* was critically or commercially successful, but a song from *Junior*, "Look What Love Has Done," which Howard co-wrote with three other people, earned Howard a Golden Globe nomination and an Academy Award nomination for Best Song.

In Knolle's 2006 interview, Reitman, who has a degree in music, a rarity for a film director, is quoted as saying, "His reputation is top-notch. He's one of two or three people who are the most sought after. His melodies are not only beautiful, but they have a beautiful emotional range that add an enormous amount to the films."[34] When speaking about Howard's musical qualities, Reitman says, "I know *Dave* is a great score because I've seen it imitated dozens of times in temp scores—you almost recognize the chordal and melodic shifts."[35] In a 1994 interview, when asked if he would work again with Reitman, Howard said, "Probably in Reitman's case, as long as there is a good script involved. I had a very good time with him on *Dave*. That was a different kind of movie for him. It was a very pleasurable experience, and we had a good time."[36] It is possible that because Reitman liked the music for *Dave* so much, they were unlikely to work outside of the comedy genre, and their collaborative relationship was not destined to last for a long period of time.

Relationships That Began after *Signs*

Howard continues to forge relationships with directors who ask him to score multiple films. Collaborations with three different directors began after Howard scored *Signs* in 2002. Howard has scored three films with Tony Gilroy: *Michael Clayton* (2007), for which he earned an Academy Award Nomination, *Duplicity* (2009), and *The Bourne Legacy* (2012); four films with Francis Lawrence: *I Am Legend* (2007), *Water for Elephants* (2011), *The Hunger Games: Catching Fire* (2013), and *The Hunger Games: Mockingjay – Part 1* (2014); and four films with Edward Zwick: *Blood Diamond* (2006), *Defiance* (2008), for which he earned an Academy Award Nomination, *Love & Other Drugs* (2010), and *Pawn Sacrifice* (2015). Howard's work with Gilroy is fully dramatic, with some action-thriller elements added, particularly for *The Bourne Legacy*, a spy movie. Howard's work with Lawrence is a bit more varied, as *I Am Legend* and *The Hunger Games* films are science fiction, while *Water for Elephants* is a romantic drama film. Howard also scored the first *Hunger Games* film, which was not directed by Lawrence. However, in wanting to keep continuity within the sound world of the film, Howard has continued scoring the series. Lawrence is listed as the director of *The Hunger Games: Mockingjay – Part 2*, scheduled for released in 2015. It would be surprising if Howard did not score that film. Howard has scored three dramas and one comedy for Zwick, with the comedy being *Love & Other Drugs*. While Howard was initially known for scoring (romantic) comedy films, his most popular work has clearly become in the drama/thriller genre.

Summary of Howard's Non-Shyamalan Collaborations

Howard's work with some collaborators resides within a single genre, like his comedic scores with Ivan Reitman, or his action-thriller scores with Andrew Davis. In other relationships, Howard worked across multiple film categories, best demonstrated through his work with Lawrence Kasdan, composing scores for comedy, romance, western, drama, and science fiction films. Joel Schumacher gave Howard a great deal of freedom to experiment with orchestration and style early in Howard's career, while other directors such as Kasdan had Howard rewrite individual cues over fifty times. While Howard got his start scoring mostly (romantic) comedy films, he gradually moved into dramatic and action-thriller films, which became much more prominent in his output. Howard never abandoned (romantic) comedy films, and his success in scoring films of multiple genres continued to create opportunities for him.

Because of Howard's work across multiple film categories, and with several directors, a number of trends come to the surface. Howard tends to forge relationships with directors who also work in specific genres, with Howard resisting a label. When these directors return to ask Howard to score their films, it is because they have been pleased with the results of his previous efforts. A second trend that is born out of these collaborations is that Howard's musical style transcends genre, and he is equally adept at writing music for an action film as he is for a romantic-comedy and a dramatic film. Through working in multiple film styles, and with multiple directors, his musical style has grown and he is able to successfully meld the genre of the film with the needs of the director and his own style. Finally, Howard recognizes that his job is to serve the film and musically realize the vision of the director. Essentially, Howard's role is to serve as the musical voice of the film, as specified by the director, and because Howard is so effective, he continued to work with the same directors again and again.

Howard initially started orchestrating music for Elton John, and through that process, learned how to work with someone else, realizing another person's musical ideas. From the middle of the 1970s through the middle of the 1980s, Howard continued working in popular music, arranging strings to accompany the typical rock ensemble. Making the leap from arranging to composing was natural for Howard. And because of the rapport that he built with several directors, he was able to realize the ideas of the director. Howard says, "I have been ready to abandon ideas when a director will step up and say, 'No, don't be so quick to move away from that. There's something really good there.'"[37] This quote points out two things. The first is that Howard is foremost a composer, so he needs to feel that his music, even in the service of a film, is adequate. The second is that his rapport with directors allows him to have an open exchange of ideas, in order to create the best music possible for the film, a concept that will be highlighted in his work with Shyamalan.

Through all of his collaborations with various directors, Howard earned a reputation as a composer who was able to realize the ideas of the director. He was able to work in multiple genres, and with various amounts of time. Almost every scoring job that he had was a positive experience, and he was recommended by nearly every director, which was how Howard landed the gig composing music for M. Night Shyamalan's *The Sixth Sense*. His successful work on *The Sixth Sense* led to his continuing relationship with Shyamalan.

Howard and Shyamalan

The most recognized and fruitful collaboration that Howard has is with director M. Night Shyamalan. Howard has scored all eight of Shyamalan's films since their first effort on the 1999 film *The Sixth Sense*. Howard has also scored *Unbreakable*, *Signs*, *The Village*, *Lady in the Water*, *The Happening*, *The Last Airbender*, and *After Earth*. While many think that *The Sixth Sense* was Shyamalan's first film, it was actually his third. Shyamalan's first two films were *Praying with Anger* (1992), a film that he made while he was a student at New York University, and *Wide Awake* (1998), a small film that did not gross $500,000 at the box office. Shyamalan's *The Visit* (originally titled *Sundowning*) opened in September 2015, but contained no original score, as its narrative is told through "found footage."

Howard was not Shyamalan's first choice composer for *The Sixth Sense*. In fact, Howard recalls coming onto the project fairly late, and scoring the complete film within six weeks.[38] Shyamalan recalls the same thing. "He came on very late in *Sixth Sense*, and we had only a few weeks to put together the score, which ultimately turned out to be amazing."[39] Shyamalan approaches each film the same way—the film will not contain music. Of course, a finished film without music is exceedingly rare, to the point where it would only exist as a novelty.[40] When Howard works with any director, he attempts to limit the amount of music in a film, beginning with the bare minimum.[41] Howard strongly dislikes the overuse of music in film, stating, "I feel that film scores are terribly overspotted. There's too much music in most movies. There's just too much music. And most of it is terrible, most of it is not saying anything. It's just there. And that's really a security blanket."[42] The process of scoring for Howard and Shyamalan involves building up from no music at all.

When they started work on *Unbreakable*, a new approach was started that they have used on every film from *Unbreakable* through *Lady in the Water*, and a process that is specific to their relationship. Howard and Shyamalan met before any filming began. Shyamalan says, "I showed him storyboards, walked him through the whole movie. I described the feeling of the movie, and I said, 'Go write down your emotion in notes.' He did that."[43] Jon Burlingame writes, "Unlike virtually every other director in the biz, Shyamalan does not 'temp' his movies. Shyamalan and Howard together work through a variety of approaches, often including multiple false starts. . . . [quoting Shyamalan] 'There's not a drop of music that's not original, not his, in the movie.'"[44]

The advantage to writing music based only on storyboards is that while Shyamalan may have an idea, Howard may create a better one, without being pushed in a particular director or musical style. Howard wrote several different versions of the Main Title music for *Unbreakable* after the storyboarding meeting. Howard recalls, "I sent a CD of four or five different ideas. My least favorite one, naturally, was the one that he really liked. That was that one that had this kind of trip-hop drum thing that went with it. It ended up working well, and people seemed to really respond to it, so what do I know?"[45] Howard's quote once again foregrounds the idea that he is willing to realize the concept of the director, rather than allow his own ego or his "best idea" to overtake his music.

Although the process of scoring to storyboards yields highly positive results, it is extremely time consuming, and can take up to six months, much longer than the time a composer typically has to score a film. The difference is that most composers score the film after it has been edited, so they are scoring to the rough cut of the film. In Howard's case, he is scoring while shooting is taking place, and adjusting while the film is in post-production. Not only does the additional time afford Howard the ability to wrestle with the music, he can also send demos of his music to Shyamalan, who can then comment on them. As a result, Howard's scores for Shyamalan's films often feature cues that have been revised several times.[46]

Unbreakable contains approximately one hour of music. Fred Karlin, in his book *On the Track*, writes, "This film is spotted relatively lightly. There is no music for most of David's (Bruce Willis') soul-searching scenes as he tried to understand his situation and considers what it all might mean to him."[47] *Signs* contains even less music than *Unbreakable*. The music is composed in such a way to only enhance the narrative, and not simply to have music throughout the entire film. Howard's stated preference for using as little music as possible is clearly noticed by scholars of film music.

Shyamalan's films typically deal with the supernatural and the unexplainable. In *The Sixth Sense*, ghosts are the issue. In *Unbreakable*, a man with super strength realizes his true calling. Aliens invade in *Signs*. *The Village* contains a "monster," but is really about trying to live in a fashion similar to one hundred years ago. The titular *Lady in the Water* crosses into our world from her home, Blue World. Plants attack humans in *The Happening*. The characters in *The Last Airbender*, based on the animated television series, can manipulate the four elements: earth, fire, water, and air. *After Earth* takes place on Earth, over one thousand years since mankind abandoned it. Howard's music in Shyamalan's films is as much of a character as any actor. Shyamalan often employs actors on a recurring basis, both leads and supporting actors, so his decision to use Howard as his composer for his films is not uncommon.

Just as an actor's performance in a role can elevate the entire film, so can music. In the collaborations between Shyamalan and Howard, Howard's music is as highly revered as the films themselves, and in some cases, because of the poor critical reception of the films, Howard's music is seen as a highlight. For example, in 2006, Howard referred to his music for *Lady in the Water* as "my most evolved score compositionally. It's the most symphonic score I've ever written, with a choral element and a fair amount of electronics as well."[48] While *Lady in the Water* was not well received by critics or audiences, Howard's score was awarded 2006's Best Film Score by the International Film Music Critics Association; people who deal exclusively in film music deemed Howard's score the best of the year.[49] Howard's work with Shyamalan has been his most prolific, and arguably, his most successful collaboration.

Conclusion

The career arc of James Newton Howard is different than most highly successful Hollywood composers. While Howard had a well-versed background in classical piano, he never formally studied composition, and only attended a university for less than two months. Instead of studying, Howard became a gigging musician, learning arranging and orchestrating on the job, particularly while working as a member of Elton John's touring ensemble. Howard's notoriety grew, and he wrote arrangements for more popular musicians, continuing to perform on piano and keyboards. His work as a studio musician led to work as a film score session player, which in turn led to his first opportunity to score a film. From that point, Howard became known as a film composer, and no longer as a session player.

Through Howard's unique experiences and background, he was able to use his skills to compose film music in a number of musical styles very fluidly, a skill that composers without Howard's rock/pop experience did not have. With each new style in which Howard was asked to score, a quick mastery came, and despite scoring many comedies early in his career, Howard managed not to be typecast.

Directors with whom Howard has worked on multiple occasions recognize Howard's ability to compose in different genres and his musical versatility. In a 1994 interview, Howard acknowledged the same thing. He said, "I pride myself on being versatile, because I think I am, and I don't say this from an egotistical point of view. I am versed in rock n' roll and classical, and I feel lucky to have benched that way because I think a lot of guys run into a brick wall when they have to deal with one or another."[50] Having the diverse exposure to all styles of music and professional performing experience, as a touring musician, as a session rock musician, as a studio film score musician, and as an arranger, gave Howard an advantage when it came to scoring films of all types and genres, and preventing becoming typecast as a composer of a single filmic style. He found success as a Hollywood film composer relatively early in his career, and has continued being successful, becoming one of the most prolific and sought-after composers of his generation.

2

Howard's Film Scoring Technique

The technique that James Newton Howard has brought to scoring films has, quite naturally, evolved over the thirty years that he has worked in Hollywood. The work that he did in his first five years of film music composition is largely different than how he approaches films now. In 2006, *Daily Variety* asked Howard to comment on ten scores that the publication had selected, using the parameters "the most popular, the Oscar nominated, and the most musically distinguished."[1] Without much surprise, none of those ten scores came from the first five years of his Hollywood career. Perhaps of greater surprise is that the three films he scored that had the highest box office gross—*The Sixth Sense*, *Pretty Woman*, and *King Kong*—are also absent from the list.

Because Howard is equally accomplished in the popular and classical worlds, he has been able to combine these two into his film scores through orchestration and instrumentation (acoustic and electronic), and through the use of rhythms commonly found in popular music. This chapter explores Howard's working processes and how they have evolved over the course of his film music career as well as his various influences, compositional and technological. Howard's unique background prepared him to approach films in multiple ways, from using temp tracks selected by the director for inspiration to having only storyboards and no aural examples at all. In order to demonstrate how Howard's music is so effective across genres and with various directors, the identifying features of Howard's style and sound will be examined. Those identifying features will present a James Newton Howard

23

"sound," present in nearly all of his mature film scores. To show Howard's compositional evolution and progress, the chapter also presents a summary of Howard's work in film on some of his significant scores, leading up to the composition of *Signs*. These films are presented chronologically because each film adds a new element or piece of diversity to Howard's oeuvre. Over the years, his style has matured. The commentary provided on each film will show how and where his compositional style elements have been used and developed over the course of his career, and will also identify when new compositional elements were added to Howard's musical box of tools.

Howard's Approach to Composition for the Screen

James Newton Howard does not have a single approach that he applies to every film. In the case of his film scores for Shyamalan's films, he writes the Main Titles first, and based on the storyboards, composes the music over a period of five to six months. This process with Shyamalan is extremely different than nearly every other director, who will often add a temp score to the rough cut of the film to give Howard an idea or direction for his music. One thing that is consistent is Howard's inclusion of technology—synthesizers—in nearly every score, both during the process of composition and in the final product.

Influences

Coming from a classical piano background, it is no surprise that Howard was influenced by composers from the eighteenth and nineteenth centuries. In terms of historical musical eras, Beethoven, Brahms, and Tchaikovsky all composed in the Romantic era, while Debussy and Ravel came out of the Romantic era into the twentieth century. It should also be noted that Beethoven, Brahms, and Tchaikovsky all composed in the German style of music, while Debussy and Ravel composed in the contrasting French style. Howard confirmed the influence of the Romantic German masters on his music in an interview conducted by Rosemary Reninger in 2000. Howard said, "I'm really a product of the whole nineteenth-century romantic idiom in classical music. That's the essence of what I do. I think I'm extremely melodically oriented. Although I adore and embrace a lot of twentieth-century and contemporary music, my orchestral sense is rooted in the nineteenth century."[2] Despite where he said his orchestral sense resided, in

2014, Howard stated that Stravinsky was a strong influence on his writing.[3] Stravinsky's influence can be heard in a number of ways in Howard's music, most notably in the changing and asymmetrical meters, and in his approach to having multiple musical threads occurring simultaneously, a technique known as stratification. In addition to growing up playing classical piano, Howard regularly attended symphony orchestra concerts in his youth, experiencing music from the great composers.

In addition to Beethoven, Brahms, and Tchaikovsky, two other significant composers from that period are Carl Maria von Weber and Richard Wagner, both known for their operas, and a thematic device called *Leitmotiv*. A Leitmotiv is a musical idea—shorter than a full theme—that recurs through an opera, and not necessarily in exactly the same fashion; some development of a Leitmotiv is expected. The Leitmotiv can be melodic, harmonic, or textural. Although the term *Leitmotiv* is commonly associated with Wagner now,[4] Stan Link, in his article on Leitmotif, writes, "The term leitmotif ('leading motif') was first used by F. W. Jähns in 1871 to describe Carl Maria von Weber's fragmentary reintroduction of thematic material in his operas."[5] Early film composers took some of the ideas of Leitmotiv and applied them to film, a technique still happening today, and one that Howard also applies to his music.[6]

The use of Leitmotiv in film is one where the technique is not applied in exactly the same fashion as Weber and Wagner used it. Stephen Meyer notes, "As David Neumeyer and others have pointed out, invoking the Wagnerian connection was a way for film music—and, by extension, the medium of film itself—to establish its cultural legitimacy."[7] By taking an element from high art, opera, and applying it to a lower art form, film, it elevated film above its low art origins. Many of the film composers of the 1930s, such as Max Steiner, Erich Korngold, Dmitri Tiomkin, and Miklós Rósza, began to codify the ways in which film music was used. Link writes, "The traditions of European art music, particularly of the nineteenth century, were naturally central to the education and experience of the many European composers laying the cornerstone of Hollywood's 'classical tradition' in the 1930s."[8] While these composers would have been familiar with the operas of Weber and Wagner, Max Steiner's view on the application of Leitmotiv shows the greatest distance from Wagner's. Meyer writes,

> During the period of so-called 'silent' film, and well into the 1930s (as Bill Rosar and others have pointed out) the practice of adding music to film had more in common with the traditions of theatrical music than with those of the Wagnerian music-drama. Indeed, Steiner's various references to Wagner have frequently overshadowed the

words of other musicians from the prewar period, who recognized ways in which the leitmotivic practice in film scoring differs from the Wagnerian model.[9]

Steiner was primarily a writer of melodies, largely due to his pre-Hollywood background in musical theater and operetta, which took him from Vienna to London to New York. As Kate Daubney writes,

> The extent of his involvement in the evolution of film scoring practice and the adoption of his techniques by other composers suggest that Steiner came to cinema scoring with a master plan for how the newest art form might benefit from the oldest. It was, however, as much circumstance as design which fostered the connection between Steiner's musical theatre and cinematic careers and led to the achievements of one of Hollywood's most prolific composers.[10]

Even Steiner's Hollywood rival, Erich Wolfgang Korngold, who did have an opera background, used a modified version of Leitmotiv. In his book on *The Adventures of Robin Hood*, Ben Winters writes,

> Korngold's commitment to thematic structures in his scores is perhaps his most obvious stylistic trait. While I would hesitate to apply the term *leitmotivic* to the film scores, with its operatic and specifically Wagnerian narrative associations, the musical structures of Korngold's film scores are dominated by a number of recurring themes. This approach can be traced to Korngold's operatic output.[11]

The thematic principles applied by early Hollywood composers became entrenched in music for films. Steiner's deformation and application of the term Leitmotiv, combined with the eagerness to legitimize the medium, led to the term becoming easily applied to film music.

Howard had the opportunity to reflect on the influence of film music composers from the 1940s to the 1960s. When asked about these composers, Howard stated that he was certainly affected by them, naming Max Steiner, Elmer Bernstein, Miklós Rósza, Jerry Goldsmith, and Bernard Herrmann as being specifically influential. Goldsmith's influence is particularly significant since Howard performed on scoring sessions for Goldsmith's music, and writes action music in a similar fashion to Goldsmith, using stratification rather than fast tempos. Howard also mentioned three of the most important scores for him, all of which were composed by Bernstein: *To Kill a Mockingbird* (1962), *The Ten Commandments* (1956), and *The Magnificent Seven* (1960).[12] The composers that Howard mentions are from Hollywood's "Golden Age," the late 1920s through the early 1960s and considered to be some of the greatest film music composers ever, often writing music that closely resembles the style of the German Romantic era.

In his interview with Michael Schelle, Howard was asked about his feelings on early-twentieth-century composers as well as the "sound-mass architects" of the 1960s.[13] Howard responded that he does like those composers, specifically naming Penderecki and Ligeti as models for his music for *Flatliners*, and that his interest in that music is part of the natural maturation and growing process through which all composers go.[14] Howard said, "I am a huge Ligeti fan, a big Penderecki fan. Elliott Carter's interesting. I really like [Howard] Hanson. . . . I am not a huge modernist, I am basically a tonality guy. Even my atonal material is tonality-based. I am pretty much rooted in tonality, and I probably always will be. I supposed even Corigliano and Goldenthal and guys like that are still tonality-based. I like those guys."[15] By naming Ligeti and Penderecki, two composers not known for their tonal works, Howard clearly demonstrates his appreciation for a specific type of atonal work that began after World War II, and a style not to be confused with the free atonality or serial styles of composers such as Schoenberg, Webern, and Berg. Tonality is necessary for the general audience to remember music. Memorable themes should be able to be sung or hummed by audience members after the film, and tonal/modal themes are far more easily remembered than atonal ones.

Howard's main popular music influence was The Beatles, as mentioned in chapter 1. Through his work in Los Angeles in the 1970s and 1980s as a studio musician, arranger, and songwriter, Howard worked in a number of popular genres. Howard was able to see and hear how each instrument fitted into the music, and how keyboards and synthesizers could be used as both melodic and accompanimental instruments. He also learned about using the synthesizer to double a part being played by another instrument, to add additional emphasis to that part. As he started to compose music for songs, he learned about structure and dealing with ending a song, either with a final chord or through fading out. The idea of endings is one that would become particularly useful in his film composition, as film cues do not always have "final" endings.

Beginning the Compositional Process

Unlike John Williams, who sketches his music by hand and demonstrates his scores at the piano, Howard writes music both on his synthesizers and writing ideas down on paper. In 2000, he said, "I do it both ways. I write a lot to paper still. When I get something that has possibilities, I'll turn off the video and turn to pencil and paper and try to compose something based around that idea, at least for eight or sixteen bars. I'll take it to a point where it sounds like it's on the right track. Then I'll go back and put that up to picture. If it's the right idea but needs editing, that's easy."[16] Writing notes on paper also forces Howard not to succumb to just playing music into the synthesizer and hoping that the result is adequate. He said, "It's much more fun to improvise perfection into your sequencer than it is to sit down and write out ideas. Ideas have to be chased, the counterpoint has to be worked out on paper, and so on."[17] Howard had clearly matured from his early Hollywood days, recognizing that a first or second effort was not always good enough. Composing melodic counterpoint is not easy—semester-long courses in counterpoint are regularly taught at the university level—and being able to visually see the music as note-against-note can allow a composer to know very quickly if what is written will sound appropriate or not.

Howard creates all of his mockups, or demos, using synthesizers. One example of why he uses synthesizers can be demonstrated through his experience scoring the film *Vertical Limit* in 2000. Howard said, "Here are the options: you can either be exhausted from creating the demo and sequencing and basically orchestrating the movie, or pick up a pencil and spend four weeks sketching, which was mind numbingly difficult and time-consuming. So at this stage I would prefer to do the demo process. I'm very fast at it."[18] Howard only had five weeks to complete the score, so spending time sketching versus working directly with demos was no contest. Howard is actually known for the high quality of his mockups. Regarding Howard's mockups for *Unbreakable*, Shyamalan said, "His mockup was so good that it was like, 'Jesus man, don't make it any better or you are going to lose the job of scoring the movie.' It's too perfect, you don't even have to score it."[19] The perfect nature that Shyamalan describes is due to the high level of attention and detail that Howard gives to the synthesizers, specifically the attacks and immediate decays.

In order to have the mockup sound as close to a real orchestra as possible, Howard manually manipulates the synthesized instruments, having some instruments enter slightly after the notated point of attack, while having others enter early.[20] To get the appropriate sound of a 110-piece orchestra, some elements of the mockup have to be doubled (e.g., unmuted string orchestra doubled with muted string orchestra). Howard says, "You shouldn't approach MIDI orchestration with the same instrumentation guidelines you'd use for a real orchestra. That's part of the secret to making mockups sound real."[21] Even in 1990, prior to scoring *Pretty Woman*, Howard was using synthesizers to write music, rather than sketching cues by hand. In a 1990 interview conducted by Robert Doerschuk, Howard said, "I generally do what a lot of people do: Put up the picture and start playing. A lot of times, I'll record into my Linn [9000], with no autocorrect, using it as a digital tape recorder so that I can go back and edit bars or delete things."[22] So even when Howard was in the early stages of his orchestral scores, his mockups began on the synthesizers.

Howard has spoken at length about his ability to write themes or tunes. In his interview with Schelle, Howard says, "Tune writing is relatively simple for me, but it's also a very intimidating problem. I approach most scores from the 'theme is king' perspective—I try to put the thematic material in perspective before I do too much else on the score."[23] Howard's quote indicates that he, like most film composers, writes the thematic content of the film first, and then finds ways to integrate the themes or Leitmotivs into various cues, as appropriate. By nailing down the thematic content first, it allows Howard to then contrast that theme with other music in the film, and change the style, instrumentation, or accompaniment of the theme. Through Howard's popular music background, it should come as no surprise that he finds "tune writing" to be easy. Writing musical themes is often the easy part of composing music. Filling in the accompaniment, harmonies, and scoring the remainder of the film is usually more difficult.

Howard's Stylistic Evolution

Many of Howard's film scores in his first five years were for comedies and romantic-comedies. Howard has said that during that period, he was "getting pigeonholed as a 'romantic' composer, which I didn't want to happen."[24] Because of Howard's extensive background in arranging strings for Elton John's band, Howard's earlier scores were, in his words, "pianistic," meaning that much of the music was composed at the keyboard and then arranged for piano, strings, and some woodwinds. Howard said, "Somebody told me early on, when I first joined Elton John's band, that if a part sounds good on the piano, it's going to sound good on the strings. To a large extent that's true. That's the guideline I used for a long time."[25] Howard's quote largely explains why many of his scores, including several in the early 1990s, rely mostly on piano, strings, and a couple of melodic woodwinds for orchestration. Howard was composing for an ensemble with which he was familiar and comfortable. Howard also explains why adding brass to his orchestrations took time, saying, "And that rule about strings doesn't necessarily apply to brass. You could have a cluster voice that sounds great with a trombone section playing it, but the same voicing on the piano is too muddy. Furthermore, a voicing that works with brass might

not sound good when strings are added."[26] Having never formally studied orchestration, another semester-long course offered at the university
level, Howard had to gradually add instruments to his work, and needed
to experiment before he finally became comfortable with a full symphonic orchestra.

When asked, in 1994, how he had evolved as a composer, Howard
replied, "I think I've gotten better as a symphonic composer. I have a
better sense of creative rhythm with the orchestra, and can expand my
thematic ideas without writing too much for scenes. . . . Film composing has been an evolutionary process for me, and I think that I've just
gotten started."[27] Howard gave this interview shortly after completing
the score for *Wyatt Earp*, which contained approximately two hours of
music. At this point, he had received Oscar nominations for *The Prince
of Tides* and *The Fugitive*, and his style was maturing with each film.
He was essentially asked the same question in Jeff Rona's interview in
2004. Howard responded,

> I think the most obvious thing for me is that I write much less pianis-
> tically. When I first started out I was a pianist, so I would write or-
> chestra parts that I could play on the piano. I don't do that nearly as
> much anymore. . . . I think less from a pianistic viewpoint now. My
> music is more evolved, more complicated in terms of the timbrel [sic]
> selections, more varied, with better orchestration and somewhat more
> tonal. My music is a little more subjective, not quite so specific, not
> quite so "on the nose."[28]

By writing less melodically, Howard's music can still manage to keep
some level of ambiguity, rather than stating a sweeping melodic theme
and telling the audience how to react to his music. Of course, Howard's
melodies can be lengthy, such as the theme in *Dave*, rather than just
short motivic fragments. As a composer, Howard possesses the skill to
write both long melodic themes and short melodic fragments, which not
all composers can do well.

Throughout his career Howard has grown, working in every film
genre, and mastering them all. When given the opportunity to score an
action film, *The Fugitive*, he did it so well that he was rewarded with an
Academy Award nomination. When given the opportunity to use indig-
enous instruments, such as the shakuhachi and taiko drums in *Snow
Falling on Cedars*, he was able to incorporate and integrate them seam-
lessly into the context of the orchestra. When Howard began scoring
animated films, first *Space Jam* in 1996, and then *Dinosaur* for Disney
in 2000, he learned how to have an extreme attention to detail. In a
2004 interview with Dan Goldwasser, Howard was asked if he ap-

proached scoring animated films differently than other films. Howard said,

> The Disney methodology is such that you'll come on board, and meet with the filmmakers—it's just very "committee." It's roundtable discussions, instead of a composer working in their ivory tower, you're just a working man among other working men. There are writers, and animators, and producers, and music supervisors, and everyone just sits around and works it all out. In each case, what I did first was the main thematic material which is difficult for me because I like the thematic stuff usually to evolve out of spending time with the movie. . . . The thing about animation is that the detail is enormous. I think it requires you to be much broader in your approach. There are iconic versions of every kind of music you've ever heard: fanfares, big band, broadly comic, broadly tragic, and all in one film. . . . Animation is really hard, but I think I learned more about orchestral writing on those projects than anything else I had ever done, so they were a rite of passage—I think it's a rite of passage for every composer![29]

Interestingly, Howard points out that while he was the composer on the film, a group of people contributed to the ideas. In order to operate successfully in that environment, Howard needed to be sure of himself and have the confidence to know that he could take the ideas from the "committee" and turn that into music that maintained his compositional voice. By resisting the urge to be solely in control of the music, Howard again demonstrated that he is flexible in his work, and willing to make adjustments in order to satisfy the needs of the director and the film. Clearly Howard's experiences scoring the animated Disney films was a positive one, and one that forced him to find solutions to musical problems, especially when the target moved so quickly within the film.

The End Credits

In most Hollywood films, the music that accompanies the End Credits is almost irrelevant, as audience members rarely stay until the conclusion of the credits.[30] Many contemporary films use songs rather than exclusively orchestral score. In those cases, the songs usually occur first, with the score relegated to filling out time at the end. The songs in the End Credits are placed there, often in hopes of selling soundtrack albums, with those songs often unavailable on an album elsewhere. Howard has a specific approach to the End Credits, which is somewhat different than most composers—he views the End Credits as part of the structure of the film, even though it's not part of the narrative. He says, "I have one philosophy about end credits, which is that I like to approach it as the final chapter of the film. It's still a viable part of the

construction of the film, kind of a last chapter, if you will. So, often-
times I like to start off with a new piece of music or something that,
certainly, eventually goes into a reprise of material from the movie.
I've been able to do that most with Night."[31] Howard has followed this
approach from early in his career.

A "James Newton Howard Sound?"

Nearly every composer, classical or film, has a signature sound or style.
It's the element that allows the audience to hear a new work and identify the composer by the specific stylistic traits. Howard has been asked
multiple times if he has a signature sound. In Schweiger's interview in
1994, Howard was asked, very directly, if his music has a specific
sound. Howard replied, "While I've endeavored not to repeat myself, I
have, by definition, done a lot of scores that sound like James Newton
Howard. I'm trying to escape that by taking chances."[32] Howard didn't
really answer the question, other than to affirmatively acknowledge that
he does have a signature sound. Howard doesn't actually say what that
sound is, or any of the elements that would go into creating the sound,
but makes clear that going forward, he will try to move away from the
signature sound, by using the word "escape." In a different interview in
1994, with Will Davis Shivers, Howard said, "To me, even when I'm
doing wildly different scores, there is a very similar quality to them and
that's style, that's why they hire me."[33]

Howard continued to avoid the question of what goes into a signature sound in Schelle's 1999 interview. Leading up to a question,
Schelle acknowledges that earlier in his career, "Howardisms" arose in
his music, but then Schelle's question has nothing to do with the signature sound, so Howard didn't answer anything about a sound or style in
that lengthy interview.[34] Jeff Rona's brief interview in *The Reel Sound*
in 2004 didn't address the issue. But in an interview with Christopher
Reynolds and Mark Brill, published in 2010, Howard gave an extended
answer to the question. Reynolds and Brill gave features of a "Howard-
ian sound" as ostinatos, drones, dissonant clusters, and other elements
before asking what Howard does to make these elements, available to
all composers, sound different in his compositional sensibilities.[35]
Howard gave a lengthy response:

> I think a strong rhythmic element is something that I've always been
> [interested in]. When I say rhythmic element, I mean electronically
> generated or acoustically generated percussion. . . . I think the hall-
> mark of what I do, and I can't avoid it even if I want to, is a very me-
> lodic kind of take on a piece, even in tiny little bits and pieces, little

motifs, "motifinal" bits, little snippets. I try to be more gestural and less "notey," but it turns out that it's really hard for me to do that.[36]

Howard finally self-defines the salient style elements that identify him: the use of percussion and the approach to generating melody motivically, rather than thematically. Howard's comments support a statement he gave in 2009 to Jeff Rona where he said, "I've tried to be less melodically driven except when I make a conscious decision to do it. Most of the time I try to be a little more vague about the implications."[37] Long melodic themes, or even melodic four-measure phrases, can be absent in favor of short melodic motifs of three to six notes. When combined with the emphasis on percussion, Howard's music sometimes avoids long melodic themes. In other films, such as *Dave*, *Wyatt Earp*, and *Unbreakable*, his music is quite melodically-thematically driven. Howard's response to Rona's question is essentially an avoidance of responding at all. He basically says, "I do X, unless I do Y," where X and Y are the only two possibilities. Like his music, Howard's responses to questions about his specific sound obscure his own style and make it difficult for a listener to pin down musical traits.

Later in the interview, Howard is asked directly if he feels as though he has a specifically identifiable sound. Howard responded,

> I hear myself in other peoples' music. I hear them replicating, imitating, which I'm always flattered about. I think I try to avoid sounding like James Newton Howard, if at all possible, at this point. I just did this little movie *Duplicity* (2009, dir. Tony Gilroy) . . . and in the end we got an interesting score, and almost the universal comment from people was: "Doesn't sound like you." And that's the best thing somebody can say.[38]

Howard clearly tries to sound different from film to film, a musical chameleon who, despite certain hallmarks, writes music to serve the film rather than serve himself. And by attempting to not sound like himself, he once again presents the idea of obfuscating his stylistic hallmarks. Howard's discussion of his own music becomes more opaque with time. In 1994, he said that style is consistent, even if the film genres are not. In 2010, he said that he can hear his style in other composers' music, but doesn't identify those hallmarks.

When asked about Howard's style, his longtime orchestrator Brad Dechter said,

> James is, to me, as good of a film composer as there has ever been. Based upon his obvious absolute mastery of music in many idioms, he has the great ability to create music for a movie, not impose music on a movie. In other words, James really creates something unique

for a film; it's not just James Howard doing a film score. He has a style. He has, in fact, many styles, in a way. I can recognize many aspects of his work throughout very disparate types of scores, because they all still have a thread of James that goes through them. But he adapts himself to the movie, and he realizes that he is serving the drama of the film. That's his job. That's how I would categorize his chameleon-like abilities. He never fails to amaze me.[39]

Dechter's statement reinforces the fact that trying to summarize a style for Howard is problematic. In fact, Dechter uses the phrase "many styles" and "chameleon-like abilities" when describing Howard's music. And like Howard so often does, Dechter doesn't address what these stylistic hallmarks might be.

So is there a "James Newton Howard sound?" To say that it uses percussion, ostinatos, and melodic motifs would not be specific enough, as many composers use those compositional techniques on a regular basis. But Howard clearly believes that there is a sound, as he hears others imitate his work, and actively tries to avoid sounding like himself. Dechter clearly hears a sound, or multiple sounds. The problem with summarizing a style is that no single score uses all of his style elements, nor does he use a single element in every score. Howard can write melodies like Tchaikovsky and Beethoven and Strauss. He can write rhythmic music like Stravinsky and Bartók. He can write motivically like Schoenberg and Herrmann. He can write homophonically, melody plus accompaniment, and he can write with multiple independent and unrelated layers of music. His music is orchestrated like Debussy and Ravel, with different colors peeking through the musical fabric. And with every film he scores, he adds a new element to his compositional "bag of tricks." But trying to find all of these elements within a single context is unlikely to happen.

One can hear identifying elements, recurring gestures, in multiple films. The percussion elements in *The Fugitive* are very similar to those in *Outbreak*. This could be due to the fact that both are essentially action/thriller films, but even the placement/spotting of the cues that use the percussive elements are similar. A three-chord progression that occurs near the end of the Main Titles in *Outbreak* foreshadows a chord progression that occurs in *The Sixth Sense*, four years later. A cue in *Dave*, where Dave interacts with the single child at the homeless shelter/school, contains a descending line of the pitches F-F-E-D-C-B♭-C. This descending line appears, though not exactly, in *Unbreakable* as G-G-F#-E-D-E. While the music in *Dave* begins on tonic and the music in *Unbreakable* begins on scale-degree 3, the similarities between the two lines, particularly with the repeated first note, are clearly recognizable. These examples are certainly not the only instances of this phenomenon, but are perhaps some of the easiest to hear. The "James Newton Howard sound" is difficult to pin down, elusive yet familiar, recognizable when it's heard but hard to define. For a composer who does his best to distance his music from himself on every project, difficulty defining a specific sound should come as no surprise.

Because of the difficulty in locating a "James Newton Howard sound," and because Howard himself will not willingly reveal his style hallmarks, there must be a reason for the mystery. Howard worked hard to avoid being pigeonholed as a romantic and/or comedy composer. He was, and is, clearly very good at composing that style of music, based on the amount of scores, and his Academy Award nominations in those genres. Howard also is able to function in any genre, moving fluidly and fluently through action, science fiction, drama, comedy, romance, and any other type of film. To clearly identify a "James Newton Howard sound" would be to reveal the subtle nuances and tricks that give his music the elements that keep him employed. Additionally, those elements, when taken on their own, are nothing remarkable: use of percussion, ostinato, short melodic motives, and syncopated rhythms. Howard may not want to reveal his stylistic sound because it would appear to be disappointing to the world, not acting as a musical Rosetta Stone, but seeming to be mundane and pedestrian. But like all great composers, Howard's music is greater than the sum of its parts.

Early Film Scores

Howard's very first film score was for a small film entitled *Head Office* (1985). This first foray into film scoring was scary for Howard. In a 1994 interview, he recalled, "I was always a little frightened of becoming a film composer. I'd have to know how to write on demand, and understand the technology of synching music to picture. But then a comedy called *Head Office* came along. I entered into it with zero expectations, and grew to love the job."[40] Howard had a strong background in music technology, as he was highly knowledgeable about synthesizers, so learning the film technology was not nearly as much of a burden as he might have initially thought. Howard's *Head Office* score is not particularly memorable. The score itself seems to be performed entirely on synthesizers, as no orchestra or ensemble is listed in the End Credits. Since Howard was familiar with synthesizers, this compositional methodology is not wholly unexpected. Unfortunately, it gives the music a very dated sound, marking it as a film clearly from the mid-1980s. The cues are very short, with six of the fifteen cues lasting less than a minute,[41] and only two cues lasting longer than two minutes. Those two cues, the Main Titles, and a sequence where the main character tries to get out of the company building at the end of the film, would be the most likely choices for longer cues, as the End Credits are accompanied by a song rather than score.

Howard's musical choices in *Head Office* and in other early scores are tame and somewhat expected. Music that accompanies more intimate scenes is predictably sultry and stylistically jazzlike, while music that accompanies physical activity is faster and in a rock style. The music in the film seems largely composed to stay out of the way and intentionally be unmemorable, particularly because so many of the cues are short. The film itself has problems because it contains too many characters, and the editing has the film continuously jumping from scene to scene. The editing doesn't allow time for longer musical cues to exist, and montage is not a film technique used in *Head Office*.

Like most composers, his first few efforts are not equal to that of the mature composer. He does acknowledge that his first breakthrough was the 1988 film *Everybody's All-American*.[42] This was one of Howard's first films where the score substantially moved beyond synthesizer-dominant scoring. In addition to the music that Howard composed— just over thirty minutes—the film featured a large number of songs appropriate to the various eras over which the film spans. Instead of Howard scoring the montage, where the timeline moves from the 1950s into the mid-1960s, a song is used, Hank Ballad and The Midnighters' "Finger Poppin' Time."

Howard's music doesn't enter until nineteen minutes into the movie, when the main character, Gavin Gray, races an African-American, who is said to be as good, or better than Gavin. In the director's commentary on the DVD, Taylor Hackford discussed the music in this scene and said,

> He [Howard] wanted to do a real Americana score, something in the area of Aaron Copland. If you listen to the score behind this sequence, it's just fantastic. And all the way through this, there are themes in this film that James created that are, I still believe, some of the most beautiful themes in modern film. He's a brilliant collaborator—we worked together on *The Devil's Advocate* after this—but this was the . . . it was me deciding that this was something I wanted to do. . . . Just listen to this score.[43]

Hackford's hyperbole notwithstanding, much of Howard's music in this film is scored using piano and strings, and the occasional melodic woodwind instrument, Copland-like, but without brass. Howard has said that much of his early film music derives from his arranging for Elton John's band, and that a string orchestra will basically sound like

it does on the piano. The love theme that Hackford mentions first occurs twenty-two minutes into the film, and follows the couple throughout the entire film. It is the music sounded at the end of the film, and by
using this theme at the film's conclusion, it clarifies that the emphasis
of the film is their relationship, and not football.

Howard scored a second sports film the following year, working
on 1989's *Major League*, a film that focuses on the misfits of baseball,
the Cleveland Indians. In addition to composing score, he also wrote
the music for two songs in the film, including "Most of All You." It is
sung by Bill Medley and is heard as a love theme for the catcher and
his former girlfriend, whom he is trying to win back. This score is
largely synthesizer-based, with almost no orchestral music in the film,
excluding source music. Much of the soundtrack is upbeat, rock-based
music, and it often accompanies montages, such as spring training practice and the Indians' pennant drive.

Howard also used the music for "Most of All You" as score. This
is the music that concludes the film, as the ex-girlfriend returns to the
catcher, the Indians win the American League's East Division, and all
former rivalries within the team are settled. Like *Everybody's All-
American*, the use of the love theme at the film's conclusion refocuses
the film and declares that the emphasis is on the relationship, with
baseball as the vehicle to reunite the former lovers.

Significant Scores from the 1990s

The decade of the 1990s is where Howard made the leap to a highly
celebrated composer. He began the decade composing the music for
Pretty Woman, and ended the decade scoring *Runaway Bride*, both
films starring Richard Gere and Julia Roberts, and both romantic-
comedies. That is certainly not to say that all that Howard scored were
rom-coms, but he did become known for excelling within that genre.
He says, "1991 was a very strong year for me, because *The Prince of
Tides*, *Dying Young*, *Man in the Moon* and *My Girl* all got released. But
I was also getting pigeonholed as a 'romantic' composer, which I didn't
want to happen."[44] The early 1990s did yield work in a number of different styles, with Howard scoring films as diverse as *The Prince of
Tides*, *Grand Canyon*, *Glengarry Glen Ross*, *Dave*, and *The Fugitive*.

Ultimately Howard broke out of the romantic(-comedy) mold, but
the genre helped him earn his first Academy Award nomination for
Barbra Streisand's *The Prince of Tides*. Working with a director who
had a strong musical background posed some difficulties. Howard says,
"Working with Barbra elevated my work ethic. It was on this film that I

started doing multiple versions (of cues). The style of that score, and its romantic quality, required a certain kind of polish and elegance that I aspired to."[45] Despite the critical success of the film's score, Howard did not feel like it was particularly representative of what he could do. In 1994, just three years after composing the score, he said,

> I hope I've left piano-sounding scores like *Dying Young* behind. It's hard for me to listen to my old music. I went to a concert where they played the end titles from *Dave* and *The Prince of Tides*, and I just wanted to crawl under the chair! My orchestrations sounded primitive and uncomfortable. Film composing has been an evolutionary process for me, and I think that I've just gotten started.[46]

Howard's scores evolved throughout the 1990s growing in scope and often stature. The films in this portion of the chapter are presented in chronological order, as each film tends to present some new aspect of Howard's compositional career.

Pretty Woman

Howard's first major work in this decade was 1990's *Pretty Woman*, directed by Garry Marshall, the film for which Howard began to earn his romantic-comedy reputation. Like *Everybody's All-American*, *Pretty Woman* features a number of songs, limiting opportunities for Howard's music. As a result, less than twenty minutes of score are heard in the film. On the official CD release, eleven songs are included, but none of Howard's score appears. In the first hour-and-fifteen-minutes of the film, Howard's cues are all shorter than one minute in length. However, once Edward (Richard Gere) and Vivian (Julia Roberts) begin to fall in love, Howard's music becomes much more prominent, and the accompanying music for their kiss becomes their love theme and dominates the remainder of the film's score. The orchestration is largely piano and strings, with the occasional melodic woodwind instrument. Although not lengthy, Howard's music is very effective at tugging on emotions when used.

The Prince of Tides

Howard's first Academy Award nomination was for his score for *The Prince of Tides*, a romantic drama. The main character is a southerner, Tom Wingo (Nick Nolte), who travels to New York to aid in his suicidal sister's physical and emotional recovery. In the process, he falls in love with his sister's therapist, Dr. Susan Lowenstein (Barbra Streisand). Ultimately, Tom returns to his family in South Carolina, and resumes his marriage and familial obligations. Dr. Lowenstein helped him deal with his past, and allowed him to feel again.

Howard's music in the film is almost exclusively tonal, melodic, and consonant. A recurring motive, A-C#-D, is present at both the beginning and end of the film, as well as when Tom returns home for a weekend. That motive represents Tom and his comfort. The motive also occurs when he arrives in New York, but with different, and more dissonant harmony, as his voice-over narration tells the audience why he doesn't like New York. Most of the melodies in the film are either played by the oboe, piano, or violin, and the orchestration features large romantic swells. A couple of cues feature a "soft rock" ensemble: guitar, keyboard, and drums—clearly a style with which Howard was familiar. Some of the most significant scenes of the film are left unscored, with the dialogue and sound effects carrying the drama. This is a result of Howard not overscoring, as the drama didn't need additional emotional emphasis from music. *The Prince of Tides* is the film where Howard began making significant and multiple revisions to his cues, and the film forced him to hone his skills to get the maximum effect from his music, in cooperation with the director. Additionally, the Academy Award nomination showed that Howard had mastered the romantic (drama) genre.

Grand Canyon

Grand Canyon is a film that weaves various unrelated events into a single narrative. As a result, the diversity of events mandated a diversity of styles in Howard's score: ambient-techno, jazz, rock, and brass fanfares are included in the music for the film. The film's narrative weaves storylines of as many as six characters, with a musical style for each one.

The most interesting aspect of the music is how the musical styles are able to instantly switch to reflect the cuts in the story, yet the flow of the music remains uninterrupted. The cue "Main Titles," the crux of the film's music, is based on a series of eight chords that are repeated multiple times. In this way, the music is somewhat similar to a Baroque passacaglia, but instead of melodic variations, each repetition adds a layer or new musical element to the previous statement. Fred Karlin writes, "Howard's chord progression is the foundation for his score, unifying the many disparate elements of this film. [Quoting Howard] 'I put that throughout the movie in unexpected places, in the middle of conversations when things would shift slightly. So that was really the tent pole of the score.'"[47] Howard's music is most effective when covering scene overlaps, as the film often jumps from place to place, character to character. At the end of the film, when several of the characters travel together to the Grand Canyon, the opening eight chords are transposed and played by a brass quintet. While the music is familiar, the style is totally different, indicating that the characters have transformed into different people. By integrating so many different styles, while tying together the film's music through the harmonic progression, Howard demonstrated his adeptness at handling multiple musical genres within one film.

Glengarry Glen Ross

Glengarry Glen Ross, based on David Mamet's play, may be most memorable for Alec Baldwin's "Coffee is for closers" speech, even though his is a relatively minor character.[48] Howard did not compose much music for the film, as the dialogue is omnipresent and percussive, so when the genre of jazz was suggested to Howard, he was a bit surprised, saying, "Music Producer Tommy LaPuma thought that a jazz approach would be a good way to go, which is very funny, because it would seem that a jazz score and a David Mamet screenplay are completely at cross purposes. I think [the jazz style] added to the sense of chaos, unpredictability and edginess."[49]

Howard uses three different jazz styles in the film. The most common, and the style heard in the main titles, is a middle-of-the-road style, relaxed, with a typical ensemble of saxophone, piano, bass, and drums. This opening music is much more rhythmically active than nearly any other moment in the film, since it does not contain any dialogue. This style, reminiscent of what one might hear in a *film noir*, often contains sustained harmonies and little rhythmic activity, in order to stay out of the way of the dialogue. As the film moves forward, a mystery does appear, so the style is justified.

The second style is a bit sultrier, more seductive, and is used when Ricky Roma (Al Pacino) is trying to close a sale in a restaurant, essentially seducing a character named Lingk. This jazz style is only heard when Roma and Lingk interact.

The third style in the film is much more frenetic, much faster, and begins with only bass and drums. It is first heard when Roma arrives at the office the morning after his sale, when the office has been robbed. He is frantic, confused, and elated by his sale, and the music both feeds on and contributes to his energy. This is the one point where the music interferes with the dialogue, as both music and dialogue are extremely active, which, in turn, adds to the chaos of the scene and situation. This was Howard's first and only exclusively jazz-oriented film score, but showed that his jazz cues from *Grand Canyon* could be sustained for the entirety of a film.

Falling Down

Howard scored *Falling Down* in 1993, a film about a disturbed man who finally snaps and goes on a rampage in Los Angeles. The tension in the film comes from waiting for Bill Foster (Michael Douglas), the main character, to react to his various situations. He goes from smashing a convenience store to killing a neo-Nazi, with the events escalating every time. He is finally killed by the police officer (Robert Duvall) who has been chasing him throughout the film.

The film is scored with mysterious and ominous sounds, such as wind chimes and gongs, as well as synthesizers combined with electric guitar, low sustained notes and dissonant harmonies. The wind chimes in the score ultimately refer back to the wind chimes located outside the house of Bill's ex-wife, in his attempt to get "home." Much of the film's music sounds mysterious and tonally ambiguous. Additionally, the music lacks melody, in an attempt to prevent the audience from viewing Bill sympathetically. As Bill is killed, the music references a Requiem, with choir and strings. Even though the film was scored in an unusual way, with Howard stating that this was one of his strangest scores,[50] his work on this film, with its action and tension, likely made composing music much easier for *The Fugitive*. The most significant aspect of the music is the way in which Howard keeps the music restrained, except when Bill lashes out. As Bill's actions become more outrageous, so too does the music.

Dave

The title character in 1993's *Dave* (Kevin Kline) is a stand-in for the President of the United States who is actually the manager of a temp agency. The music associated with Dave is a waltz, often with the melody played by the clarinet. This is one of the earliest significant instances of triple-meter ($\frac{3}{4}$) music in Howard's scores and the waltz becomes the primary music in the film. The melody is in the Lydian mode, rather than major or minor. Since Dave is a person who wants to help make things better, the waltz, exceptional in its meter and its mode, is what allows the character to be exceptional.

Cues are often initiated by the snare drum, particularly when people are walking through the White House. Howard also wrote a love theme for Dave and the First Lady (Sigourney Weaver), based on a three-note ascending gesture, G-A-D. This theme is heard twice more in the film, first when she sees Dave walking away from Washington, and then at the end of the film, when she walks into Dave's temp agency. As they kiss, the music is fully orchestrated for the first time.

Though *Dave* is not a romantic-comedy like *Pretty Woman*, those aspects permeate the film score, particularly through the orchestration of the waltz, which can be described as whimsical. *Dave*'s director, Ivan Reitman, is aware of the quality of Howard's score, citing its use in temp scores in multiple films.[51] While Howard may not have been initially proud of the score for *Dave*, he changed his mind. In a 2010 interview with Christopher Reynolds and Mark Brill, when asked what movies and scenes he was the most proud of, Howard said, "I like the score to *Dave* (1993) a lot, oddly enough."[52] Howard seemed surprised to like his work, but enough time had passed that he was able to reassess and reappraise the score, and finally enjoy it.

The trajectory of the End Credits mirrors the film, as Dave comes to Washington, captures the joy of helping, falls in love, and quietly leaves. In this case, the music that Howard used in the End Credits is the most memorable in the film, leaving the audience with not only the arc of the film, but with the music that they will remember.

The Fugitive

In 1993, Howard earned his second Academy Award nomination for his music from *The Fugitive*, for which he had little time to compose. Commenting in 1994, Howard said, "About 95 minutes of music. . . . For me, it's the most music I've ever written in a film. I had about eight weeks to do it and I could've easily used more."[53] A few months later, Howard said, "That score was effective in driving the picture, but I have a lot of reservations about it. I had eight weeks to do over 90 minutes of music. I don't think it's one of my greatest scores. But a lot of people say it's my best work."[54] Revisiting the score in 2006, Howard was a bit more candid, calling it, "An exercise in terror for me. It was my first big blockbuster thriller. I regarded half of that score as a failure. I didn't know how to make an orchestra do the things I wanted an orchestra to do."[55] Howard's comments indicate that he was still unhappy with his music, unlike his reassessment of his music for *Dave*.

Howard's score for *The Fugitive* is one of his earliest examples of a significant use of dissonance and tonal ambiguity, as well as rhythm and texture being more important than melody. Laurence MacDonald writes, "Howard's melodic ideas are of secondary importance to the score's driving rhythms, which enhance the film at every turn."[56] The music reflects the ongoing tensions of the film: Did Richard Kimball (Harrison Ford) kill his wife? If not, who did? Will Kimball be caught by Deputy Gerard (Tommy Lee Jones)? Will Kimball solve the puzzle of his wife's murder? The intensity in the film is portrayed through an orchestra that is constantly in motion. Rapid runs on the piano, percussion, layering of different orchestral timbres, and quick changes in texture propel this intensity.

Howard also uses Leitmotiv in the film, using a four-note motive, E-B-D-A, at various points in the film. Another Leitmotiv, what director Andrew Davis referred to as the "Kimball Theme," is heard several times during the film, and is heard as the End Credits begin.[57] This Leitmotiv is a bit more intricate, as Kimball and his situation are complex. Instead of a single musical line, a bit of counterpoint is present to show the facets of Kimball. Howard composed a bass line similar to a chaconne, except that the bass line is not always consistent. The melodic line on top of it is syncopated, with the longest note of each measure of 1 falling on beat two.[58]

A montage cue that incorporates rock and jazz elements, and is much less typically orchestral, is used to propel the narrative and the intensity of the film. Speaking about the montage scenes, Davis says, "James's music sort of ties it [the montage] all together."[59] In summarizing his feelings on the music, director Davis stated, "I feel that the score is an incredibly important part of this movie, and I was very lucky to work with James on it."[60] The work was strong enough that Davis would hire Howard to compose music for *A Perfect Murder* five years later.

The final cue segues into the End Credits, which immediately begin with a statement of the Kimball Theme. The music then changes to the love music, back to the Kimball Theme, a brief statement of chase music, and finally to a fully orchestrated Kimball theme. Clearly the main character is Richard Kimball, even though more people may remember Deputy Gerard from the film. Howard's music reinforces who the film's protagonist is.

Wyatt Earp

In 1994, Howard scored the three-hour western epic *Wyatt Earp*, which follows Earp through his youth, his first marriage, his time in Dodge City, and the events in Tombstone before ending on a ship in Alaska with his wife Josie. When interviewed in 1994, shortly after completing the score, he said, "I probably listened to every western soundtrack ever written to see how other composers did before me, especially since *Wyatt Earp* was my first score in the genre," and named Alfred Newman's score for *How the West Was Won* as a model.[61] Howard also said that he spent about five months working on the film's score, which contained nearly two hours of music.[62] With the amount of time that he had, Howard was constantly reworking the cues, both because he was unsatisfied, and because director Lawrence Kasdan was not satisfied. Howard said, "Larry liked my work, but he made me rewrite a wagon chase cue 87 times! That's more than I've ever changed a piece of music for any director, including Barbra Streisand."[63] While Howard was not starting over with his cues, he would make small changes, attempting to capture the exact desire of Kasdan.

As the film is a western, that style of music would certainly be invoked, as well as the music of American composer Aaron Copland, who somewhat defined the sound of the American West.[64] This was not Howard's first attempt at invoking Copland's style, as he had done that earlier in *Everybody's All-American*. So, in an attempt to separate his music from that of Copland's, Howard wrote multiple cues in $\frac{5}{8}$ meter. Concerning the asymmetrical meter, Howard said, "Actually I kind of got stuck in $\frac{5}{8}$ meter and had trouble getting out of it for years. I would feel like I was in four and I was really in five. You get so used to it. It starts to feel so comfortable. But when someone else hears it for the first time, it has a limping quality to it. I ended up writing $\frac{5}{8}$ in *Wyatt Earp*, which was probably a big mistake."[65] Howard's use of $\frac{5}{8}$ can be traced back as far as his solo album from the 1970s, and asymmetrical meter continued to feature in films from this time period, including *Outbreak* and *Waterworld*.

Howard's music contains several Leitmotivs that return during the course of the film. The music for the Main Titles is one of those motives.[66] Played by the horn, it invokes Copland and the epic nature of the film, while also representing the wide-open spaces of the nineteenth-century American West. This motive returns multiple times, including when the family moves across the Great Plains, and when the Earps move to Tombstone. A second Leitmotiv is first sounded when Wyatt's father tells young Wyatt about lawless men. The motive is later sounded for Wyatt, who has been thrown in jail. Howard also wrote a love theme, initially heard when Wyatt and Urilla, his first wife, seek shelter from the rain in an empty house. The theme, played by the English horn, is sounded again for their wedding night. Despite Wyatt's relationship with Maddie Blaylock, the love theme is not sounded while he is with her. It returns when Wyatt shares his memory of Urilla with Josie, his future wife.

When asked what it was like to score a western, Howard responded, "[W]hat worried me most was coming up with a memorable theme, because any film that wants to be an epic has got to have a great piece of music. . . . I think it's one of my best efforts, and am really happy with the main title."[67] At the time, *Wyatt Earp* was the most music that

Howard had ever composed for a single film. Howard had a chance to reflect on his score in 2006 and called it, "The greatest musical opportunity of all time. I took a decidedly un-Western approach to it. There was a big romantic epic quality to the music, which I think was OK. (It features) the best love theme I ever wrote, my favorite one still."[68] Howard clearly was proud of his work just after completing it, and still pleased over a decade later. Despite the film's relative lack of critical and commercial success, Howard's score was quite effective.

Outbreak

The 1995 film *Outbreak*, about an Ebola-like outbreak in a small California town, featured music similar to that of *The Fugitive*. This is due, in large part, to the fact that both films are essentially action films. Like *The Fugitive*, much of the "chase" or "running" music in *Outbreak* is not melodically based, but texturally and timbrally based. While Howard does write a melodic theme for the relationship between Sam (Dustin Hoffman) and Robbie (Rene Russo), melody is not what drives the score. Howard said, "I think I'm only lately getting away from that [being too thematic] or becoming able to write freely. I think that it's really all about counterpoint—more counterpoint and less melody. Just dig into the texture of the music rather than the melody or the theme."[69] The melodic themes present in *Outbreak* are often accompanied with identifying instruments or textures, since the melodies are often no more than a few notes, rather than lengthy themes. One of these identifying elements is the meter often used to accompany the American military, $\frac{5}{4}$. He has said that the asymmetrical meter is indicative of the military being out of alignment with what should be done versus what is actually being done.[70] Another is the music specific to the "host," the monkey that has both the virus and the antibodies to the virus. The music sounds hopeful and mysterious, involving a (synthesized) celesta.

With *Outbreak*, Howard's approach to orchestration changed. Until then, Howard would essentially orchestrate the entire score, leaving only proofreading and notational adjustments for his orchestrators. Regarding *Outbreak*, Howard said, "There was just no time for me to orchestrate. . . . I had to write eighty-five minutes of music in five weeks. There was just no way in the world that I could have copied it out! So what I did was give my sequences to my copyist, who created a midi-file extraction and output my demos, which are pretty complete and extremely elaborate."[71] Due to his deadline, Howard had to give his orchestrators more control, but because Howard's mockups are so close to complete, the job of the orchestrators is easier, as much of Howard's orchestration is done before it reaches his orchestrators.

The significant use of percussion, coupled with the use of asymmetrical meter, is what sets this score apart from previous films. Howard's use of nonmelodic instruments strongly represents the militaristic nature and character of the film, and the asymmetrical meter comments on the "correctness" of the actions of the military. *Outbreak* is also the film where Howard began relinquishing complete control over his orchestrations; he has never returned to his original approach.

My Best Friend's Wedding

My Best Friend's Wedding was the first of four films that Howard scored for director P. J. Hogan. It also earned Howard his third Academy Award nomination for Best Score. The film is a romantic comedy, but one where Julianne (Julia Roberts) attempts to break up the wedding of her best friend Michael (Dermot Mulroney) and his fiancée Kim (Cameron Diaz). Howard's score fits his previous work in the genre, sharing similar orchestrations with films such as *Pretty Woman* and *Dave*. The music is primarily scored for piano, strings, and woodwinds, with the clarinet or oboe often playing the melody. However, Howard's music for *Wedding* is more mature than his earlier work in the genre. His music accentuates the angle that Roberts's character takes in trying to split up the engaged couple, portraying her feelings and intentions, playing up her mischievous acts, emphasizing her jealousy, and telling the audience when she regrets her actions.

In a further level of sophistication, two of Howard's cues stylistically resemble the High Classical music of Mozart and Haydn. The third movement of Mozart's *Eine kleine Nachtmusik*, K. 525, is used early in the film in a scene where Roberts stumbles into wedding preparations. She is now actively trying to stop the wedding. The diegetic music of Mozart will give way to the nondiegetic music of Howard. When Howard, as pseudo-Mozart, uses this style, it is when Roberts tells lies about Mulroney to Diaz, in an attempt to split them up. Howard called this score "My favorite romantic comedy score since 'Dave.'. . . One of my more touching compositions (occurs) toward the end, a solo piano piece when she [Julia Roberts] admits that she wishes she would have been with Dermot Mulroney."[72] Howard's music in the romantic comedy genre had fully matured, as evidenced by his quote about the "touching" music. He no longer felt embarrassed about his earlier "piano scores," which seemed to dominate his writing for this type of film, and this maturity earned an Academy Award nomination, something that his work on *Pretty Woman* and *Dave* failed to do. The score demonstrates Howard's absolute mastery of the genre.

Snow Falling on Cedars

Howard's score for the 1999 film *Snow Falling on Cedars* was perhaps his most effective at that point in his career. The film's plot concerned Kazuo (Rick Yune), a Japanese-American man on trial for the murder of an American fisherman, Carl Heine. Howard's music utilizes traditional Japanese instruments, such as taiko drums, various gongs and wind chimes, and a shakuhachi, a transverse flute, to incorporate the ethnicity of the Japanese immigrants on San Piedro Island in northern Washington. Howard also used choir and various electronics, which, along with sound effects, makes for a fascinating sound design. As much of the film deals with the mystery of how Carl was killed, Howard's music is often tonally ambiguous, even ominous, with extended passages of low sustained pedal tones to enhance the tension.

As the film's director Scott Hicks has stated, the film's temp track contained examples from Polish composer Krzysztof Penderecki[73] and American composer Philip Glass.[74] Estonian composer Arvo Pärt's work *Fratres* may have also part of the temp track as well.[75] Like much of Penderecki's, Glass's, and Pärt's music, Howard's score rarely contains points of resolution. Cues are often left sounding tonally incomplete or unfinished, with endings only made clear through crescendos or the use of specific instruments.

Howard again makes use of Leitmotiv, both melodically and instrumentally. The solo cello seems to represent Kazuo, as it is heard, most notably, when he is testifying in his own defense, and again, when the charges against him are dismissed. Howard also incorporates a four-note motive, usually sounded on the pitches C-B-D-C.[76] This motive is heard when Ishmael (Ethan Hawke), a reporter, is involved with Hatsue (Yûki Kudô), before the war; she is now Kazuo's wife. The motive represents their illicit love, from young adults through when she sends him a letter during the war ending their relationship. In the director's commentary on the DVD, the first time the motive is used, Scott Hicks says, "James Newton Howard's score here develops the mantra of this young love story in the most extraordinary way."[77] In what would foreshadow Howard's score for *The Village*, an arpeggiating violin is also used multiple times in the film.

As a result of the film's narrative strategy, which contains flashbacks and is not told linearly, Howard's score contains more contrapuntal music than any other score to this point in his career. Howard said, "With *Snow Falling on Cedars* I worked so hard writing things out. I spent weeks working on the string counterpoint. Consequently it's some of the least 'James Newton Howard' sounding music I've ever done. That's a good thing!"[78] The more contrapuntal music is, the more technically complex it is, and the music's complexity reflects the complexity of the film. Howard is quoted as saying, "It's probably the least linear movie I've ever done," and shares similarities with his score for *Grand Canyon*.[79] Hicks had previously used Howard's music for *Grand Canyon* as temp tracks, and was interested in using a repeated harmonic pattern in *Snow Falling on Cedars* like Howard had done in *Grand Canyon*. Howard said, "That can be the greatest challenge of all, to recreate something you've done before without it sounding like the same thing."[80] The chord pattern musically connects the various threads of the film, aiding the nonlinear narrative of the film.

The End Credits in *Snow Falling on Cedars* depict the scene of a dead man in the water near his boat, the snowstorm during the trial, Ishmael's memories of the war, and the essence of mankind. While Howard has said that longer melodies tend to tell people too much about what to think about the onscreen action, Howard's End Credits remove any confusion about what was really important in the film.

Howard's score has been critically praised, with Jonathan Kaplan of *Film Score Monthly* naming the score one of the best of 1999.[81] Various online soundtrack review sites celebrate this score, including Film Tracks, rating it four (out of five) stars.[82] In the 2010 interview with Reynolds and Brill, Howard discussed his pleasure with his music: "There's a scene in *Snow Falling on Cedars* I like, which is the summation for the defense by Max von Sydow, that sequence that's kind of a montage of him walking on the beach, and the choral bit. I think that's a really nice moment."[83] In his reflection with Burlingame in 2006, Howard said about *Cedars*, "I'm very proud of that score . . . a really good example of a director pushing me to come up with alternate solutions to situations. It was an extraordinarily beautiful movie that I was very close to. It seems that the ones that matter the most to you get the least attention."[84] Director Hicks states, "I think that James Newton Howard just created the most extraordinary atmospheric cues throughout the film."[85] Howard's score received acclaim from the director, the composer, and the film score community. Even though the film was not as successful as had been hoped, the score for *Snow Falling on Cedars* is a watershed moment in his compositional career.

Conclusion

Like many Hollywood composers, James Newton Howard uses the same musical compositional techniques available to everyone. Howard makes significant use of Leitmotiv (or theme) in his film scores, but also makes use of three- and four-note motives that are significantly shorter than a Leitmotiv. He also uses techniques such as ostinatos and pedals as ways to sustain intensity and suspense without writing music that might get in the way of a scene, like Stravinsky or Jerry Goldsmith. Most importantly, Howard's use of rhythm and percussion separate him from other composers. Very few film composers have Howard's background in popular music, and he makes use of that background with syncopated rhythms, orchestral and electronic percussion, and asymmetrical meters, particularly $\frac{5}{4}$ or $\frac{7}{8}$. Additionally, Howard's background as a classical pianist gives him insight into the developmental process of composers from the nineteenth century. Howard is familiar with how motives can be manipulated over the course of a piano movement or full piece, and uses that knowledge to his advantage when dealing with his own music.

Howard is reliant on technology for his film scores, entering most of his information digitally via synthesizers. Howard can compose while viewing a rough cut of the film, and can edit and add tracks all from the comfort of his studio. His orchestrators can then turn the demos into a fully realized orchestral score.

Howard's mixed background gives him advantages in working in Hollywood, because he is able to score in any film genre. His music has covered styles as diverse as jazz, blues, and urban rock, as well as orchestral music for romantic comedies and Westerns. He has composed music that utilizes ethnic instruments when necessary, and accentuated action and thriller films with his chase music. His use of percussion sets him apart from nearly every other composer, particularly in those action sequences.

Howard has benefitted from choosing the right projects when they have been offered to him. Some of these projects resulted from existing relationships with directors, while others can be attributed to working on a solid film. Being asked to compose music for *Pretty Woman* advanced his career, particularly in the romantic comedy genre, and within the same decade, he had mastered music in those films to the extent that he earned an Oscar nomination for Best Score. He scored *The Fugitive*, in part, due to his relationship with director Andrew Davis. His score for *Dave* contributed to a commercially and critically strong film. He began the 1990s as a relative newcomer to big-budget Hollywood films, but by the end of the decade, James Newton Howard was a well-known composer working in Hollywood. His work with Shyamalan, and his other work in the 2000s would elevate his name to one of the top film composers in the business.

Trying to isolate or articulate a style specific to James Newton Howard is a difficult proposition at best. His work is widely diverse, both in terms of genre and in terms of orchestration. He has composed

scores that are fully electronic, fully acoustic, and everything in between. He has composed music for all genres of films, defying being
typecast or pigeonholed into one or two genres. He has been asked directly about the elements that go into his style, and how he himself
would classify his style. Most of these questions have been deflected
and left unanswered. He finally relented, saying that he is a melodic
composer, even in short motives, but that statement doesn't clearly articulate style. Howard's unwillingness to answer the question is similar
to living composer Arvo Pärt, who rejects questions regarding his style
from interviewers. With Pärt's music (which Howard closely replicates
in *Snow Falling on Cedars*), there is a certain element that cannot be
explained or isolated, but denotes his music as clearly his. Pärt is un-
willing to give up his secret. Howard is much more of a moving target,
pleased when he "doesn't sound like himself," chameleon-like in his
ability to change musical style and film genre, a composer who is more
interested in serving the best interests of the film and the director than
he is on imposing his own musical fingerprints. James Newton Howard's "style" is what is best suited for his current project.

3

Historical and Critical Context of *Signs*

Science fiction films have been a staple of Hollywood filmmaking since early cinema. In the 1930s and 1940s, many of the classic monster films were made, such as *Dracula, Frankenstein, The Invisible Man, The Wolf Man,* and *King Kong.* These films all invoke a level of supernatural, something that cannot be explained by science, but is still of this world. Many science fiction films are centered on space travel, and when the monsters are no longer from Earth, they are aliens. Within the science fiction genre, the alien invasion film, a subgenre, exists as its own type of film. In the majority of these films, an alien invasion is a bad thing for humanity, as the aliens look to conquer the planet, often to create a new home or to pillage and harvest Earth's natural resources. The atomic age greatly accelerated these fears, for if we could destroy our own planet, why couldn't another species? The alien invasion subgenre of films became prominent during the 1950s, when some of the best films of that subgenre were made, such as *The Day the Earth Stood Still* and *Invasion of the Body Snatchers.* Invasion films continue to be made, with *Pacific Rim* (2013) and *Edge of Tomorrow* (2014) as recent examples.

Every science fiction film abides by its own internal logic, meaning that ground rules are established early in the film, and the narrative of the film should derive from these ground rules. As viewers of a film, we are asked to suspend our beliefs in reality and accept the reality presented by the film. In *Signs,* the audience is asked to accept a number of science fiction elements: an alien invasion that has the potential to be hostile, advanced technology and camouflage, and belief in a divine entity or spirit (God). As discussed later in this chapter, the most

51

significant of those elements is the belief in God, since the film's central character has lost his faith.

Signs wrestles with issues of faith and belief, of family and protection, and of salvation from deep loss. Elements from science fiction and horror films are recalled in *Signs*, drawing on films such as Alfred Hitchcock's *The Birds*, for its element of unexplained events, George Romero's *Night of the Living Dead*, for the supernatural and for the claustrophobia within a house, and the original *Invasion of the Body Snatchers*, for its lengthy periods of suspense.[1] While not quite as critically revered as the most celebrated alien invasion films of the 1950s, *Signs* is viewed quite favorably, with a positive rating of three out of every four reviews, and was extremely commercially successful. As a post-1990 alien invasion film, it is one of the most successful films in the genre, not relying on a multitude of special effects and CGI and not utilizing an overabundance of music, like many of those films. It is a serious and dramatic film that still displays elements of humor and tenderness, and while the elements of action that drive so many other films are absent in *Signs*, the tension is present through the passages of suspense, and through the avoidance of clearly seeing an alien until the conclusion of the film. *Signs* also contains a significant element of religion and faith, as the protagonist searches for signs that God is present, watching over him and his family. The audience even views the farmhouse and the town through the God's-Eye View, indicating His presence. While *Signs* contains elements of the supernatural, those events are not so far-fetched that they could be impossible, like in most science fiction films.

This chapter provides a brief history of the alien invasion film, identifying significant science fiction elements in these films. These elements will be shown to be common to both earlier films and *Signs*, creating a canon of works to which *Signs* can be compared. *Signs* will also be critically evaluated on its own merits, through reviews and through secular and religious comparisons. Through these critical comparisons and observations, *Signs* will be situated within the science fiction canon, showing that the film itself deserves to be discussed alongside some of the best films within the alien invasion canon.

A Brief History of Alien Invasion Films

Prior to 1945, films about alien invasions were rare, but the fascination with space travel and otherworldly creatures was common. As early as the 1860s, Jules Verne wrote about voyages of the fantastic: to space, underwater, and to the planet's core in such stories as *From the Earth* to the Moon, *Twenty Thousand Leagues Under the Sea*, and *Journey to the Center of the Earth*. Attempts were made to adapt these stories, referred to as *Voyages Extraordinaires*, for the stage. When moving pictures were created in the 1890s, a new medium became available to writers and directors. In his book *Hollywood Science*, Sidney Perkowitz refers to Georges Méliès's 1902 film *Le Voyage dans la Lune* as "the first true science fiction motion picture."[2] Little of early film centered around science fiction. Instead of exploring space, pre-1945 films tended to feature supernatural creatures, often based on fiction from the nineteenth century. Films such as *Nosferatu* (1922), *The Phantom of the Opera* (1925), *Frankenstein* (1931), *Dracula* (1931), *Dr. Jekyll and Mr. Hyde* (1931), *The Mummy* (1932), *The Invisible Man* (1933), and *The Wolf Man* (1941) defined the early horror genre and were popular with audiences. During the 1940s and 1950s, the invasion film exploded in popularity. Several sources, including Vivian Sobchack's *Screening Space* and Patrick Lucanio's *Them or Us* discuss alien films and space films in detail.[3] In order to position *Signs* within the alien invasion canon, a short history of alien invasion films will be given, beginning with films from the 1950s, as they codified the genre and display characteristics seen in *Signs* as well as contemporary invasion films.[4]

Introduction to Science Fiction Films

Science fiction literature of the nineteenth century was visionary, excited by the possibilities that science could open to humanity, but after atomic explosions in Hiroshima and Nagasaki in 1945, "SF writers were neither as optimistic about nor unafraid of science as they previously had been, and their stories and novels reflected their age and anxiety."[5] After seeing the aftermath and repercussions of that weapon, the fear that a nuclear war could occur was on the minds of everyone, including filmmakers and writers. The post-atomic world saw the birth of critically acclaimed science fiction films. In her book *Screening Space*, Vivian Sobchack writes, "In this context, it must also be remembered that although the SF film existed in isolated instances before World War II, it only emerged as a *critically* recognized genre *after* Hiroshima. . . . The film genre, emerging when it did, had no roots in the philosophical attitudes of the nineteenth century."[6] Since film did not need to tether itself to earlier times, it was able to seize on contemporary fears, topics, and issues. The result was the production of several highly acclaimed science fiction films, particularly those in the subgenre of alien invasion. Not all aliens in these films attempted to destroy humanity, but that was the most common fear portrayed.

Science Fiction Films of the 1950s

The year 1951 saw three great science fiction films: *The Thing from Another World, The Day the Earth Stood Still,* and *When Worlds Collide.*[7] *The Thing from Another World* is based on the 1938 novella "Who Goes There?" by John Wood Campbell, Jr., one of the most significant science fiction authors of the twentieth century. Perkowitz writes that *The Thing* "tells of an unearthly creature whose spacecraft has crashed in the Arctic, a big, strong, mobile plant that ferociously seeks human blood. Aliens have figured in film after film ever since, right up to *War of the Worlds* (2005)."[8] The secondary issue in *The Thing* concerns the quest for answers. Perkowitz states, "Like Dr. Frankenstein, this cold-blooded scientist, [Dr. Carrington], puts the search for knowledge above human concerns. In the midst of the Cold War between the United States and the Soviet Union, his portrayal represents a contemporary reaction to the nuclear science that had destroyed Hiroshima and Nagasaki and might destroy the world."[9] In the film, Carrington is willing to sacrifice human life in order to attempt to communicate with The Thing, going so far as to try to protect it after it kills people on the military base. Through the depiction of the hostile alien, the being that kills and cannot be reasoned with, an element of horror was introduced alongside the science fiction elements.

In *The Day the Earth Stood Still*, an alien named Klaatu, along with his robot Gort, travel to Earth in an attempt to get humanity to disarm itself of nuclear weapons. The film is based on the short story "Farewell to the Master" written by Harry Bates in 1940. Klaatu's appearance closely resembles humans. "Not only is he like us outside and inside (only better, with a longer life span and marvelous powers of recovery), he also looks good in both a futuristic, nicely tailored silver jump suit and ordinary Earthling wear."[10] Humanity does not listen to Klaatu, and ends up shooting him; he is temporarily revived by Gort. In his departing speech, Klaatu warns the people of Earth that if they want to be part of the galactic community, they must behave in an appropriate fashion.[11] Klaatu doesn't just speak to the characters in the film, but also to the audience viewing it. While Klaatu is not hostile, he is perceived to be threatening. The film aligns with *Signs* in that both films ultimately acknowledge that there is a presence watching over the people of Earth. In *Signs*, the presence is divine, watching over humanity with a parental instinct; in *The Day the Earth Stood Still*, the presence is the galactic community.

One of the earliest and best known science fiction novels to incorporate an alien attack on Earth was H. G. Wells's *War of the Worlds* in 1898, made even more famous in 1938 with Orson Welles's radio broadcast adapted from the novel. The novel was the basis for a film adaptation in 1953. *War of the Worlds* (dir. Byron Haskin) transported Wells' Victorian-era London to "present day" southern California. Like so many films of the time, a primary source of anxiety was the presence of the atomic bomb, which is ineffectively used as a measure of desperation against the Martians. Ultimately, the Martians, who cannot be defeated with weapons, are defeated by bacteria, the most basic of organisms. They are hostile, have no place for religion, and are insistent on destroying humanity. Their technology is so advanced that the world's military cannot harm them at all, including through the use of a nuclear weapon.

Invaders from Mars (dir. William Cameron Menzies) was also released in 1953.[12] As children's fears and nightmares are dismissed by adults, so too is young David's claim of seeing a flying saucer land near his house. David finally convinces the local astronomer of the presence of the saucer, and he, in turn, convinces the army to take action. The saucer is destroyed before it can depart, and David is seen in bed, waking much as he did the first time, indicating that what we have seen is a dream. But then, the saucer from his dream lands in the same place as before. The audience is left trying to figure out if David is once again dreaming, trapped in a nightmare, or if he was having a premonition of an actual alien invasion. Again, the hostile aliens use their advanced technology to take over the planet, with the military intervening to stop them. The Martians do not want to destroy the planet, but they want to control, and potentially overrun it. In this way, the aliens in *Invaders from Mars* are very similar to the aliens in *Signs*, who have no intention of destroying the planet, but want to kidnap people for some horrific purpose. A common theme in all four of the films is the intervention of the military, with varying levels of results.

Much like the unstoppable force portrayed by the Martians in *War of the Worlds*, the title alien from 1958's *The Blob* (dir. Irvin Yeaworth) could not be destroyed. The title creature crashes to Earth in a meteorite, and begins consuming everything it touches, both people and objects. As it consumes, it grows. The two teens who spotted the arrival of the meteorite are dismissed, with the adult authorities believing their story to be nothing more than a teenaged prank. The Blob only responded to cold, so it was successfully frozen and airlifted to the Arctic, where it is dropped. But the film concludes with the words "The End," which reform into a question mark, as the musical accompaniment, triumphant and final, shifts to an unresolved dissonant harmony.

The 1956 film *Invasion of the Body Snatchers* (dir. Don Siegel) is based on the 1954 novel, *The Body Snatchers*, by Jack Finney. In the film, a doctor is told by a number of his patients that their loved ones have been replaced, and dismisses it as simple hysteria, even though his voice-over narration tells us he believes something is wrong. The following evening, the doctor finds replacement versions of himself and others emerging from what appear to be large seed pods. The doctor even sees truckloads of these seed pods being delivered to the town. The suspicion is that people are replaced by the "pod people" when they fall asleep, and these "pod people" are physical duplicates, but lack any emotion or sense of individuality. The doctor escapes the town by making his way onto a highway, screaming at the passing motorists, "They're here already! You're next! You're next!" No particular being appears to be in charge, as the pod people have a hive mentality, attempting to spread from the initial point of entry. No mention is made of their origin, nor do they possess any particular technology, other than the pods. They do tell the humans that the conversion process is painless, intimating friendly intentions, even though their goal is clearly hostile. The film contains few special effects, closely aligning *Body Snatchers* with *Signs*.

Science Fiction Films of the 1960s and 1970s

The 1960s saw few alien invasion films of consequence. NASA's space exploration and race to the moon was more interesting than fiction. The closest thing to a significant invasion film in the 1960s would be 1968's *2001: A Space Odyssey* (dir. Stanley Kubrick) because of the alien intelligence that appears via the monolith.

When Steven Spielberg's aliens invaded Earth, it was not to overthrow it, but to connect and communicate with it. *Close Encounters of the Third Kind* (1977) featured a communion with aliens instead of invasion, and also featured tremendous visual effects with an outstanding original score. John Williams's score did not win the 1978 Oscar, losing to his own score for *Star Wars*. In *Close Encounters*, a number of humans who had been abducted are returned, and Roy Neary (Richard Dreyfuss) willingly travels with the aliens away from Earth. The spirit of exploration and wonder of the universe are paramount in the film, as opposed to the paranoia and destruction of so many of the films of the 1950s. The intentions of the aliens remain unknown until the conclusion of the film, when the aliens are revealed to be explorers, and not hostile. Spielberg's next alien film was 1982's *E.T.: The Extra-Terrestrial*.[13] Once again, the aliens are not hostile; the titular creature is a botanist who accidentally gets left behind on Earth, forming a bond with a young boy named Elliott. The most aggressive characters in the film are the military, occupying Elliott's home and trying to experiment on *E.T.* Spielberg's films changed the intentions of aliens from hostile to explorers, and made that element possible in invasion films.

Science Fiction Films of the 1990s

Invasion films of the 1980s tended to be cheap campy films, such as *Killer Klowns from Outer Space* and other B-Movie fare. Most attempts at serious films are unmemorable, but the 1990s brought about a number of films that resurrected the genre from the scrap heap of Saturday afternoon and late-nite UHF programming, including *Independence Day* (1996, dir. Roland Emmerich), *Mars Attacks!* (1996, dir. Tim Burton), *Men in Black* (1997, dir. Barry Sonnenfeld), and *Starship Troopers* (1997, dir. Paul Verhoeven). Both *Independence Day* and *Mars Attacks!* are invasion films, where the aliens' objective is to take over Earth. The spaceships in *Independence Day* hover above all of the world's major cities and destroy them. Additionally, the alien ships and the individual fighters are protected by a field that renders all weapons against them ineffective, including nuclear weapons, connecting the film to *War of the Worlds*. The aliens are defeated when the mother ship is destroyed and the group on which the film has focused manages to bring down a ship over the Nevada desert.

Tim Burton's *Mars Attacks!* is intended to be campy in terms of its appearance, as an homage to the B-movies of the 1950s. The Martians hide their intentions to colonize Earth, and after disintegrating hundreds of influential politicians and celebrities, the Martians attack monuments and iconic buildings across the world. They are defeated as their heads explode when forced to listen to loud music, an absurd winning mechanism, but the film is not meant to be serious. Both *Independence Day* and *Mars Attacks!* are typical in that the aliens want to destroy humanity and take over the planet, but *Mars Attacks!* contains much more humor than *Independence Day*.

Men in Black concerns a secret government agency that deals with aliens who live on Earth. An alien "bug" crashes on Earth in an attempt to steal "the galaxy." The two Men in Black, J and K, have to prevent the bug from leaving Earth with the galaxy. In this film, the hostility is caused by a single alien, as Earth serves as a neutral planet. The aliens live on Earth, assimilating into everyday life, and causing few problems on a daily basis. The conflict only occurs when the bug lands on the planet, exhibiting hostility and aggression.

Starship Troopers is an example of humans bringing the fight to another planet. The mobile infantry travels to the Klendathu system because of long-distance attacks from the alien bugs, which is why the film can be considered as an invasion film. Ultimately, the "brain bug" is captured, with a psychic military officer informing everyone, "It's afraid. It's afraid!" *Starship Troopers* makes no secret of its commentary on fascism, with propaganda shorts inserted into the film. Unless action is taken, the result in both *Men in Black* and *Starship Troopers* is that Earth will be destroyed. These aliens do not negotiate.

Science Fiction Films since 2000

Since 2000, the majority of alien invasion films have been huge spectacles with large budgets and the expectation that they will reach "blockbuster" status. These films include *Men in Black II* (2002, dir. Barry Sonnenfeld), *Transformers* (2007, dir. Michael Bay), *District 9* (2009, dir. Neill Blomkamp), *Battle: Los Angeles* (2011, dir. Jonathan Liebesman), *Cowboys & Aliens* (2011, dir. Jon Favreau), *Super 8* (2011, dir. J. J. Abrams), *Pacific Rim* (2013, dir. Guillermo del Toro), and *Edge of Tomorrow* (2014, dir. Doug Liman).[14]

Both *Super 8* and *District 9* are set in the past. *Super 8* takes place in West Virginia in 1979, while *District 9* is set in Johannesburg, South Africa in 1982. Both films show aliens who are in distress and want to get home, not take over the planet, but are still treated with disdain, suspicion, and hostility.

In some invasion films, the objective of the aliens is clear. In *Battle: Los Angeles*, the aliens are here to take water from the oceans and then to eradicate humanity. The aliens in *Cowboys & Aliens* are in the Old West to not just discover humanity's weaknesses and eliminate them, but also to mine for gold. Unsurprisingly, with questionable motivations, neither film received very positive critical reviews.

Two factions of aliens, Autobots and Decepticons, are at the center of *Transformers*. The Autobots, the good cybernetic organisms, want to work with humanity to defeat the Decepticons, who want to destroy Earth to rebuild their home planet of Cybertron. Monsters, known in Japanese as "Kaiju," appear in the Pacific Ocean through a dimensional portal in the floor of the ocean in *Pacific Rim*. In order to defeat the Kaijus, humanity builds enormous machines called "Jaegers," the German word for "hunters." In the film, it is learned that the Kaijus are not arbitrarily attacking but that they are exploiting the Jaegers' weaknesses in order to conquer humanity and take over the planet. The aliens in *Edge of Tomorrow* are referred to as "mimics," and their invasion begins in Europe. Following a victory at the Battle of Verdun, humanity feels like it has the upper hand against the mimics, until a ground offensive on the French coast destroys the human army. Through killing a mimic "alpha," Cage (Tom Cruise), acquires the ability to reset the day when he dies, and, like in a video game, is able to get a little bit further each time. The mimics are controlled by a creature referred to as the "omega." Cage and his military company leave in the middle of the night, and are successful in killing the omega and winning the war. The motivations of the aliens in these films are to eradicate humanity and take over or consume the planet.

Summary

The vast majority of alien invasion films, which initially became popular in the 1950s, demonstrate a level of hostility from the invaders, often with the aliens trying to conquer the planet, or destroy enough of humanity to appropriate Earth's natural resources. The aliens in *Signs* fit this model quite well. The films that do not depict aliens as hostile are rare, but audiences respond to them, as both *Close Encounters* and *E.T.* set box office records: *Close Encounters* was the highest grossing movie from Columbia Pictures at its point of release, and *E.T.* held the global box office record from 1983 to 1993. As special effects improved, alien invasion films often became more dependent on these effects, leading to a lack of critical acclaim for many of these films. However, because of the spectacle and possibility of extraterrestrial life, the subgenre of the alien invasion film has remained strong for over sixty years, and shows no signs of slowing down any time soon.

Where does *Signs* fit within this genre? Like most invasion films from the 1950s, *Signs* is not reliant upon special effects; most of the film occurs in and around the farmhouse. Spaceships are seen, but only on television, and only at night, when their lights are on. This sets *Signs* apart from most of the invasion films in the 1990s and 2000s. It is intended to be serious, separating it from *Mars Attacks!* The aliens are not on Earth because they wish to communicate with humans, as in the Spielberg films. Instead, they are hostile, intending to "harvest" people and take them back to their home planet. *Signs* also contains a sense of horror, not just that the invasion is occurring, but the horror at Graham having lost his faith. The element of horror likens it to *The Thing*. However, the horror in that film was that the alien could be anywhere, and in the 1982 remake of *The Thing*, it could be anyone or anything. The horror in *Signs* is different, since the aliens don't formally attack until the full invasion actually occurs, and the television switches to an "off-the-air" graphic. *Signs* is just more than an invasion film, as it deals with deeper issues. *Signs* even more closely aligns itself with *The Day the Earth Stood Still*, because of its minimal special effects, dialogue-driven story, and its message. The message in *The Day the Earth Stood Still* is that the rest of the galaxy will be watching to see Earth's decision to give up its warring ways. In *Signs*, the being doing the watching is God, as Graham eventually finds his faith again and learns that someone is watching out for him, and for everyone. *Signs* shares characteristics with several of the films within the science fiction genre and alien invasion subgenre, but is different enough that the film can be considered to be unique within both the genre of science fiction and subgenre of the alien invasion film.

Religious Elements in *Signs*

Faith in a divine being is a central issue in *Signs*. However, the religious aspects of the film were not always reviewed positively. Even when media reviews did not always see the value in highlighting religion within the film, the arena of Christian film scholarship has made significant contributions in engaging with *Signs*.

Principal shooting for the film began outside Philadelphia on September 12, 2001, the day after the attacks on the World Trade Center in New York City. The film was released on August 3, 2002, slightly before the one-year anniversary of the attack. As a result, much of the scholarship that utilizes religion focuses on the tight-knit family unit in the film, as well as the issue of belief and doubt in God and dealing with troubling situations. One such book is *The Gospel according to Hollywood* that devotes a significant portion of its opening chapter, "Faith and Belief," to addressing *Signs*.[15] Greg Garrett writes, "A wondrous example of these two evidences of God—the marvelous everyday and the extraordinary marvel—comes together in M. Night Shyamalan's *Signs*."[16] Garrett even discusses the origin of the word "signs," coming from the New Testament Greek word "semeia," which generally translates as "signs," and quotes the Book of John, 4:48, where Jesus says, "Unless you see signs and wonders you will not believe."[17] This verse is almost the same as the question Graham poses to Merrill: What kind of a person are you? Are you the type that sees signs, sees miracles, or do you think that people just get lucky? The emphasis on the titular word is not by accident. Garrett writes,

> Shyamalan says that he and cinematographer Tak Fujimoto conceived of the entire movie as a metaphor (a sign, if you will), 'a conversation between God and this one man,' and he notes that the title, like most good titles, has multiple layers of meaning. It refers to the elaborate crop circles created as navigation devices by the invading aliens descending from outer space, as well as to 'the existence of signs from above in a kind of heavenly manner' for a man who has lost his faith and desperately needs to know that 'there's somebody out there' still watching over him.[18]

After his wife's death, Graham has only seen signs that God is not present, and has looked for ways to avoid God's presence in everyday elements. Garrett writes, "In the faith of his family, and in the belief that grows out of the events of the film, Graham comes again to have faith that there is a God, and to recognize that if this is true, we must believe in the dark times as well as in the times where there is evidence as far as the eye can see."[19] Garrett's statement can be taken in reference to the 9/11 attacks, in that despite the horrific tragedy of that day, the belief in God should be the one constant, the unwavering knowledge that someone is looking out for us.

Ecclesiastes, Job, and *Signs*

Other works of Christian film scholarship liken *Signs* to specific books of the Bible. Robert K. Johnston's *Useless Beauty* views various films via the Book of Ecclesiastes, while Cheryl Exum's chapter "Do You Feel Comforted?" in *Foster Biblical Scholarship* compares *Signs* to the Book of Job.[20] The Book of Ecclesiastes focuses on taking joy in life, even though our actions are ultimately meaningless. Events are predetermined, so when a positive event occurs, take joy in it, for God has provided that joy, but because events are predetermined, daily actions are performed in vain. In Johnston's chapter on *Signs*, "Can God be in This?," he frames the question as, "Where is God in the evil and tragedy of life?"[21] Johnston then proceeds to view the film as three connected stories: a film about an alien invasion, a film about a family suffering from the loss of the matriarch, and a film about the absence/presence of God. Johnston describes the two basic elements common to Shyamalan's first three films: the struggle to make sense of events in life and the significance of family as safe refuge from the world.[22] Those elements comprise the bulk of the Book of Ecclesiastes.

A more familiar portion of the Bible to most people is the Book of Job. Through the blessings of God, Job is wealthy, but has it all taken away and is made to suffer. Job is rewarded at the end of the Book for his faith with even greater blessings than before. Through Job's suffering, the question can be asked: Why do bad things happen to good people? The common thread between Ecclesiastes and Job is the search for wisdom, dealing with "Why" questions, so while the content may seem different, the prevailing themes in the two Books are quite similar. Cheryl Exum's chapter compares the two protagonists, Job and Graham. Like Job, Graham is blessed with a wife, children, and a farm, and is a "man of God." But when his wife is taken from him, he does not understand why. Unlike Job, Graham turns his back on God, first denying His existence, then cursing Him before having his faith restored at the end of the film. Exum writes, "Ultimately what brings about a change in Graham, as in Job, is a *deus ex machina*: in Job's case, the appearance of God; in Graham's, it is not so much the appearance of extraterrestrials as their hasty, unanticipated departure."[23] Exum then takes on the ending of *Signs*, arguing that "Graham's existential dilemma—either there are no coincidences or we are all on our own," is disappointing to viewers, because it cages the positions of the issue too antithetically, and in order to have his son's life saved, his wife had to die.[24] Ultimately Graham sees signs and miracles again. Exum concludes by showing the epilogues to be quite similar: "[They are] brief, the hero is no longer defiant, and he is restored to his previous way of life."[25] The brief epilogue in *Signs* has no dialogue, and the musical cue from the film's climax, "The Hand of Fate Part 2," continues into the epilogue. Graham is seen putting his collar on and smiling, his children's laughs heard in the background. Exum writes, "Both *Signs* and the book of Job make us aware of the precarious lot of humanity in a world that is now and then bewildering and unaccommodating."[26] Graham and Job are certainly similar characters, and their journeys do share some parallels. However, while Job essentially loses everything, Graham does not, and while Job does not completely give up on God, Graham does for a significant amount of time, both before the film begins, and during the film's narrative. Only in the presence of signs does Graham find his way back.

The academic religious community has critically commented on *Signs*, relating Graham's struggles to specific books of the Bible, and on the journey of the "hero," from belief to disbelief and back. While the religious element of the film was not necessarily advertised in the promotion of the film, it is certainly significant to the narrative and significant enough to spark academic work on the film and its relationship to both modern society and Biblical thought.

Shyamalan as a "Hot" Director

Shyamalan made two films, *Praying with Anger* (1992) and *Wide Awake* (1998), before his breakthrough with *The Sixth Sense* in 1999. Through the critical and commercial success of *The Sixth Sense*, he was nominated for Oscars for Best Direction and Best Original Screenplay, and the film was nominated for Best Picture. *The Sixth Sense* immediately propelled Shyamalan into the upper echelon of directors.

Immediately, Shyamalan was viewed as a hot young director and writer, and was involved, at times, with several productions. In 2000, he was in talks with Steven Spielberg to write a script for a fourth Indiana Jones film, but couldn't make it work at the time. Instead, Shyamalan went on to write the screenplay for *Signs*.[27]

The success of *The Sixth Sense* hinged on the ending twist, that Dr. Malcolm Crowe (Bruce Willis) had been dead since the opening of the film. When Cole (Haley Joel Osment) tells Dr. Crowe his secret—that "I see dead people. Walking around like regular people. They don't see each other; they only see what they want to see. They don't know they're dead"—Cole is in a hospital, the lights in the room are out, and he has the blanket pulled up to his chin. The clue that Dr. Crowe is dead is the blanket, as the film has established that the temperature drops when Cole closely encounters a ghost. Following this admission, Cole continues to treat Dr. Crowe as though he's alive, keeping the twist still secret. The locking of Malcolm's basement office, his inability to speak with his wife, and her new suitor can all be explained by the marital problems that Malcolm believes that they are having. It's only at the end of the film, when she is watching their wedding video and has fallen asleep that we see her cold breath, and she asks, "Why did you leave, Malcolm," that we learn that he actually died in the shooting shown at the start of the film. In her article "Mind-Tricking Narratives," Cornelia Klecker uses the titular term to be synonymous with the phrase "brilliant plot twists."[28] She writes,

> When we look at the landscape of mainstream film in recent years, meticulously designed narratives that force the audience to participate actively and lead up to the final mind-boggling plot twist have been extremely popular. M. Night Shyamalan is probably the most famous director in this trend in film, and his *The Sixth Sense*, released in 1999, is definitely the best-known and, with about a $300 million box office gross in the United States alone, the most successful representative.[29]

Audiences and critics alike initially loved the film, and that allowed Shyamalan the freedom to make his next film, *Unbreakable*.

According to Michael Fleming of *Daily Variety*, Shyamalan received "$10 million upfront for" *Unbreakable*, and the deal, "which included $5 for his spec script, broke the spec auction record."[30] While *Unbreakable* was received relatively positively by critics, the domestic box office was disappointing, as it did less than $100 million.[31] The results led some to wonder if *Unbreakable* was simply an example of the "sophomore slump," or if Shyamalan would ever have a huge hit again. Disney believed in Shyamalan. Fleming wrote,

> "In what is believed to be an eight-figure deal, Walt Disney Pictures has made a preemptive purchase of 'Signs,' a thriller with supernatu-

ral overtones that M. Night Shyamalan wrote and will direct in the
fall. The studio moved quickly to keep Shyamalan in the fold after
his first two Disney efforts, 'The Sixth Sense' and 'Unbreakable,'
collectively grossed nearly $1 billion worldwide. Shyamalan deliv-
ered the script to studio brass on Saturday. Peter Schneider, Nina Ja-
cobson and Dick Cook read it quickly, and came to terms with
Shyamalan's UTA agents and attorneys by early the following morning."[32]

It is clear from the Disney executives that they believed that they had a
huge film on their hands, and wanted to ensure that they would be the
ones promoting the hot director.

The teaser trailer for *Signs* used much of the music that would end
up as the "Main Titles" cue, and created a strong buzz about the film.[33]
With good publicity leading up to the film's release, Shyamalan was
featured on the cover of *Newsweek* at the time of the film's release.
Aside from a single sentence that mentions *Signs* and directs readers to
the review later in the magazine, the story "Out of This World," written
by Jeff Giles, focuses exclusively on Shyamalan, his background, his
motivation, and his family. Giles includes statements in his story such
as "director M. Night Shyamalan is proving himself to be our next great
storyteller," and "Shyamalan is every bit the movie buff that the '70s
auteurs were. His idols are unapologetically pop, though: not Fellini,
Bergman and Kurosawa, but Hitchcock, Lucas and Spielberg."[34] Giles
tells his readers that Shyamalan is a student of cinema, but also wants
to appeal to mass audiences through films that feature strong family-
units and good story telling. Giles also writes, "Now he's [Shyamalan]
attempting to turn his name into a brand, like Spielberg, so that on
opening weekend audiences will converge not to see a Mel Gibson or a
Bruce Willis movie, per se, but an M. Night Shyamalan movie with
Gibson or Willis in it."[35] Giles's story largely focuses on Shyamalan's
work getting into Hollywood, and experiences from his first two films,
Praying with Anger and *Wide Awake*, neither of which was successful.
Giles writes, "Shyamalan himself regards the 'Wide Awake' fracas as a
pivotal moment in his career,"[36] and Shyamalan then made a blockbuster film, with inspiration from his idols. Even without mentioning
much about *Signs*, it is clear that he wants everyone to go see the film,
because he likes Shyamalan the person, as well as Shyamalan the writer
and director.

Multiple publications wrote previews/reviews/career summaries
about Shyamalan and *Signs*. It would be expected that they would be
published prior to release of the film, in order to build the appropriate
level of anticipation. However, the article in the *National Review*, by
Austin Bramwell, was published in mid-September, a full month after

the film was released. The article discusses such points as Shyamalan's view of the nobility of people, "tropes of popular mythology," and his positive view of religion.[37] Bramwell then gets to the heart of the article and writes,

> The central theme, however, of Shyamalan's movies, is not so much what this strange truth is, but what to do with that truth once we find it. . . . Shyamalan shows, in other words, how only with the characteristically male virtues can we cope with the knowledge of who we are. One of these virtues is courage . . . another virtue is loyalty. . . . In this respect, his movies turn out to be unwittingly Christian.[38]

In addition to *Signs* being his mostly overtly religious film, Bramwell states all of Shyamalan's films have been filled with religious elements, and that his characters demonstrate, and succeed, because of masculine traits.

In contrast, the article "Ominous Signs," which appears in *Film Journal International*, places its focus on Shyamalan's thoughts on acting and viewing films.[39] Shyamalan gives his thoughts on these topics, stating that he wants his audience to understand and travel the same path as his characters, but wants people to undertake multiple viewings of his films. *Entertainment Weekly*'s article "Night of the Living Dread," by Daniel Fierman, is an interview with Shyamalan and commentary on the director, his first two films, and the path that he took to make *Signs*. Fierman gives some background on Shyamalan's life, his family, his first two films, and his success with *The Sixth Sense*. But Fierman takes the time to document Shyamalan's struggle with *Unbreakable*. He writes,

> *Unbreakable* kills Night Shyamalan. It just kills him. His brown eyes go dull and droopy talking about the movie, the one that was supposed to cement his status as a great filmmaker hybrid. . . . Just listen to the director for five minutes and he'll almost convince you what a disaster it was: Audiences didn't get it. He was too early with the comic book thing. He and Disney made the wrong marketing decisions. Even the title dripped hubris. What's worse, he didn't see it coming.[40]

In the carnage of the film, at least in Shyamalan's mind, Fierman writes that Shyamalan took a vacation. "He mulled over what went wrong. He considered his family and his faith in his own ability. He lay on the beach. And within weeks, he had started *Signs*."[41] Fierman closes the article by quoting people around Shyamalan, who all give an absolute vote of confidence in his work, including Mel Gibson, who "settles for just one word: 'Genius.'"[42]

With Shyamalan touted as the next big thing in Hollywood, and delivering on that promise with *Signs*, he was able to choose his films. His next film, 2004's *The Village*, received less critical acclaim, but still made over $100 million in the United States and over $250 million worldwide. The "twist" ending upset a number of critics, and Shyamalan was criticized for lazy writing. *The Village* is the film where Shyamalan's star began to fade. After working on the screenplay for *Lady in the Water* (2006), it was offered to Disney, as his previous films had been, but Disney rejected it. Verbal sparring ensued, and Warner Brothers ended up as the distributer.[43] The film performed poorly at the box office, making less than $45 million domestically, and suffered under crushing critical reviews and poor word-of-mouth reviews. *The Happening* (2008) received even worse reviews, but did better at the box office than *Lady in the Water*, taking in approximately $65 million domestically.[44] 20th Century Fox, willing to take a chance on Shyamalan after his previously disappointing efforts, distributed *The Happening*.

An essay published in 2010 by Kim Owczarski, "Reshaping the Director as Star," addresses Shyamalan's position as the driving force that would make audiences see a film that he directed, rather than actors as the driving force.[45] Much of the issue for Shyamalan is to which pole he might be pulled: the pole of popular success (i.e., box office receipts) or the pole of critical success (i.e., screenwriting, more artistically driven). Owczarski writes,

> I argue that the image of the director as star is a contradiction between competing discourses of what constitutes mainstream filmmaking. M. Night Shyamalan's image as a star director not only defined him as part of the mainstream Hollywood machinery but also defined him as working *against* it. The ability of Shyamalan's image to mediate these conflicts ultimately defines the limited terms available for director stardom within the contemporary filmmaking landscape.[46]

Owczarski highlights the problem that is often applied to musical groups and performers: sacrificing artistic integrity for commercial success. Owczarski states that Shyamalan has often been praised for his original ideas, and that he is able to navigate between film as an art and film as a business, comparing him as a director to Spielberg, and comparing *The Sixth Sense* to other "cultural phenomena" as *The Exorcist*, *Jaws*, and *The Godfather*.[47] She then writes, "By producing, writing, and directing films that were not only commercial successes but also critical ones, Shyamalan's image as a 'star' filmmaker in his early career carefully negotiated the line draw between Hollywood filmmaking as art versus business."[48] Stars drive audiences to see films, and in the promotional materials for *The Sixth Sense*, the film's star, Bruce Willis, was featured on the poster as Shyamalan was a foreign name to moviegoers. On the poster for *Unbreakable*, Shyamalan's connection to *The Sixth Sense* is clearly stated. On the *Signs* poster, the film is marketed as "M. Night Shyamalan's *Signs*," although the lead actor's name, Mel Gibson, is also featured prominently at the top of the poster. Owczarski writes, "Beginning with *Signs*, the promotional materials begin to reflect a possessory credit for Shyamalan. With *The Village* and *Lady in the Water*, Shyamalan's name is the only name listed, an indication of his star stature."[49] As Shyamalan's films became successful, and audiences began to have expectations about what they would see, the actors became less important than the writer-director-producer of the film. But following the commercial and critical failures of *Lady in the Water* and *The Happening*, Shyamalan's name was featured much less prominently on the posters for *The Last Airbender*, and not at all on posters for *After Earth*.[50] For a time, and during the period of *Signs*, Shyamalan was most certainly a star director.

The *Signs* Screenplay

The screenplay for the film is not available commercially, but is available for academic purposes.[51] The screenplay is 116 pages long and includes scenes that were not included in the final cut of the film. Much of the first two pages of the screenplay did not make it into the film. These two pages introduce the audience to Graham, who is brushing his teeth, and Merrill, who wakes up, upon hearing the screams of children, and "stands in his red bikini briefs and looks around bewildered."[52] The screenplay contains a scene, just before Bo walks into her room claiming that there's a monster outside her window, where Graham has a "conversation" with his dead wife. The existence of this scene explains why Bo asks her father if her mother ever answers when he talks to her. Graham later has a "conversation" with Colleen about the possibility of aliens that was cut from the film and would have occurred just before Graham's encounter with the alien in the cornfield. The longest passage cut from the screenplay is when Graham and Merrill are boarding up the house, and realize that they forgot to board up the attic trapdoor in the ceiling of the upstairs hallway. After Merrill keeps it closed for a short period, Graham wedges a piece of a door between the wall and the trapdoor, keeping it closed enough to get somewhere else in the house. Graham then tells his children the story of how he dislocated Merrill's arm when the two of them were kids. This story follows the two birth stories that he tells each of his children.[53] Graham ends the story by apologizing to Merrill, which, perhaps he never did as a child.

Screenplay Ambiguities

Details, such as what Ray Reddy looks like, the description of the alien chatter on the baby monitor, the presence of alien eyes, and minor changes in dialogue, are changed between the screenplay and film; these types of changes are to be expected. The description of Ray Reddy is only that he is "a thin, thirty-year old man."[54] No hair or eye color is mentioned, no distinguishing facial features are stated, and Reddy's race is undefined. Because of the lack of specificity in describing the character of Ray Reddy, it allowed Shyamalan himself to play the part.[55] Shyamalan discussed this role in an interview found on the DVD extras. He said,

> The decision to act in the movie is one of combined terror and desire to try to do more in my movies and be more personal, make the movies more personal, and a desire to express myself in different ways: writing, directing, acting. And I felt like there was this role that I really, really connected to when I wrote it, and so I was terrified to do it, and if I failed this, I would hurt the movie.[56]

Previously, Shyamalan had played Dr. Hill in *The Sixth Sense*, a physician who examines Cole after the incident at the birthday party. In *Unbreakable*, Shyamalan played a drug dealer at the stadium where David works as security. In both films, Shyamalan is only shown in one scene, and the roles are minor. In *Signs*, Shyamalan's character is seen three times, and additionally heard on the phone in another scene. Reddy is first seen by the Hess family from a distance in town, with Morgan asking, "Is that him?" Later, Reddy, in conversation with Graham, recalls the event leading to Graham's wife's death, saying, "It was meant to be," and then apologizes to Graham for the pain he caused. Reddy cannot bear to look Graham in the eye, so he continues to look forward from the driver's seat of his car while speaking to Graham. Shyamalan's acting in this scene was strong.

In the film, the alien conversation heard on the baby monitor near the car sounds like clicks that are exchanged back and forth. The screenplay reads,

> The voice-like sounds are not words but more like grunts and gurgling like someone drowning. The sounds are being created by inhales, not exhales. A sequence of these sounds in one tone is followed by silence and then the second tone begins another sequence

like a conversation. . . . The tones escalate in volume. . . . The sequence of sounds becomes shorter and faster. The tones become harder, angrier. The silences almost gone. The voice-like tones reach a loud feverish pace, almost violent and then we hear a click and they're gone.[57]

This description of the alien chatter sounds menacing on paper, but the clicks and sounds that ended up as the alien voices sound much more disturbing in the film than one might imagine the voices as described in the screenplay. The sounds in the film invoke something lizard-like, something very distant from humanity, and much more violent and hostile.

A final change from the screenplay to the film concerns the gender of the police officer. Cherry Jones plays Officer Paski in the film; her character's first name is Caroline. In the screenplay, Officer Paski's first name is Edgar.

Changes from Screenplay to Screen

The dialogue changes are usually small and don't change plot points. For example, when Merrill is in the recruiting office, the recruiter asks him why he's not in the pros, "making stacks of cash and having your toes licked by beautiful women." The screenplay says "making stacks of cash and getting handfuls of T and A," which is cruder, but the final version is more memorable, and lightens a heavy discussion about alien and military reconnaissance, referred to as "probing." Another dialogue alteration to the screenplay is when Merrill tells Morgan that nerds probably made the crop circles with other nerds.

A significant change between the screenplay and final cut of the film occurred in the scene where Merrill is shown grabbing some items from the guesthouse, and then throws a rock into the cornfield, waiting for it to be thrown back (à la *E.T.*). When nothing happens, Merrill enters the main house. In the screenplay, Merrill is moving a number of objects into the main house. After he drops some items, including a baseball, he searches around for a rake, and unscrews the end of it from the handle. Merrill then tosses the ball in the air, swings at it with the rake handle, like a baseball bat, and misses. He tries a second time, swinging harder, and misses again. On his third attempt, "he yells as he swings. He rips the air with the wooden stick so fast it blurs to the eye," and misses a third time.[58] After looking forlorn, Merrill gathers his belongings, and unexpectedly tosses the ball in the air one final time. He whirls around, swings, and crushes the ball, with the ball clearing "at least four or five hundred feet of crops."[59]

One of the biggest omissions from the screenplay is the presence of the flashbacks when Graham falls asleep. The first is after Graham talks to Merrill, asking him, "What sort of a person are you?" The second is when Graham falls asleep in the basement after Morgan has his asthma attack. The other large omission from the screenplay is the absence of the final scene in the film, where Graham is seen in his ministerial collar, with the indication that time has passed. Perhaps Shyamalan felt it necessary to further demonstrate that Graham had found his faith again, rather than leaving it open to interpretation. The *Signs* screenplay corresponds fairly closely to the finished film.

Critical Reception of *Signs*

Signs premiered in the United States on August 2, 2002. The film's initial reviews were generally positive. As might be expected, several national publications published reviews on or about the date of release. Additionally, Shyamalan was the focus of the cover story of *Newsweek*'s August 5, 2002, edition. The website Rotten Tomatoes lists *Signs* as 74% fresh, out of 226 reviews.[60]

National Reviews

One of the most positive reviews comes from Roger Ebert, who gave the film four-out-of-four stars. Ebert writes "M. Night Shyamalan's 'Signs' is the work of a born filmmaker, able to summon apprehension out of thin air. When it is over, we think not how little has been decided, but how much has been experienced. Here is a movie in which the plot is the rhythm section, not the melody."[61] Ebert is clearly enamored with the film because he describes its "genius," and writes, "The purpose of the film is to evoke pure emotion through the use of skilled acting and direction, and particularly through the soundtrack. It is not just what we hear that is frightening. It is the way Shyamalan has us listening intensely when there is nothing to be heard. I cannot think of a movie where silence is scarier, and inaction is more disturbing."[62] Ebert is clearly a fan of Shyamalan's work, praising his earlier efforts, and likening *Signs* to a Hitchcock film, in terms of "play[ing] the audience like a piano."[63] Music is rarely addressed in film reviews, and Ebert's is no exception. In fact, Ebert speaks of silence as being more terrifying than sound, not unlike the tagline from the film *Alien*: In space, no one can hear you scream.

The longest newspaper review was written by A. O. Scott of *The New York Times*. Scott's review is not as positive as Ebert's, but Scott does praise Shyamalan's filmmaking ability, saying, "Mr. Shyamalan is a master of control, with a sure grasp of the classical filmmaking lexicon. His suspense sequences build slowly and elegantly, and he is adept at evoking dread through shifting camera angles and careful manipulation of the frame."[64] But Scott does not fully buy into the film, writing, "Skillful as he is, Mr. Shyamalan is undone by his pretensions. . . . The lesson that 'Signs' imparts–have faith!–is ubiquitous in the culture . . . [b]ut Mr. Shyamalan never gives us anything to believe in."[65] The review of the film comes across as neutral, perhaps on the negative side of neutral, with some positive and some negative issues highlighted. Scott does make one mention of music in his review, stating, "Anyone who has seen 'The Sixth Sense' or 'Unbreakable,' Mr. Shyamalan's two most recent features, will enter 'Signs' with heightened attention, a state intensified by the velvet orchestral stab of James Newton Howard's opening music."[66] Unfortunately this is the only mention of music, or really of sound in Scott's review.

Todd McCarthy's *Variety* review begins "*Signs* is all smoke and mirrors,"[67] and then questions Shyamalan's technique of repeating the successful ending in *The Sixth Sense*. McCarthy also has problems with the way in which Gibson's character struggles to find his faith. He writes, "Spiritual overlay of Graham's struggle to reclaim his faith has a sympathetic pull to it, but the issue is treated simply and schematically, without meaningful probing."[68] Despite McCarthy's objections to the film's storyline, he does have praise for some of the film's facets. "Craft contributions are first-rate, from Larry Fulton's immaculate production design and Tak Fujimoto's handsome lensing to Barbara Tulliver's precision cutting, James Newton Howard's supportive score and the fine visual effects."[69] From just these three reviews, it should be clear that critics' opinions ranged from thoroughly excited to extremely frustrated with the film.

Other national publications, such as *Entertainment Weekly*, *Rolling Stone*, and *Newsweek* all published reviews of the film. *Entertainment Weekly*'s Owen Gleiberman called the film "a very well-crafted tease,"[70] closing his review with, "Shyamalan, at his best, has a sixth sense for how to transport an audience, but there are moments when he could use an infusion of common sense. B-"[71] His review makes one mention of Howard's score. Gleiberman writes, "For a while, the portents are captivating. The credits feature slashing violins reminiscent of the *Psycho* soundtrack."[72] Gleiberman is referencing the famous Shower Scene with its repeated stabbing string gestures; the Main Titles in *Signs* contain string "stabs," but not as abundantly or in as rapid of succession as in *Psycho*. In spite of the possible confusion, Gleiberman writes positively about the music, even if it is only the first ninety seconds.

Peter Travers's review in *Rolling Stone* is much more positive than McCarthy's. In the opening paragraph of his review, Travers refers to the film as a "dazzling white-knuckler" and then goes on to write, "For me, *Signs* transcends all [those problems] through the sheer force of its storytelling and the faith in things beyond the tangible that Shyamalan brings to the battle between good and evil."[73] Like many other reviews, Travers mentions the music stating, "Coupled with the dark chill of Tak Fujimoto's camera lighting and the *Psycho* jangle of James Newton Howard's score, *Signs* jolts you, again and again."[74] The connections between Hitchcock and Shyamalan also make it easier to compare and connect the music between those films.

None of the other major national reviews of the film were enthusiastic, instead ranging from neutral to disliking *Signs*. The reviews use the word "auteur" in relation to Shyamalan, albeit in a questioning manner, and many reviews foreground the religious aspect of the film.[75] Only one other review of the film makes any mention of music, and that appears in the journal *Sight & Sound*. In her review, Kim Newman writes,

> Though Mel Gibson replaces Bruce Willis as the family man troubled by a sundered marriage and the paranormal (here, invading aliens), this third go-round for the M.N.S. formula hits the now obligatory beats: soul-revealing conversations in kitchens, adults taught life lessons by insightful children, night-time prowling in shadowy houses with the odd sudden scare, grown men riven by emotions that can't be expressed verbally, apparently off-topic speeches that turn out to be plot hinges, a blue-grey colour palette rarely relieved by splashes of colour (Tak Fujimoto returns from *The Sixth Sense*), and an evocative and unsettling James Newton Howard score.[76]

Like so many other reviews, the mention of music is simply in passing, and without any sort of critical comment. However, it is certainly atypical to expect a strong level of criticism of music within a review of a film, so any mention of music implies a certain level of successfulness on the part of the music, as the reviewer was at least aware of its impact.

The "Twist" Ending

After Shyamalan's two major films, each with twist endings, critics and audiences began expecting endings with some sort of twist. In *The Sixth Sense*, the twist was that Dr. Malcom Crowe (Bruce Willis) had been dead the whole time, and that the only person who could see him was Cole (Haley Joel Osment), the young boy who could see dead people. In *Unbreakable* David Dunn (Bruce Willis) was actually a "superhero," located and identified by Elijah Price (Samuel L. Jackson), who also went by the villainous moniker, "Mr. Glass." Shyamalan's three films that followed *Signs*—*The Village*, *Lady in the Water*, and *The Happening*—also had twist endings.

The overarching question in *Signs* is: Does a greater power than humanity exist, and if so, does it care about us? Graham even asks the question, "Are you the type of person who sees signs, miracles, or do you think that people just get lucky?" After his wife died, Graham believed that no one was looking after humanity, and he used his wife's final words, "Tell Graham to see. And tell Merrill to swing away," as evidence that her brain was randomly firing, and not giving final instructions. The twist in *Signs* is that nothing that happened was an accident. Bo's obsession with leaving water glasses around the house allowed a defense against the alien intruder. Morgan's asthma didn't allow any of the alien's poison to get into his lungs, and Graham finally "saw," and told Merrill to "swing away," attacking the alien with his record-setting baseball bat. All of those elements were interconnected in such a way that Graham found his faith again in a divine power; they couldn't simply be random events.

This twist is the element of the film about which most critics complained. Many saw the ending as contrived, as well as an inelegant way of trying to tie up the various threads throughout the film. In contrast to those critics, the conclusion to *Signs* can be viewed as affirming, because for Shyamalan, the existence of a divine overseer is real, and while the reasons for Graham's presence of faith may perhaps be a bit untidy, those reasons were necessary for the film's narrative. Without Bo having a problem with her drinking water outside of the house, it wouldn't have made sense. Without Morgan's asthma attack in the basement, his lungs wouldn't have remained closed.

M. Night Shyamalan's third film, *Signs*, was both a commercial and critical success. Based on domestic and global box office numbers and critical reviews, *Signs* is Shyamalan's second most successful film, trailing only *The Sixth Sense*, which at the time of its release, was in the Top Ten all-time box office grosses.[77] The biggest complaint from critics was the tidiness of the ending. To many critics, the "twist" seemed too easy, and not explored to the depth that it could have been. Few critics made any comment regarding the music in the film. The film continues to be shown on a regular basis on cable stations to people who enjoyed it the first time in the theater, and to people who are seeing *Signs* for the first time on television.

DVD Reviews and Additional Criticism

When the DVD was released in February 2003, three additional reviews were published, two of which make no mention of the actual features on the DVD. One of these is Lucius Shepard's critique of the modern American horror film in his article "Signing Off."[78] His article contains a brief synopsis of the film, mentioning that,

> [I]t borrows its setup from one of the most famous and effective of all horror movies, George A. Romero's *Night of the Living Dead.* In both *Dead* and *Signs* a group of people are trapped inside a Pennsylvania farmhouse while outside, evil creatures attempt to break in and kill them, creatures whose incidence is not localized but part of a worldwide crisis.[79]

Shepard's main problem is not that the film itself is particularly problematic, but that as a horror film, it is ineffective and unbelievable. It is unclear why Shepard chose *Signs*, a film not primarily intended to fall within the horror genre, to complain about the state of American horror films, but that is his purpose in the review. The second review that makes no mention of the DVD features is written by Scott Brown in *Entertainment Weekly*. In three very short paragraphs, Brown complains about the film and gives it a B- grade, the same grade as Gleiberman's original review.[80]

The one publication that does critique the DVD presentation is *Sound & Vision*. Josef Krebs's review gives the movie 3½ stars, and the DVD 3½ stars; both ratings are out of a possible 5 stars.[81] Half of the review concerns the film, while the other half describes the features of the DVD, particularly praising the 5.1-channel mix.[82] Krebs even mentions the music in the film, beginning his review by writing, "From the opening notes of its score—borrowed from Saint-Saëns's *Danse Macabre*—*Signs* goes all out to draw you in and begin the turning of the screw. Composer James Newton Howard then switches to a Bernard Herrmann-like theme that points you straight toward the film's main influence, Alfred Hitchcock."[83] While the opening notes in *Signs*, D-A-E♭, are the same as the first three notes from *Danse Macabre*, they are not presented in an identical fashion. The A-to-E♭ tritone in *Danse Macabre* is accomplished through the use of scordatura, the tuning down of a string lower than is typical, a technique not employed in Howard's score.

The academic journal *Film Quarterly* contains the longest review of the film, at over seven full pages. Michael Sofair's review of *Signs* was published in early 2004, nearly a full eighteen months after the film was released. The length of time between the film's release and the published review enabled Sofair to have viewed *Signs* multiple times, allowing his review to be much more analytical than those that would appear in magazines and newspapers, and able to discuss more issues with the film. Sofair negatively addresses the flashbacks in Shyamalan's previous films before stating that the "flashbacks continually intrude of the present in *Signs*, operating as a kind of frame that subliminally distorts, and threatens to overwhelm, perception of the aliens,"[84] which is odd because they only occur three times, with the first two begin quite short. His review ends with discussion of the God's-Eye View (GEV), a camera angle from the perspective of the sky. Initially, the GEV is from the perspective of the aliens, even though the audience is not yet privy to that knowledge, but at the conclusion of the film, the GEV is restored to that of God, as the Hess family is restored to its appropriately functioning level and Graham is restored to a minister. But to Sofair, the ending is not as tidy. "Like all of M. Night Shyamalan's characters, Graham ends up morally reconfirmed but psychologically unchanged. . . . Graham cannot accept being the object of such an unknowable gaze [as God's]."[85] This is a much bleaker view of Graham than nearly any other reviewer. Also, unlike other reviews, Sofair does not encourage or discourage readers from seeing the film as that is not his primary objective, and is irrelevant because of the date of publication of the review. In some ways, it is difficult to view the review as typical since it contains no critique of acting or of cinematography. Instead, Sofair's review deals more with analysis of Graham and the issues with which he is coping. This makes sense though as the review was published in an academic journal, and not a magazine or newspaper. The readers of an academic journal are looking for a different type of analysis than a reader of a newspaper wondering if he or she should go see that film.

Critical Approaches to the Films of M. Night Shyamalan, edited by Jeffrey Andrew Weinstock, was published in 2010. The book contains thirteen essays, many of which focus on themes present in multiple films of Shyamalan's, such as the family in crisis, masculine crisis, and issues of religion. The collection is broken into three sections, with the third containing essays that specifically address each of Shyamalan's six films, except for *Signs*. However, in the first section of the book, subtitled "Narrating Shyamalan, Narrating Culture," *Signs* is addressed in all six of the essays; the film is not treated like an afterthought, despite its absence in the final section of the book.[86] *Signs* is critically investigated from several different angles, and the book is a valuable source of information and insight. Curiously though, the terms "music," "score," and "Howard, James Newton" are not found in the book's index, indicating a complete absence of the discussion of music in any of the thirteen essays. This absence conforms to standard reviews of the film: unless the review's point of departure is the music, then music is rarely referenced, if at all, which is disappointing because of the interest that both Shyamalan and Howard have in ensuring the success of the music in the films.

4

Sounds of Science Fiction and Shyamalan

In her book *Screening Space*, Vivian Sobchack dedicates chapter 3 to the sounds of science fiction. In addition to dialogue, she spends a considerable amount of time discussing both music and sound effects. While sound effects are significant to film, her discussion of music in science fiction film, which she refers to as "Music of the Spheres," is more relevant to this book.[1] She writes,

> One might suppose that the SF film—because of its narrative and thematic preoccupation with the 'future,' with innovation, with 'otherness'—would utilize music in a different way than do other film genres. . . . Unfortunately, however, what is notable about most SF film music is its lack of notability, its absence of unique characteristics which separate it from music in other films. Not only does most music from one SF film sound like the music from another SF film, but most of the music sounds like all of the music from most other narrative film.[2]

What Sobchack is saying is that there is nothing particularly special about music in science fiction films; there is no overriding music ideal that significantly separates music from that of any other narrative film genre. Cara Marisa Deleon agrees, writing, "The genre [of science fiction] asks the audience to accept and understand words from strange and unusual planets, people, and objects, new technologies, foods, and life forms. One might propose that due to its subject matter, the science fiction musical score might solely reflect a world that is unfamiliar and strange. This, however, is not the case."[3] Deleon's reasoning for this is that the audience needs to feel familiar with the music, since they will be unfamiliar with the on-screen material.[4]

Sobchack does make sure to extract some of the excellent film scores in the genre, stating, "Of course, on occasion, depending one can only suppose on a film's budget, commercial promise, and artistic intent, a big musical name has been seduced into the genre—very often, with atmospherically good, if not always innovative, results."[5] Dimitri Tiomkin's score for *The Thing from Another World* and Bernard Herrmann's work on both *The Day the Earth Stood Still* and *Journey to the Center of the Earth* are acknowledged in the group of outstanding scores. Sobchack closes the section in her book by writing, "Had such musical giants as Herrmann been an available resource to the SF film, perhaps the incidence of inventive and experimental music might have been higher than it was."[6] Deleon argues against Sobchack's position, writing,

> This does not explain why such well known composers such as John Williams and Danny Elfman may slightly play with 'science fiction' sounds while composing scores for science fiction films, but when action needs to be progressed or emotion conveyed they revert to the basic structure that is present across genres. It is the need for viewer navigation that promotes such familiarity.[7]

Music in science fiction film generally operates in a fashion similar to any other genre, cueing emotion and supporting the narrative, while using conventional sounds and instruments to keep the audience in familiar aural territory when the film is in unfamiliar visual territory.

A significant element to how music functions in science fiction films is the aural designator of "the other," or in the case of the films covered in this chapter, "the alien." While these films are clearly of the genre of science fiction, a horror element exists, through the manifestation of the alien being. Neil Lerner quotes film scholar Robin Wood, who, when discussing music in horror films says, "normality is threatened by the monster."[8] This monster must be represented through sounds that are abnormal. One approach is to musically emphasize the alien with strange and unfamiliar instruments, thus setting the alien apart from humanity through orchestration. This approach has been taken, most notably with the theremin as the alien instrument. James Wierzbicki writes, "Like the various ethnic Others who preceded it to the screen, the suddenly ubiquitous and conceptually graspable alien/mutant Other of the postwar years demanded a sonic calling card. With no anthropological materials to guide them in their search for a musical stereotype, Hollywood composers turned to technology."[9]

Since beings from another world had not yet been encountered, but could be in the future, the natural inclination was to use "sounds of the future" to accompany these beings, sounds and music that would not immediately seem tethered to Earth. A second approach is to use conventional orchestration but use unfamiliar harmonic combinations. The alien other is clearly set in opposition to the tonality of humankind, and by using unfamiliar harmonies, the intentions of the aliens can remain ambiguous to the characters within the film and the audience.

The first part of this chapter will look at the music in the films discussed in the previous chapter. In many ways, the films from this decade present the apex of electronic music in science fiction film, but not in all cases. The science fiction film score after John Williams represents a substantial break from the practice of those films of the 1950s, not least of all because the electronic instrumentation was rarely used. Alien invasion films after 1990 are often action/adventure/science fiction hybrids, and the music for these films reflects that hybrid nature. The role, function, and sound of music in these alien invasion films leads into the second part of the chapter, which discusses the approaches that James Newton Howard takes in composing music for his Shyamalan films *The Sixth Sense* and *Unbreakable*.

The Sounds of 1950s Alien Invasion Films

The group of films from the 1950s discussed in chapter 3 all contain scores that accentuate the otherness of the aliens. Of that group, the film with the best-known score is *The Day the Earth Stood Still*, with music by Bernard Herrmann who, to that point in his career, was a three-time Oscar nominee (*Citizen Kane*; *The Devil and Daniel Webster*, which won; and *Anna and the King of Siam*). Herrmann had also scored *The Magnificent Ambersons*, *Jane Eyre*, and *The Ghost and Mrs. Muir*.[10] Before scoring *TDTESS*, Herrmann had only scored dramatic films and had not yet begun working with Hitchcock.

As *TDTESS* became an iconic film, so did its score, which makes use of the theremin from the outset of the film, an electronic instrument that produces sounds based on the distance from two antennae. The sound is eerie and otherworldly.[11] As Rebecca Leydon writes, "The film's score is often noted for the prominent role it assigns the theremin, a vintage electronic instrument."[12] However, the otherness of the alien visitors is not limited to the theremin. Herrmann scores the film's overture with two theremins, as well as two Hammond Organs, electric violin, electric cello, and electric bass to create his electro-acoustic orchestration. This orchestration has multiple effects. Leydon writes,

"First, they perform an alienising function—including the alienness invoked by xenophobia and anti-communist hysteria; second, they epitomise the sounds of science—including science gone horribly wrong; and finally, they mark off a space of numinosity, associated with Klaatu's 'sacred' mission and that of the 'priestly' scientists."[13] It is easy to see "science gone wrong" in the atomic bomb and Klaatu's message about war and destruction, and have those concepts aurally manifested by the electrified instruments that not only reinforce science run amok, but also the nature of the visitor, despite his appearance.

In addition to the theremin and other electrified instruments, Herrmann uses other techniques such as polychords, string and timpani glissandi, and a collection of four notes known as an all-interval tetrachord, which has a prime form of (0137).[14] About the all-interval tetrachord, Leydon writes, "It is a particularly rich sound, and is often used by composers to evoke a sense of chromatic saturation."[15] Because of the use of that particular tetrachord, as well as several half-step relationships in the score, Herrmann's music is tonally ambiguous, meaning that a tonal center could be present, but it is unclear what pitch it may be. Leydon's conclusion is that Herrmann's score "both accentuates the astonishing alienness of the world it depicts and exposes the classical Hollywood score as a nostalgic construction of false unity."[16] The alien "other" is aurally signified through a lack of a clear tonal center, as well as unusual and atypical instruments. Since *TDTESS* was one of the earliest invasion films, it would seem that others in the genre would follow its lead. That was not the case, as Deleon writes, "While effective by itself, Herrmann's score was not successful enough to completely change the approach of scoring for the science fiction film, which would support the diegetic world rather than simply supporting viewer comprehension."[17] Later composers used more conventional orchestration to signify the alien "other."

The Thing from Another World, also released in 1951, was scored by Dimitri Tiomkin. Tiomkin, like Herrmann, was a highly acclaimed composer of scores for dramatic films, particularly those of Frank Capra's. Tiomkin composed the scores for Capra's *Lost Horizon*, *Mr. Smith Goes to Washington*, *Meet John Doe*, and *It's a Wonderful Life*, among others. Tiomkin scored a number of Hitchcock's films, including *Strangers on a Train* and *Dial M for Murder*, and like Herrmann, Tiomkin was an Oscar nominee; Tiomkin had five nominations before he scored *The Thing*. After *The Thing*, Tiomkin earned his greatest acclaim composing for Western films such as *High Noon*, *Giant*, *Rio Bravo*, and *The Alamo*.

Tiomkin's music for *The Thing* tends to avoid melodies and instead focuses on dissonant harmonies and unusual timbres. When the crashed UFO is introduced, the music includes a theremin as well as high-pitched instruments that play repeated harmonies rhythmically resembling Morse code. The theremin is present to denote the alien "other" while the dissonant harmonies highlight the tension. Some of the most effective music occurs near the end of the film. As Laurence MacDonald writes, "There are two especially dramatic scenes with boldly dissonant music. The first involves an attempt to incinerate the alien and the second is the film's chilling climax. When the creature is destroyed by electrocution, the score's instrumental effects are joined together in a grand splash of sound."[18] Large passages of the film contain no music, in some ways enhancing the tension, since the titular Thing is silently lurking in various places around the Alaskan base.

Like Herrmann's score, the alien other is specifically signified through the use of the theremin, as well as dissonant harmonies and unusual instrumentation and timbres. Herrmann and Tiomkin were both highly recognized and successful composers before their respective science fiction scores, and both were strongly associated with a specific genre after 1951—Herrmann with Hitchcock's suspense films and Tiomkin with Westerns—which leads to the conclusion that great composers write great music, regardless of the genre, and that science fiction film music generally works the same way as all other film music, emphasizing the emotional content and narrative of the film.

Raoul Kraushaar scored 1953's *Invaders from Mars*.[19] Unlike Herrmann and Tiomkin, Kraushaar is not nearly as recognized as a film composer. Kraushaar's music essentially has two different styles: one style for the music of the town, which is tonal, peaceful, and calm, and the other for the Martians, which always involves a wordless choir and is noticeably dissonant. The primary struggle in the film is that the young boy, David, recognizes what is happening, but the adults, those in power, simply take David's initial fears as the unfounded fears of a child. Before the adults in the town acknowledge that something is amiss, the music reflects the peaceful hamlet, a typical 1950s town where everyone knows each other; the music is primarily string-based. In contrast, whenever the Martians attack, or after a person has been placed under their control, an eerie wordless choir accompanies the orchestra. Typically, a wordless choir accents the magical and mysterious, but since it dissonantly accompanies the Martians, it is clearly meant to accentuate the frightening nature of the situation.

Martians also invaded Earth in 1953 in *War of the Worlds*, with a score by Leith Stevens. Sobchack makes particular mention of the sound effects used in *WOTW*, stating, "While the mechanical Martian warships emit whining rays which sound like the product of angry rotors (the shape of the ships beg for biological analogy and animalize the machine), the Martian probes sound (and look) like electronic snakes mechanically hissing."[20] These are the most memorable sounds in the film. Philip Hayward writes, "Irving Pichel's big-budget version of Wells' *War of the Worlds* (1953) was also noticeable for its high-impact soundtrack. In addition to Leith Steven's [sic] score, the most dramatic audio moments were provided by Harry Lindgren and Gene Garvin, who created startling sound effects for Martian screams and death-rays from processed analogue sounds."[21] The importance of the sound effects in *War of the Worlds* appears to trump the film's score through discussion by multiple authors.

The music for the film is appropriate, but not extraordinary. In 2006, the *Journal of Film Music* issued a Festschrift covering Leith Stevens.[22] Many of Stevens's own writings appeared in the issue, along with an article by the journal's editor, William Rosar, entitled "Music for Martians: Schillinger's Two Tonics and Harmony of Fourths in Leith Stevens' Score for *War of the Worlds*." In it, Rosar states, "What is striking about the score is its mostly very sober character. There is nothing fanciful about it, and at times it has an almost mundane quality. Stevens ostensibly scored the film much as he might have scored a contemporary drama of its day."[23] Rosar's quote falls in line with Sobchack's statement about the lack of avant-garde film scores, despite the subject material. Stevens depicted the alien "other" by using unusual instruments, but not theremin. Stevens used Novachord, Stroh viola, and tuned water glasses. Additionally, Stevens used quartal chords, harmonies whose notes are spaced a fourth apart, rather than typical triads, whose members are spaced a third apart. He even uses chords whose roots are a tritone apart, essentially subverting any sense of tonality. Rosar writes, "Stevens departs in an interesting way from his notion of using melodic ideas to define characters by instead primarily using *harmony* to characterize them."[24] As for the absence of the theremin, Rosar relates the quartal harmonies, paired with the use of brass, as an Ersatz for the theremin. The identifier of the alien "other" in *TDTESS* and *TTFAW* was replaced by a typical orchestra timbre but unusual harmonies and harmonic relationships.[25]

Carmen Dragon composed the music for *Invasion of the Body Snatchers*, which is not avant-garde or revolutionary in any way, nor does it emphasize the alien "other." The main title music begins with a pedal point and timpani roll before a dissonant attacking chord corresponds to the film's title, demonstrating how terrifying the film will be. When the female protagonist, Becky, is introduced on-screen, a lush string-based melody enters, indicating a potential love interest for Dr. Miles Bennell. As Dr. Bennell pulls the blanket off of the unfinished pod person, the music imitates the main titles. The music is appropriately tense and dissonant, but follows standard cultural codes and strategies for the entirety of the film.

The score for 1958's *The Blob* was composed by Ralph Carmichael, while Burt Bacharach composed the song heard at the film's opening. Because of the style, tone, and lyrics of that song, the audience should have nothing to fear, even though the lyrics implore us to "beware of the blob." The majority of music functions exactly as it would in any other film: lush melodies for the love theme, building tension through repeated notes and pedal point, accented attacks for emphasis, and dissonance for the unknown. At the end of the film, the titular Blob is dropped in the Arctic and the music ends with a flourish indicative of victory, but when the words "The End" transform into a "?," the consonant major triad turns dissonant; perhaps the Blob isn't defeated after all?

The 1956 film *Forbidden Planet* is musically significant, but is an outlier when compared with the other films discussed so far, both because of its music and because it is not really an invasion film. James Wierzbicki's book on Louis and Bebe Barron's music for *Forbidden Planet* is part of the Scarecrow Film Score Guide Series, and provides a critical framework for discussing the music in the film. In addition to providing analysis of the Barrons' score, both as it functions in the film and as it exists in an isolated soundtrack recording release, Wierzbicki also provides a great deal of history regarding the use of electronic sounds in film, not limited to *Forbidden Planet*. The film's score represents the maximum saturation point of electronic music in science fiction film.

In addition to providing futuristic sounds in *Forbidden Planet*, Wierzbicki provides a history of the use of the theremin in film, noting that its earliest uses often-accompanied abnormal psychological states. He writes, "The theremin was featured in Miklós Rósza's scores for *Spellbound* (1945), in which the instrument's quivery sound is associated with the hallucinations of one of the protagonists, and *The Lost Weekend* (1945), in which the sound is tied to the main character's alcohol-fueled ravings. . . . A link between its characteristic timbre and abnormal states of mind [was] thus established."[26] Through its Hollywood associations with unusual and abnormal mental states, the leap to the theremin's association with alien beings, creatures that are unfamiliar and terrifying, can be seen as logical and expected.

In addition to Wierzbicki's book specific to *Forbidden Planet*, Sobchack and Rebecca Leydon single out the film for its use of electronic instruments. Leydon writes,

Forbidden Planet is regarded as the first feature-length film to employ electronic scoring throughout; moreover, the music was pro-

duced in one of the very first studios to combine electronic sound
generation with the technologies of magnetic tape. . . . It thus played
an important role in anchoring the signifying relationships between a
new category of musical sounds and their narrative connotations.[27]

And in confirming Sobchack's general statement that science fiction
film music functions the same way that all narrative film music does,
Leydon writes, "In retrospect, the pairing of the film's futuristic images
with electronic music seems entirely suitable but amid the dominant
musical practices of Hollywood in the 1950s, the Barrons' music is
singularly anomalous."[28] Lisa M. Schmidt acknowledges how atypical
Forbidden Planet's score is, fully comprised of electronic sounds. She
writes, "*Forbidden Planet* is unusual among 1950s representations of
outer space (specifically) and technological exploration (generally) in
that it has a fairly optimistic view of 'what lies beyond.'"[29] While the
theremin and other electronic sounds were used in 1950s alien invasion
films, the more common use of music was to use the standard orchestra
and orchestral sounds in an attempt to both keep the audience grounded
while still signifying the alien "other."

Science Fiction Music and the
Influence of John Williams

In 1977, John Williams scored two science fiction films, *Close Encounters of the Third Kind* and *Star Wars*, both of which became musically
and culturally significant. The five-note motive from *Close Encounters*
is most prominently sounded on the pitches A-B-G-G-D. This five-note
motive became ubiquitous in popular culture, as those notes were associated with aliens and outer space, in the same way that the shrieking
violins from *Psycho* became culturally associated with someone crazy.
In his article "The Major Tritone Progression in Recent Hollywood
Films," Scott Murphy writes, "It is appropriate that this survey begins
with John Williams' score for *Star Wars* (1977), which helped to re-
store the orchestra as the primary performing ensemble for science-
fiction and adventure scores, and conspicuously draws on Holst's *Planets* along with music of other composers such as Elgar and Korngold."[30] Like *Star Wars*, *Close Encounters* is lushly scored in a late-
Romantic era style, with clear melodies and music that establishes time,
place, and mood. Williams's approach is a stylistic break with the approaches of the composers of invasion films in the 1950s in two ways.
First, the size and scope of Williams' orchestration is much larger, thus
producing a different sound. Second, by scoring a hybrid ac-

tion/adventure/science fiction film such as *Star Wars*, Williams did not need to overtly represent the alien other, because when dozens of characters are depicted as alien, that difference is no longer important. Williams also uses dissonance and tonal ambiguity to represent the alien "other" in *Close Encounters* rather than using instruments to signify it. Some of this is due to trends in art music that developed during the 1960s. Neil Lerner writes,

> The *Close Encounters* score employs several characteristic techniques of high musical modernism, including aleatoric passages and the use of tone clusters, in addition to the overarching modernist musical eclecticism championed by Richard Strauss in 'Der Rosenkavalier.' . . . Spielberg's seemingly inevitable movement from darkness to light, from mystery to enlightenment, from suburb to celestial paradise, is powerfully underscored as the music shifts stylistically from cues with a pointed lack of melody early in the film (emulating the progressive/modernist tone cluster pieces of György Ligeti and Krzysztof Penderecki) to later cues featuring a clear, familiar melodic theme (frequently Disney's *When You Wish upon a Star*), harmonised with a post-Romantic tonal language. The score thus sets up the more experimental musical style as strange by associating it with the aliens, and ultimately it rejects this modernist musical language, substituting tonality for atonality just as it substitutes a non-descript heavenly existence for middle-American materialist banality.[31]

Since the actual alien encounter doesn't occur until the end of the film, the audience does not know if the aliens are benevolent or hostile, and Williams uses this to his advantage. Concerning this aspect of the score, Lerner writes,

> Williams also plays with certain modernist vocabularies in order to emphasize the frightening nature of the aliens (before we learn their true benevolent intent, they are set up as mischievous and even menacing: they mess up our refrigerators and steal our children). . . . Extreme dissonance, unfamiliar timbres and atonality have long been associated with representations of negative states and emotions, and Williams' use of this post-serial atonal vocabulary here acts only to heighten the sense of terror associated with the abduction.[32]

Rather than using the theremin as the instrument that designates psychological abnormality, as Rósza did in the 1940s, Williams uses dissonance and sound mass to convey these feelings. Additionally, the use of the theremin became so closely associated with alien beings during the 1950s that trying to use the theremin for a different purpose in an alien invasion/science fiction film would likely have been unsuccessful.

As a result, Williams had to turn to harmony and orchestration to present the ambiguity of the aliens' intentions.

When the alien crafts land at Devil's Tower, they are greeted with the five-note motive, played on a synthesizer, with an oboe sound. We see the scientist play the keyboard, and hear that the timbre of the oboe is associated with humans. The aliens respond with the timbre of a tuba, clearly creating a sense of the "other" through the opposite timbres. When the craft begins to open, Williams uses dissonance to convey the fear and mystery as to who or what is behind the door. But when the faces of the little aliens are juxtaposed with the face of the young abductee Barry's, we are told that these aliens are nothing to fear, and the music changes. Williams accompanies the final moments with strings and choir; the music has returned to tonality, and all has been reconciled.

Through the success of Williams's music for *Star Wars* and *Close Encounters*, Williams's approach to scoring science fiction films became popular. In an interview in 2014, James Newton Howard acknowledged the score for *Close Encounters* as one of his favorite John Williams scores, so Williams's work clearly affected Howard, both as a younger composer and into the present day.[33] Through his space music, Williams used atonality to convey the sense of the "other" and then diffused the negative nature of the "other" by using tonality to reconcile the negative effect of the earlier music, techniques that could be used in any genre.

Science Fiction Music since the 1990s

The invasion films of the 1990s and 2000s generally feature hostile aliens attempting to destroy humanity, the planet, or our "way of life." Spectacle and special effects play a significant role in these films, and as a result, the action portion of the action/science fiction hybrid is emphasized. Regardless of what position humanity finds itself in, we know that ultimately we will prevail before the film ends.[34] Beyond winning, our "way of life" will continue, interrupted, needing to be rebuilt, but it will continue.[35] Because the ending is never in doubt, a composer can effectively use the idea of dissonance ultimately returning to consonance and tonality by the end, following a musical approach similar to Williams. The elements of fantasy and humor play a role in many of these films, both in the dialogue and in the music, but the prevailing style is one of a typical action film. The use of electronic music, notably the theremin, was now seen as passé, a relic from decades ago, the B-movies with poor special effects and Saturday after-noon television airings.

Murphy's article deals with a particular relationship between two major triads a tritone apart.[36] Murphy provides nineteenth-century ante-cedents for how the two harmonies are employed and provides several examples from science fiction films as early as the 1950s. Murphy moves chronologically and cites both *Men in Black* and *Starship Troopers* as using the major tritone progression. But like nearly every other film, the orchestration is accomplished by using traditional in-struments, and only the harmonic relationships are somewhat unusual. The chords themselves, major triads, are fundamental to harmony, so they are not extraordinary in any way, nor is their use intended to des-ignate anything as "other." Murphy's article supports the argument that science fiction music, particularly recent films, functions and is scored in a way similar to any other genre.

In *Independence Day*, scored by David Arnold, much of the film's thematic music relates to humanity's triumph over the alien invaders. In one scene, the Americans are sending Morse code messages around the world, and each nation that is shown gets its own "ethnic" music, par-ticularly the Russians. "Otherness" is depicted by not being American, and therefore, not having the capability to form a workable plan to de-feat the aliens.

The Danny Elfman-scored *Men in Black* functions typically in terms of narrative support. The most recognizable theme bears his rhythmic style, and moves almost exclusively in half and whole steps, and mainly serves to identify the titular Men in Black. The music is somewhat jazzy, reflecting the urban setting of New York City. The alien "bug" is not given a theme. Instead, it is mostly accompanied with dissonance and string shrieks.

Basil Poledouris's score for *Starship Troopers* emphasizes two qualities: the awe-inspiring sense of outer space, and the militaristic nature of the human army. The wonders of space are musically depict-ed through the use of chromatic mediant relationships, as these harmon-ic relationships seem to momentarily suspend the prevailing tonality and propel the film into a mythic realm. The human army is depicted using all of the typical elements that are associated with the military: snare drum, loud brass, and dotted rhythms found in marches. When the "bugs" finally attack, the music uses a repeated timpani note that feels as though it will never stop, followed by pointed attacks, angular lines, and no strong sense of melody. In some ways, the music reflects being in the middle of a military firefight. But when the "brainbug" is captured, the music incorporates both the music of space and the mili-tary music in one final victorious exultation.

The exception to the 1990s films is *Mars Attacks!*, also scored by Elfman. As mentioned in the previous chapter, the film itself is a spoof of the 1950s invasion films, and even directly references films such as *Earth vs. the Flying Saucers* and *Invaders from Mars*.[37] *Mars Attacks!* is another film in the director-composer duet of Tim Burton and Elfman. Philip Hayward claims that "all of these [Burton-Elfman] films have featured original and ambitious uses of film music and soundtrack. Burton's background in animation is significant here, since the animated feature film has a rich history of inventive soundtrack work and of colourful musical composition."[38] Elfman, through virtue of Burton's background, has been given perhaps more latitude in terms of atypical or nontraditional scoring procedures, methods, and orchestration. Hayward writes that Elfman reworked multiple scores of science fiction films from the 1950s, and that "Elfman's score for *Mars Attacks!* takes its cue(s) from Bernard Herrmann's music for *The Day the Earth Stood Still* (which Elfman has cited as *the* inspirational point for his career as a film composer)."[39] The expectation, then, is that Elfman's music in *Mars Attacks!* will operate similarly to Herrmann's.

Like most composers, Elfman often uses Leitmotivs to identify characters and accentuate their presence on screen. But in *Mars Attacks!*, the vast number of human characters are not given time to develop and earn their own music. As a result, the most commonly seen character is a Martian—and here, it doesn't matter which one because they all function to destroy anything that moves. Hayward writes,

> As Elfman has emphasised, *Mars Attacks!* – as a studiedly *un*-heroic film – resists such a standard approach, since the most prominent 'characters' are the scandalously amoral, anti-heroic Martian hordes. For the Martians' 'signature' sound, Elfman augmented an orchestral march sequence with high-set choral sounds (used both texturally and rhythmically) and melodic lines played on the theremin. . . . Indeed Elfman has acknowledged that when writing the score for *Mars Attacks!* he frequently replayed Herrmann's film music.[40]

And like *TDTESS*, the theremin is heard in the title sequence; in *Mars Attacks!* we are shown a fleet of flying saucers, immediately demarcating the sound of the theremin music with the visual image of the Martian invaders. Even though the instrumentation of the theremin is atypical, the scoring procedures for the film are typical.

Music for films such as *Transformers* and *Battle: Los Angeles* follows the typical plan of action/adventure scoring, using little to no electronic sound, and emphasizing the heroic roles. *Pacific Rim* and *Edge of Tomorrow* continue the use of traditional scoring and context in their music. Action sequences are scoring in ways that audiences would expect, and the alien "other" is not depicted through "alien" instruments, but through specific, sometimes dissonant sounds.

The science fiction films of the early 1950s used electrified instruments, and significantly used the theremin in particular. Later in the decade, the theremin became a cliché, the obvious aural indicator of alien life or worlds. Composers had to find a way to represent the alien "other" while using familiar instruments. Due to new approaches to composition in the world of art music, techniques such as sound mass, passages of atonality or tonal ambiguity, and aleatoric music kept audiences searching for musical stability, while associating the musical instability with the alien "other." As will be shown in Howard's scores for *The Sixth Sense*, *Unbreakable*, and *Signs*, his orchestration is typical of both a nineteenth-century orchestra and of standard science fiction, eschewing electrified instruments. Like other composers, Howard's representation of the "other" changed from film to film, depending on a film's specific needs, but he still musically acknowledges the "other."

The Sounds of Shyamalan

Shyamalan's first three major films all deal with aspects of life beyond what is visible and known, and are all scored by James Newton Howard. However, none of the three films have the same orchestrating team. *The Sixth Sense* was orchestrated by Jeff Atmajian, Brad Dechter, Robert Eihal, and Howard. *Unbreakable* was orchestrated by Atmajian, Dechter, and Howard, and *Signs* was orchestrated by Atmajian, Dechter, and Pete Anthony, who also conducted the recording sessions for all three films.

A large element of what separates the three films is in its melodic-motivic content. Howard recalled a phone conversation that he had with Shyamalan when the 2000 Academy Award nominations were revealed, and *The Sixth Sense* was not nominated. Howard said,

> He called me up and said: 'See?' and I said: 'See what?' He said: 'The music wasn't singular. The music did not have a singular quality. It was okay, it served the movie, but it didn't have a life of its own.' And he's right, in a way. It served the movie incredibly well. But it's not like you could hear one note of *The Sixth Sense*, and go: 'That's *The Sixth Sense*!' As opposed to *Signs*—you know that's *Signs*.[41]

The music in *The Sixth Sense* doesn't contain lengthy themes or melodies, but it complements the narrative, the tension, the mystery, and the anxiety of the film, and does contain recurring elements.

Commonalities in *The Sixth Sense, Unbreakable,* and *Signs*

A typical gesture in Howard's Shyamalan music is to use a repeating, somewhat arpeggiating line of eighth notes in the piano. In the cue "Vincent Gray" from *The Sixth Sense,* the piano accompanies the chordal Leitmotiv as seen in example 4.1.

Example 4.1 – *The Sixth Sense,* Piano and accompaniment in mm. 23-26 of "Vincent Gray"

A second example appears near the start of the film:

Example 4.2 – *The Sixth Sense,* "Run to the Church," mm. 2-4

In the cue "Main Title" from *Unbreakable,* a similar moving piano line appears at the beginning of the cue:

Example 4.3 – *Unbreakable,* Piano in mm. 1-4 of "Main Title"

Both piano lines provide moving "melodies" above the static harmonies to keep the music active. In both examples, the moving line helps to clarify the tonality, or at least, the prevailing harmony. In example 4.1, the prevailing harmonies of C# minor and C major, respectively, are being outlined, with the third note in every four-note group operating as a non-chord tone. The *Unbreakable* example demonstrates a firm grasp of two-voice counterpoint, while maintaining a repeating and unchanging piano part. The melodic notes marked with parentheses show the notes that are outside of the prevailing harmony in example 4.3. While the harmonies in the *Unbreakable* example and the "Run to the Church" example from *The Sixth Sense* are not that similar, the way in which the melody is written demonstrates an eerie similarity between the two. The asymmetry of "Run to the Church" indicates that something is deeply wrong, as opposed to the square four-measure phrase from *Unbreakable*.

While the piano in *Signs* doesn't arpeggiate or have continuously moving notes often, one occurrence is toward the end of the cue "Throwing a Stone," where the three-note motive is not used, and the piano plays a descending line over a sustained brass harmony. Example 4.4 provides a reduction of the music.

Example 4.4 – *Signs*, "Throwing a Stone," mm. 91-92

While this example only occurs once in *Signs*, as opposed to multiple times for the examples from *The Sixth Sense* and *Unbreakable*, it shows that a constantly moving piano line over a sometimes static harmony will be used at some point in a score for a Shyamalan film.

It is certainly unexpected for similar thematic gestures to appear across films that are unrelated, but one such example exists between *The Sixth Sense* and *Signs*. In *The Sixth Sense*, a short Leitmotiv that I have called "Help" appears once Cole figures out how his gift can be used to help the ghosts, and helps Cole not to be afraid of them. This Leitmotiv, with its harmonic reduction, is shown in example 4.5.

Example 4.5 – *The Sixth Sense*, "See You Tomorrow," mm. 17-19

The orchestration, rhythms, and pitch content are nearly identical to a moment near the end of the final cue in *Signs*, "The Hand of Fate, Part 2," which is shown in example 4.6.

Example 4.6 – *Signs*, "The Hand of Fate, Part 2," mm. 57-60

While the pitch content between the two examples is nearly the same, each emphasizes a different harmony. In the example from *The Sixth Sense*, the horn melody outlines the key of G major, based on the open leap from D to G, the metric prominence of G, and the outlining of the G major triad—G-D-B—at the end of the melody. However, this melody is largely harmonically supported by CM and Em triads.

The example from *Signs* uses nearly identical pitch content, but this melody outlines C major, based on its recurring leaps from G to C, outlining *sol* and *do*. This example also contains a much slower harmonic rhythm, using only two chords over the span of four measures. In both films, the music is used to signify a resolution. In *The Sixth Sense*, the resolution is that Cole has learned how to use his gifts to aid the dead. In *Signs*, the resolution is that Graham has regained his faith and returned to the ministry.

All three scores make use of techniques such as sound mass, tone clusters, and aleatoric passages, and all share a similar orchestration. The biggest difference between the music in the three films is that *Signs* is clearly derived from the three-note motive, while *Unbreakable* tends to focus on longer melodies and themes. *The Sixth Sense* focuses on small motivic gestures, but not at the same obsessive level as *Signs*.

Orchestration and Compositional Techniques for *The Sixth Sense*

The score uses conventional orchestration in order to get the eerie sounds from the music to accompany the sights and sensations of the supernatural. It is unlikely that *The Sixth Sense* would be classified as a science fiction film, as it deals with ghosts and the ability to communicate with them, but Howard avoids electrified instruments anyway. The

woodwind section is typical, with three flutes, two oboes, three clarinets, and two bassoons. Additional commonly doubled instruments are
also used. The brass section uses six horns, four trumpets, four trombones, and a tuba. Celesta and (synthesized) piano are used, as well as
two harps and an array of percussion instruments. The strings are comprised of twenty-eight violins, twelve violas, ten cellos, and eight basses. A choir is used in some cues as well, ranging from only men to only
women to the full four-part SATB choir.

Even though the orchestration is quite standard and similar to a
late-nineteenth-century orchestra, specific techniques are used to create
the atmosphere and tension in the music. For example, in the "Main
Title" cue, the violas and cellos are given their own five- and four-note
patterns, respectively, and given instructions to play those notes, "in
any order, random tempi," and play them *sul ponticello*, to bow at the
bridge of the instrument, creating a scratchier sound than normal.
Flutes, clarinets, and harps are also provided with collections of notes
to be played at any tempo, creating a sense of repetition, but one of
great unease. This type of music is called aleatoric, which Fred Karlin
and Rayburn Wright define in *On the Track* as "music that contains
chance performance elements, usually with pitch and timing of notes to
be decided by the performers."[42] To continue the atmosphere of tension, tone clusters in the horns and vibraphone are added, and a superball is rubbed on a gong, while a suspended rivet cymbal is played with
a brush swirl.

Concert composers have used aleatoric passages such as these
since the middle of the twentieth century. Composers like Witold
Lutosławski and György Ligeti have instructed players to bend pitches,
to play repeated passages at any tempo, and to use extended techniques
in their works. It is unclear how often aleatoric passages are used in
film music, but they are more common than most people might think,
largely because of the effect that these musical passages can have on
the visual element of the film. Another type of aleatoric music, sound
mass, is used by Howard, with strings and voices playing a chromatic
aggregate of pitches between two points. Howard employs this technique in the cue "Cole's Secret." The violas begin on three pitches—C,
E, and F—and are instructed to gradually bend their respective notes
until all twelve notes are sounding at once. When an exact pitch is unclear in film music, often more tension is created, and in order to emphasize the mystery and terror of the interaction with the ghosts in *The
Sixth Sense*, various scenes use this musical tension. Howard first used
sound mass, both vocal and instrumental, when composing the score
for *Flatliners* in 1990, a film that had living people interacting with the
dead, then used the technique again for *The Sixth Sense*.

Use of Leitmotiv in *The Sixth Sense*

The music in *The Sixth Sense* contains a number of Leitmotivs. One of the first Leitmotivs heard in the film is simply an alternation of two chords, a C# minor triad, followed by a C major triad, shown in example 4.1. This Leitmotiv is first heard in the "Main Title" cue, and then in the following cue, "Vincent Gray," who is Malcolm's former patient who has broken into the house. Over the course of the film, this Leitmotiv is heard six times. It does not appear at the same pitch level each and every time, nor would that be expected. At its most fundamental level, the Leitmotiv is an alternation of a minor triad with a major triad whose bass note is a half-step lower. This Leitmotiv is utilized to acknowledge the presence of ghosts. Of its six uses, two are during the opening and ending credits, two are directly associated with Vincent, and the remaining two are associated with Cole. When Cole reveals his secret that he sees dead people, the two chords are present. They appear again when he attends Kyra's funeral, and her ghost gives him the video of her mother poisoning her. The two chords have an otherworldly feel to them, as C# minor and C major are not functional in the same key. On the first two hearings, it is unclear what the Leitmotiv means, but when Cole says that he sees "dead people," the audience immediately understands the connection, reflecting back to when Vincent asks, "Do you know why you're afraid when you're alone? I do."

A second Leitmotiv, what I am calling "Something Is Wrong," is played by the piano, a single melodic line with varying orchestration in its harmony. The three-measure pattern is notated in the score with changing meters of $\frac{3}{4}$, $\frac{2}{4}$, and $\frac{3}{8}$, shown in example 4.2. When this is first heard, Cole runs from his apartment to a church. Like the "Ghost" Leitmotiv, this Leitmotiv is also heard six times over the course of the film, including in the End Credits. While the melody is tonal, the meter is what makes the Leitmotiv memorable, as it is uneven. The effect of the asymmetry is that the audience feels as though something is not right. The melody is innocuous, pleasant, but the presence of the $\frac{3}{8}$ measure upsets the expected repetition of the $\frac{3}{4}$ measure. On its first appearance, it accompanies Cole, and the audience should feel that something is wrong with Cole, even though nothing should be. The visuals add to this, as Cole puts on large glasses that do not have lenses, like a disguise. Every time the "Something Is Wrong" Leitmotiv is used, it emphasizes that the natural state is upset, notably when Cole hands the videotape to Kyra's father, and he watches his wife poison his daughter. This Leitmotiv is also heard twice during the End Credits, first, as the initial material, then accompanied by the two chords of the

"Ghost" Leitmotiv. When those two are used in combination, the message is that something is wrong because of the presence of ghosts. Additional examples of Leitmotivs in *The Sixth Sense* include the music heard in the cue "Help the Ghosts." Malcolm suggests to Cole that perhaps the reason he sees ghosts is that he has the ability to help them fulfill one last act, wish, or desire. Cole takes this to heart, and interacts with Kyra, the little girl who was poisoned by her mother. The music is first heard when Malcolm tells Cole a story about a doctor who tried to help a boy and wasn't able to, but is trying again. It returns when Cole soothes his mother during a nightmare, when Malcolm helps Cole, and they part, and finally, when Malcolm helps his wife let go. The "Help" Leitmotiv is shown in example 4.5.

A final example of Leitmotiv is used for Malcolm and his wife. It is a tender melody first heard when Malcolm sees that she has left their wedding video on, and shown in example 4.7.

Example 4.7 – *The Sixth Sense*, "Love" Leitmotiv

This "Love" Leitmotiv returns twice: first, when Cole tells Malcolm to talk to her when she's asleep, and then when Malcolm decides to leave, stating, "I needed to tell you something." The final two times, the "Love" motive is paired with the "Help" motive, as Cole helps Malcolm talk to his wife, and then Malcolm helps his wife move on with her life. Howard's use of Leitmotiv in *The Sixth Sense* helps to create a tightly knit score, and one that informs the audience, providing clarity outside of the aleatoric, unclear, and eerie music that is also present in the film.

Orchestration and Compositional Technique for *Unbreakable*

The orchestration of *Unbreakable* places very little emphasis on woodwinds. Instead, strings, brass, percussion, harp and piano, and choir are privileged. The choir, like in *The Sixth Sense*, is used sparingly and wordlessly. When the choir is used, for example, in the "Main Title" cue near the start of the film, the bass voices enter wordless and at a *pianissimo* dynamic, sustaining a low note. Other parts of the choir—tenors, sopranos, and boy sopranos—layer on top of the basses. Finally, the altos enter and the full choir is split into six parts and then seven, roughly doubling what is occurring in the string parts, but tim-

brally different. All parts sing a single syllable, either "ah" or "oh," as
the choir does not have lyrics. The other significant difference is the
presence of a synthesized drum groove. This electronic drum does not
appear in the score of the "Main Title" cue, but its aural presence is
unmistakable. Because of the electronic drums, the acoustic percussion
has less of a presence, both in this cue, and throughout the film. In spite
of these specific differences, the size and scope of the orchestra for
Unbreakable is roughly the same as *The Sixth Sense*.

Use of Leitmotiv in *Unbreakable*

Unbreakable is very different, since it contains multiple contrasting and
recognizable Leitmotivs, mostly melodic with one textural. The textural
Leitmotiv is largely based on a drum groove, reminiscent of hip-hop,
with low brass accents. This theme occurs twice in the film. It occurs
during the Main Titles, and then again when David goes to the train
station and touches people, having visions of what they've done wrong.
The music is intended to represent the character of Elijah Price, as he
directs David to go to the train station, and can represent the urban location of Elijah's art gallery.

The "Heroic" Leitmotiv, associated with David, is heard more than
ten times in the film, often beginning on different pitches. The Leitmotiv opens with a leap of an ascending perfect fifth, and continues to
climb stepwise to the octave. In its most clearly heroic usage, it begins
on D♭ (or C#), utilizing the Dorian scale, as shown in example 4.8.
However, the tonic triad is harmonized with an F rather than the F♭
from the Dorian scale, allowing the tonic triad to be major, rather than
minor.[43]

Example 4.8 – *Unbreakable*, "Heroic" Leitmotiv

Neither the pitches F or F♭ appear melodically. This type of harmonization for a modal scale containing a minor third scale-degree is not uncommon, particularly for "heroic" themes. A well-known example of
this is the "Fellowship" theme from the *Lord of the Rings* Trilogy,
composed by Howard Shore. The melody uses the pitches of a C Aeolian (or natural minor) scale, but is harmonized almost entirely by major
triads, including a major tonic triad.

The heroic theme is first used about eighteen minutes into the film,
played by a solo cello, as David is wearing a rain poncho and standing

in a tunnel in the football stadium during a rainstorm. Even though it is not clear what the Leitmotiv means from this initial use, it clearly foreshadows the latter section of the film, where David saves two children from an intruder, while wearing a poncho in a rainstorm. The theme begins on the pitch G♭. Over the course of the film, the Leitmotiv begins on the pitches (in order) G♭, G, G and C (in the same cue), B, D♭ (full hero), B, F, A, B, E, and D♭. The orchestration and harmonization change depending on the situation. In some cases, David is acting as a hero. In other scenes, David is spending time with his wife, fulfilling his familial duties as his son views him as a hero. At the end of the End Credits, the theme occurs one final time, beginning on the pitch D♭, like the first fully orchestrated version during David's flashback. This final statement connects the end of the film to David's original moment of heroic recognition.

The second melodic Leitmotiv contrasts with the heroic theme in terms of both its orchestration and its contour. This theme, heard no fewer than ten times in the film, is much softer and much sadder than its heroic counterpart, and is heard as the initial melodic material in the film. The theme descends stepwise from scale-degree 3 to scale-degree 7 before coming back up to scale-degree 1, as shown in example 4.9.

Example 4.9 – *Unbreakable*, "Sadness" Leitmotiv

It is the musical representation of the sadness that David admits to Elijah that he regularly feels. As a result, it is sounded numerous times during the film, even preceding or following the heroic theme. This theme is most commonly heard in the key of E minor. While it is primarily associated with David's sadness, it often accompanies scenes where Elijah is on-screen. Howard sometimes combines the heroic and sadness Leitmotivs, as he does in the cue "The Orange Man," where David defeats the intruder. Initially, the heroic theme is presented, as the children pull David out of the swimming pool. The music indicates that the hero has risen from, what should have been, his demise. David then attacks the intruder, putting him in a chokehold. As David gains superior position and withstands the counterattack from the intruder, the sadness music is heard, not because David is sad, but because his sadness is being replaced through his heroic act. Other times, the sadness Leitmotiv occurs first, as happens in the scene at the train station where David searches for someone to help. The sadness music represents David's confusion and uncertainty about what he is about to do, but ultimately his heroism guides him to act.

Howard also uses shorter Leitmotivs, with one in particular a four-note gesture. This motive occurs first when young Elijah is sitting in his room, in fear of the outside world, and is heard for the final time when David shakes Elijah's hand, realizing that Elijah is a master criminal. The motive only occurs when Elijah is on-screen, and contains an interval that has been associated with evil since the Medieval period, a tritone. Example 4.10 presents this Leitmotiv.

Example 4.10 – *Unbreakable*, "Evil" Leitmotiv

The descending leap between the last two notes is the tritone, which gets its name because it contains three whole steps. Howard's use of the tritone with young Elijah isn't particularly significant at the beginning of the film, but when it is used at the end of the film, the audience recognizes, along with David, that Elijah is the villain, and the tritone emphasizes his nature. Retrospectively, the audience can see that young Elijah, learning about the nature of good and evil, and his nickname of "Mr. Glass," is beginning his path. Howard gives away the film's twist without the audience even realizing it.

The various themes that occur in *Unbreakable* do not appear in every cue, nor should they. *Unbreakable*'s heroic theme is not used unless something truly heroic or revelatory is occurring in the film. The timbre and accompaniment change based on the situation and the self-realization of David's potential to be a super hero. Likewise, the hip-hop beat and the sadness theme are reserved for specific situations within *Unbreakable* as well.

While all three of Howard's Shyamalan films, *The Sixth Sense*, *Unbreakable*, and *Signs*, share a basic orchestration, the musical approaches are different between all three. *Unbreakable* contains several longer themes, while *The Sixth Sense* and *Signs* focus on shorter motives. Multiple Leitmotivs are used in *The Sixth Sense*, as opposed to *Signs*, where nearly all of the music is derived from a three-note motive. Despite the orchestral similarities, each film has its own style.

Critical Reception of the *Signs* Soundtrack CD

The official release of the CD soundtrack contains thirteen cues from the film. The five cues omitted contain large passages of music used in other cues. The cues on the soundtrack appear in their entirety, even though they do not necessarily appear that way in the film. For example, the cue "First Crop Circles" begins in m. 32 in the film. The cue "Death of Houdini" is essentially comprised of some of the unused measures of "First Crop Circles."

Additionally, the tracks of the soundtrack are not presented in chronological order. Of the thirteen tracks on the soundtrack, their chronological appearance in the film is as follows: 1, 2, 3, 7, 6, 5, 4, 8, 9, 10, 11, 12, 13. The first three cues and the final eight cues appear in the correct order, but cues 4-7 are out of order. Chronologically, cues 3 and 4 are "Roof Intruder" and "Recruiting Office," both of which use the same musical material, so placing them back-to-back on the soundtrack would be a poor decision.

The reviews of soundtrack CDs, particularly those that just involve score, are often limited to the online universe of blogs, often with reviews by people who listen almost exclusively to film scores, but not necessarily with the critical training that would be expected from a print publication (journal, newspaper, trade magazine, etc.). Multiple reviews can be found online for the soundtrack, but with varying publication dates. For example, the review at MainTitles.net (film music community) was originally published on December 29, 2010, over eight years after the soundtrack was released.[44] Thomas Glorieux certainly praises the recording, making statements such as, "**Signs** above anything else is so brilliant, that with little Newton Howard [sic] can do so much."[45] Certainly the writing is less acceptable than would be expected in a print publication.

A similar online review can be found at the website Soundtrack.net. This review was published on August 24, 2003, a little more than a year after the soundtrack was released,[46] and was written by Andrew Granade, currently Associate Professor of Music at the University of Missouri at Kansas City, but a graduate student at the time of the review. His first sentence is, "Let's get one thing straight and out in the open: Hitchcock and Herrmann would be proud."[47] Granade then provides background on the relationship between the film directors before writing, "Howard's score for *Signs* is his best collaboration with Shyamalan to date." Granade references composers Ligetti [sic] and Penderecki when referring to the film's opening cue, as well as American composer John Adams, speaking about Howard's use of "postminimalist language." He reserves his biggest praise for the end of the review, stating, "Howard's incredible reliance on one theme and its complete exploitation is one of the best examples of musical minimalism I have heard in a movie score, yet he uses percussion to accentuate the action and key relationships to establish tension and release so well that it rises above any pedantic classification I could provide."[48] Granade provides a much deeper review than often appears on a website such as this, but that is due to his scholarly background rather than listening almost exclusively to film scores.

The website Filmtracks.com is another website of similar stature to Soundtrack.net. The biggest difference with the review on Filmtracks is that it was published on September 1, 2002, barely one month after the release of the soundtrack.[49] In the first sentence of the review, Christian Clemmensen writes, "In the lengthening list of films representing the collaboration between Shyamalan and composer James Newton Howard, **Signs** is not the strongest or the weakest, but it is a somewhat predictable entry."[50] This seems like an odd statement to make, as Howard's score is unlike anything he had ever composed. The review is directed toward film score aficionados, as the review mentions "Howard collectors." The summary statement of the review is that "the score's detraction is its inability (logically) to express itself clearly until its closing moments, leaving many bare moments of empty space," and gives the soundtrack a three-star rating (out of five).[51]

Perhaps the most well-known journal that deals exclusively with film and television music is *Film Score Monthly*. The review of *Signs*, written by Doug Adams, appeared in the September 2002 issue of the magazine.[52] Adams is clearly excited about the score, as the review received an entire page in the journal, as opposed to the one or two columns (out of four on a page) that most reviews get in *FSM*. The first sentence of Adams's review is, "*Signs* represents a breakthrough for James Newton Howard."[53] Adams then spends a large amount of time summarizing how Howard, prior to 1999, had been somewhat of a generic film composer, but with his work with Shyamalan, Howard's music became more personalized and more substantial, but by using the phrase "generic film composer," Adams very inelegantly reinforces the concept that Howard's style was easily adaptable across genres.

About Howard's work with M. Night Shyamalan, Adams writes,

> From a musical standpoint, these [Shyamalan] films have provided Howard with what his career had been lacking: a home base of operations. . . . Each Shyamalan picture has allowed Howard to dig deeper into the construction of the drama and to connect more seamlessly with the film. . . . After nearly 20 years of scoring films, Howard has finally been allowed to establish a signature approach, as recognizable as a score by Elfman, Goldsmith, Williams, or Barry. Howard

seems to have become bolder with each passing Shyamalan project; each outing is more and more personalized. And suddenly the general public has taken notice.[54]

Adams's statement about Howard finally being allowed "a signature approach" is curious, as he never goes any further into that statement. That statement is also preceded by the acknowledgment that by consistently working with Shyamalan he has a "home base." Whether Adams realizes it or not, he is intimating that Howard's music has become recognizable because of his work on Shyamalan's films. The statement that "each outing is more and more personalized" is also curious, as the music in *Signs* is based on a single three-note motive, and that motive is used almost obsessively throughout the film. Howard admits to writing "motifinally" but no other film score uses a single motive again and again to the extent that it is used in *Signs*. It is unclear how the use of a single motive is representative of Howard's most personalized score.

After spending about 40 percent of the review setting up the significance of Howard's music, Adams begins on the actual review of the music in *Signs*, which emphasizes the three-note motive. Adams even mentions the scordatura tuning, and identifies the opening three pitches (D, A, E♭), before stating, "Howard quickly reassembles his D A E♭ trichord into a three-note motive, A D E♭, which is spun into a swirling whirligig exploration of the three pitches. The overture so forcefully burns the rising notes into the audience's mind that each time they return we recall that forceful first statement and await their explanation."[55] The "Main Titles" cue creates the intensity that persists throughout *Signs*, and Adams describes how the orchestration treats this motive over the course of the film, including when the three-note motive changes to become C, G, and A♭. But Adams still has to provide the conclusion to the review, and writes,

> But portent without payoff is a tease, and eventually Howard has to swing away. The score's ominous tones create a long-form build up of tension, and every ounce of amassed angst is directed toward *Signs'* penultimate sequence. This sequence makes good on the expansive promise of the overture as the two motives of the score are melded together into an enormously powerful statement that's violent and moving in equal measure.[56]

Adams connects the music from the opening of the film to its climax, rarely a connection that is made in various reviews of the music in *Signs*. He saves his highest praise for the final paragraph in his review:

> Hollywood Records' album requires attentive listening, and there's always the risk that something this subtle may go over the heads of

some listeners. As is becoming apparent, James Newton Howard can provide something much more than a big theme, loud horns and exotic percussion. This is the work of a distinctive stylist. I only hope that the high-profile nature of the score will persuade more filmmakers to come to Howard seeking his voice, allowing him to apply his notions as well as his skills. *Signs* is one of Summer 2002's best scores. Don't miss it.[57]

Adams points out the quality of the orchestration, the subtlety of the music, and the overall high quality of the score itself. Even though Howard previously earned three Academy Award nominations for Best Score, Adams implies that *Signs* is Howard's best score because it now bears Howard's individuality and voice throughout the full film.

In its annual "Best and Worst of the Year," *Film Score Monthly* assessed the best and worst scores from 2002. Writers Jon and Al Kaplan rated Howard's *Signs* score as sixth best of the year, following Howard Shore's score for *The Two Towers* and four scores by John Williams. The Kaplans also awarded the second-best Main Title to *Signs*, stating, "Kudos to the short and despicable M. Night Shyamalan for creating the main-title sequence for the express purpose of showcasing Howard's score."[58] Jeff Bond awarded the "Cue of the Year" not to the Main Titles, but to the music at the end of *Signs*, "The Hand of Fate." Bond writes, "Let's face it: This is the sort of music that hooked most of us on movie scores. Howard's *Signs* starts off with a bang, spends the bulk of the movie subtly, insidiously chipping away at your psyche, then launches this magnificent piece of redemptive wonder that has it all—suspense, propulsive action, transforming awe and an incredibly satisfying denouement."[59] Bond clearly recognizes the significance of the final ten minutes of the film's music, referring to it as "unimpeachable."[60] Bond did not call *Signs* the score of the year, but isolated this one cue as the best cue composed in any film of 2002. It is a significant statement considering it was competing with all of Shore's work on *The Two Towers* and all of Williams's work, not to mention the multitude of films released that year! The various contributors to *Film Score Monthly*, the premier journal in the field, all recognized the greatness of Howard's score for *Signs*.

Conclusion

In the early days of science fiction film, the signification of the alien "other" was musically expressed through the use of unusual instruments, "alien" to the typical orchestra. The instrument of choice was the theremin, which was used in Hollywood films of the 1940s to denote negative psychological issues. James Wierzbicki writes,

> It seems that for Rósza and the other composers of scores for suspense films in the late 1940s, the theremin was primarily a vehicle by which to convey musical ideas whose emotional signification had to do not so much with timbre as with specific combinations of pitches and rhythms. For composers of scores for science fiction films in the 1950s, however, the theremin and kindred instruments served an additional purpose. Not only could electronic instruments add color to musical themes associated, in the traditional manner, with important entities within the filmic narrative; the very *sound* of electronic instruments took on a function that in film music had hitherto been unexplored.[61]

But the "alien" sounds had to be grounded in some sort of familiar music, and as a result, the majority of music in these 1950s films turns out to be standard music, grounded in tonality, recognizable, comforting. The theremin continued to be used in invasion films of the 1950s, but as more of these films were produced, the quality of the standards and special effects fell. The inclusion of the theremin then became a cliché, a signifier of the B-Movie status of a film. The alien "other" would need to be musically announced in a new way.

Electronic instruments fell out of favor, and standard scoring methods became the typical sound of space. In the 1970s, John Williams revitalized the score through a lush Romantic era style sound and orchestra, a style that continues through to the present day. This sound represents the "normal," the idealized concept of life. In order to differentiate this music from the "other," Williams used techniques made popular in concert music of the 1950s and 1960s—sound mass and aleatoric music—and the dissonance and lack of firm tonal grounding made this style of music appropriate for the ambiguity of alien intentions, while also sounding thoroughly unfamiliar without the stigma of electronic instruments. This sound and style has an effect on Howard's scores, particularly for his first three films with M. Night Shyamalan, where the "other" is signified through the use of dissonance and lack of tonal center.

In the way that Howard is stylistically difficult to identify, due to his ability to work in any musical style, the ability to juxtapose the melodic and the rhythmic is a large part of his music in the Shyamalan films. But the idea of challenging the audience through the musical score is one that Howard takes to heart. Much of the music in *The Sixth Sense* is dissonant and nonmelodic. The brief moments of melody are often tender ones. The film is the same: very tender and loving, but happens to involve ghosts. *Signs* deals with the family unit. A global alien invasion occurs, but we only see how it impacts one family. Howard uses a repeating three-note gesture throughout the film, one that rarely has tonal grounding or accompaniment. Periodically Howard composes musically tender moments, breaking up the intensity and anxiety, and ultimately composed a great conclusion for the film.

Despite the score for *Signs* not being recognized with an Academy Award nomination, several critics viewed the music extremely favorably. The cues that were most commented on were the "Main Titles" and the music at the conclusion of the film, "The Hand of Fate." In newspaper and magazine reviews of the film, when music was mentioned, it was the "Main Title" cue. The cue clearly made an impression on both film and film music critics. The reception of the score was initially strong. Howard mentioned something that he does think about is how his music will sound apart from the film, and if his music will have a life beyond the film.[62] He clearly hopes that people will listen to his music outside of a film. This is an element that keeps him looking for new solutions to scenes and situations, challenging him to write creative and exciting music.

5

Sketching and Scoring *Signs*

The process of spotting and composing music, connecting cues through melodic-motivic material, knowing when *not* to add music to a scene, and orchestrating music is one that should take a great deal of time. However, this process generally takes no more than two or three months, and sometimes even less. One extreme example of the compressed time frame is Graeme Revell's work on *Lara Croft: Tomb Raider*, where he was given only six days to compose the music for the film.[1] James Newton Howard had much more time to work on the music for *Signs*. He composed the "Main Titles" before shooting on the film began on September 12, 2001, and the recording sessions for the score were held at the very end of May 2002. While approximately nine months elapsed between the beginning of the project and the end, Howard was not exclusively composing music for *Signs*.

This chapter examines the processes and materials that went into creating the music for *Signs*, beginning with the cue list and orchestration for the score. The orchestration will be compared with Howard's other Shyamalan scores, *The Sixth Sense* and *Unbreakable*, as will the use of Leitmotiv or motive. Because Howard consciously tries not to overspot films, the choices made regarding the absence of music will also be addressed.

The largest portion of this chapter is dedicated to the process of moving from MIDI sketch, or mockup, to orchestrated cue. Final versions of the sketches exist for every cue, and in some cases, earlier sketches were also available. The term "sketch" is a bit of a misnomer when it comes to Howard's music. The level of detail in his mockups is tremendous, as he often assigns specific parts to specific instruments. In other cases, parts are written for "woodwinds" or "strings," leaving the orchestrator to determine how that music is ultimately realized. The mockups also make use of effect patches, or "Fx," which have to be converted from a MIDI sound to acoustic instruments.

The orchestrators who work for Howard have much more fine-tuning to do in turning the mockups into fully orchestrated cues, rather than orchestrating a melody with a harmonic accompaniment. The mockups also show how his orchestrators have to change or alter these sketches, adding doublings, percussion, dynamics, articulations, performance instructions, and, in some cases, additional musical lines. Finally, in the instances where multiple mockups are available for the same cue, insight is gained into how the final versions of cues differ from earlier versions, and even from the sketches. In order to best demonstrate the tendencies of each of the three orchestrators—Pete Anthony, Jeff Atmajian, and Brad Dechter—the sketches are grouped by orchestrator. In doing this, certain tendencies of each person come to the surface and show how each person works, but also how the three orchestrators are able to assimilate their respective styles and work to ultimately produce a sound coherent with Howard's concept. The archival materials of sketches and fully orchestrated cues come from the James Newton Howard Collection at the University of Southern California's Special Collections.[2]

The Cue List for *Signs*

The music for *Signs*, as composed, covers 57:14, a little over half of the film's running time. Howard wrote eighteen cues, plus the "End Fix," which was unused. Table 5.1 provides cue title, length, and orchestrator, where PA is Pete Anthony, BD is Brad Dechter, and JA is Jeff Atmajian.[3]

Orchestration of *Signs*

The film's orchestration is typical to what might be encountered in a late-nineteenth-century orchestral work, and employs exactly one hundred musicians. The expected woodwinds—three flutes, two oboes, three clarinets, and two bassoons—are all present. The flute players double on piccolo, alto flute, and even alto recorder, while the English horn part is doubled by the second oboist. Bass clarinet and both E-flat and B-flat contrabass clarinet are used, and contrabass bassoon is often played by the second bassoon player. In addition to the typical wood-wind section, two ocarinas are used in multiple cues, which is highly irregular. An ocarina is a flutelike instrument, producing an unusual flute or whistle sound. The instrument notably appears in the opening cue, "Main Titles," and only plays sustained notes, contributing to the cue's mystery and dissonance.

Cue	Title	Time	Orch	Date Recorded
1m1 v2	Main Titles	-	PA	Unused
1m1 v4	Main Titles	1:45	PA	31 May
1m2 v6	First Crop Circles	3:17	BD	29 May
1m3 v10	Death of Houdini	0:34	BD	30 May
1m4 v3	Roof Intruder	2:19	PA	28 May
2m1 v12	Crop Circles in India	-	BD	Unused
2m1 v14	Crop Circles in India	3:42	BD	31 May
2m1A v2	Recruiting Office	2:08	PA	28 May
2m2 v3	Pizza Parlour	1:17	BD	30 May
2m3 v2	Baby Monitor	1:12	BD	29 May
3m1 v7	In the Cornfield	5:39	JA	28 May
3m1 v8 Alt Insert	In the Cornfield Alt	1:50	JA	28 May
3m2 v5	Interesting Developments	2:01	PA	30 May
3m3 v1	Through the Telescope	2:16	BD	31 May
4m2A v5	Brazilian Video	2:00	JA	31 May
4m5 v9	Throwing a Stone	5:42	JA	29 May
5m1 v10	Boarding Up the House	3:05	JA	29 May
5m2 v14	Into the Basement	5:19	JA	29 May
5m3 v10	Asthma Attack	3:57	JA	28 May
6m1 v43	The Hand of Fate Part 1	5:34	JA	30 May
6m2 v3	The Hand of Fate Part 2	3:37	JA	30 May
End Fix	Signs End Fix		JA	31 May

Table 5.1 – Complete Cue List for *Signs*[4]

The brass section calls for six horns, three trumpets, and four trombones. Instead of a tuba, which is only used in two cues, the score calls for a cimbasso, an instrument with a lower range than a bass trombone, but with a trombone sound, and a bass trombone. Aside from the use of the cimbasso, the brass section is completely typical.

In addition to timpani, quite a bit of percussion is employed, both pitched and unpitched. Xylophone, marimba, vibraphone, and crotales are used from the pitched side of the percussion, while typical instruments such as snare drum, bass drum, tam-tam, and suspended cymbals are called for, as well as less typical instruments, such as anvils, and hollow pipes. Additionally, extended techniques, such as rubbing a superball on a tam-tam for the desired effect, as in the cue "Into the Basement," using bows to produce sound from suspended cymbals, or using birch mallets to hit the rim of the bass drum rather than the head, as in the cue "Main Titles" are used.[5] Two harps and a piano complete the percussion section. The use of two harps is almost exclusively a twentieth-century orchestration practice, often associated with the music of French composers such as Debussy and Ravel (and Stravinsky, as he was active in Paris in the 1900s and 1910s). One anomaly in the score is that bass drum and cymbals are referred to by their respective Italian names: *gran cassa* and *piatti*. Certainly no need exists for this, and concert scores of the nineteenth and twentieth centuries would not mix-and-match the languages of the instruments in the score. The first appearance of the bass drum in the score, in the "Main Titles" cue, is abbreviated as "G.C."[6] While every performing percussionist would recognize that "G.C." means "bass drum," it just seems to be an unnecessary language change, particularly when everything else, except the cymbals, are identified in English.

The string section appears as is expected: violin I and II, viola, cello, and bass. The numbers of players for violin, viola, cello, and bass are 32/16/10/8. Soloists are often used, and those moments are designated in the score by the words "solo" or "soli," when two players are needed.

In addition to the standard recording of the orchestra, additional parts were prerecorded. These parts are limited to woodwinds, piano and harps, and one final instrument, kantele, was also part of the prerecorded music. A kantele is a traditional Finnish plucked instrument that is similar in nature to a zither. The instrument can be heard in four cues: "Crop Circles in India," "Through the Telescope," "Brazilian Video," and "The Hand of Fate Part 1."

The similarities between the orchestrations for *The Sixth Sense*, *Unbreakable*, and *Signs* are clear. Most notably, Howard scored *The Sixth Sense* and *Signs* almost identically, in terms of numbers and the types of instruments that he used. The biggest differences are in the exact percussion instruments, and the absence of choir in *Signs*. The woodwind, brass, and string sections are nearly identical between those two films.

Despite the relatively large size of the one-hundred-person orchestra, sixty-six of those players are on strings, two-thirds of the ensemble. Pete Anthony, Howard's lead orchestrator and conductor at the time of writing, commented that the color contrast of the orchestra was designed to evoke an older sounding score, such as one from a Hitchcock-Herrmann film, while still sounding contemporary and indicating the intensity of the film.[7] His statement about the orchestration evoking an older era is in line with the films and directors that Shyamalan cited as influencing *Signs*—*The Birds*, *Night of the Living Dead* (1968, dir. George Romero), Hitchcock, and Spielberg—all of which are at least one generation removed from Shyamalan. The size of a film orchestra used to be sixty to seventy players. With this in mind, Herrmann's score for *Psycho* was exclusively strings, which would have been about the number of string players, sixty-six, that Howard used in *Signs*. Additionally, Howard and his orchestrators had very few moments where the full power of the one-hundred-piece orchestra was actually used. Much of the orchestration features strings with soloistic lines in the winds and brass, rather than a large, full-sounding symphonic wind section. All of the orchestration choices were clearly made in line with the objective of sounding both timeless, and newer, nearly as tonally grounded as the music could be.

Use of (Leit)motiv(e) in *Signs*

Howard's score for *Signs* is different from any of his previous scores, most notably because of the reliance on a single three-note motive used throughout the film. In fact, there is only one cue, as it is used in the film that does not contain this motive. The three-note motive clearly dominates the score, but because it is used so often, and in such great repetition, referring to it as a Leitmotiv seems inappropriate.

While additional music is present in *Signs*, those elements rarely return in a significant way. For example, during the cue "Into the Basement," Graham tells Bo the story of how she was born, and the music is tender and gentle, an outlier in both the context of the overall narrative and in the context of the immediate moment, as the aliens are trying to break into the house. One musical element that does return occurs in two cues, "Roof Intruder" and "Recruiting Office." While the cue contains a three-note gesture, with the same rhythm as the three-note motive, it is not the same because the first note is repeated. Ultimately, a third discrete pitch appears, making it a variation on the three-note motive. During "Roof Intruder," the gesture is sounded as Graham and Merrill discuss what to do about the person on the roof, as ultimately they chase him around the house. While the gesture is being used, it is not ominous or foreboding. In its return in "Recruiting Office," SFC Cunningham tells Merrill that he believes "they" are probing, providing reconnaissance and intelligence about their surroundings, "for the rest of them." The music connects the two events. Since it is only used twice, the music in "Roof Intruder" and "Recruiting Office" cannot be considered to be a Leitmotiv.

The only other musical material used more than once in the film is a gesture that appears in brass instruments, and it also appears twice. The gesture, which creates an expanding wedge, is first heard in the horn in mm. 46-50 of the cue "Throwing a Stone." This gesture appears in example 5.1.

Example 5.1 – "Throwing a Stone," mm. 46-50
Wedge-shaped contour in the horn parts

As this music is sounded, Merrill, who has been watching television reports, utters, "It's like *War of the Worlds*." When this gesture appears for the second and final time, it is played by the trumpet, and is transposed higher. The rhythm of the final two notes is slightly changed, but the gesture is unmistakably the same. It appears in mm. 111-115 of the cue "Into the Basement," as the aliens are banging on the door, but not trying to get inside. This second musical statement is more pessimistic than the first, despite the higher register. Just after this musical moment, Morgan states that the aliens are likely good problem solvers, and will find a way in.

The audience is supposed to take what Merrill said about *War of the Worlds*, and apply it to the aliens in *Signs*. While the aliens in both films seem unstoppable, the most pedestrian of elements will defeat them. In *War of the Worlds*, bacteria defeated the Martians. In *Signs*, water will defeat the aliens. The music is not really a Leitmotiv, since it is referential and dependent upon knowledge of the film *War of the Worlds*. Since the music depends on outside knowledge, it does not fully function within the narrative of *Signs*.

Because no other material outside of the three-note motive returns in the film, it can be concluded that Howard's music for *Signs* does not contain Leitmotivs and is not constructed Leitmotivically or thematically, just motivically. Recalling Howard's quote used earlier in chapter 2, the music in *Signs* is an example of Howard's strong use of motive, rather than theme. While some cues do contain lengthier melodic material, that is not the primary compositional idea in *Signs*.

The difference in thematic approaches in *The Sixth Sense*, *Unbreakable*, and *Signs* reinforces the idea that Howard's approach and style changes from film to film, and that his "style" is the one that best suits the particular project. The reliance on a single gesture, repeated over and over throughout the score, is entirely unique in Howard's compositional output. Prior to *Signs*, Howard never composed film music largely derived from a single gesture, and this, again, shows Howard's chameleon-like skills in writing music that "sounds like James Newton Howard" versus music that is best suited for the particular film.

Characterization of the Three-Note Motive

The three-note motive (or TNM) forms the basis for the music in *Signs*. Nearly every cue uses it, but it does not always appear the same way. In an interview on the *Signs* DVD, Howard said,

> The 'Main Title' that you see over the opening of the movie was written before the movie was ever shot. And it's based on a three-note motif. Dee-dee-dee, dee-dee-dee. . . . [Howard sings the motive] and that motif is reprised throughout the movie in all kinds of benevolent, hostile, threatening, mysterious kinds of ways. It was not specifically written to be the 'Main Title.' In fact when we [Howard and Shyamalan] first listened to it, evaluated it, we wondered, if in fact, there was anywhere in the movie for this music to exist, although we both thought it was somehow related. I think it was kind of a stroke of genius because it starts the movie off in such a mind blowing way, and I, just the level of intensity—it's unexpected. What it does is, it sets up a context of expectations, so you know, that what you're listening to in the 'Main Title' is going to happen, sometime in the movie. You just don't know where, and you don't know quite how. It informs people about what they're about to see.[8]

Howard is aware of how important the TNM is to the entire score, and how it transforms, both in terms of pitches and in terms of emotional content. He uses the adjectives "benevolent, hostile, threatening, mysterious" to describe the various statements of the TNM, which also demonstrate how it changes and evolves throughout the film. The words "tender" and "ominous" can also be added to the list to describe the use of the TNM in various places.

Table 5.2 shows how the cues correspond to the four adjectives used by Howard in his statement from the previous paragraph. The way in which the TNM is used in the "Main Titles" doesn't return until an alien is actually shown in a broadcast video from Brazil. Following this, the hostile and threatening TNM returns when the Hess home is attacked. In Howard's quote, the first and last adjectives are benevolent and mysterious, respectively. Those are the two adjectives that best classify the use of the TNM throughout the film. Of those two, mysterious is the most common, as the reason for the presence of the crop circles is unclear, and the true reason for the presence of the aliens is not revealed until most of the way through the film.

Cue Title	Adjective
Main Titles	Hostile, Threatening
First Crop Circles	Benevolent, Mysterious
Death of Houdini	Benevolent, Mysterious
Roof Intruder	Mysterious
Crop Circles in India	Uncertain, Mysterious
Recruiting Office	Mysterious
Pizza Parlour	Ominous
Baby Monitor	Mysterious
In the Cornfield	Benevolent, Mysterious
Interesting Developments	Ominous
Through the Telescope	Benevolent, Mysterious
Brazilian Video	Hostile, Threatening
Throwing a Stone	Uncertain, Benevolent, Mysterious, Tender, Ominous
Boarding Up the House	Hostile, Threatening
Into the Basement	Mysterious, Hostile
Asthma Attack	Ominous, Mysterious
The Hand of Fate Part 1	Hostile, Threatening, Triumphant
The Hand of Fate Part 2	Benevolent, Mysterious, Tender

Table 5.2 – Characterization of TNM in Cues in *Signs*

Howard's statement about "informing people about what they're about to see" is also significant. Regarding main title music, film scholar Claudia Gorbman writes,

> As background for opening titles, it [music] defines the genre; and it sets a general mood. Further, it often states one or more themes to be heard later accompanying the story; the distinctness of the melody can cue even the nonmusical listener into this promissory function, setting up expectations of the narrative events to follow. Finally, opening-title music signals that the story is about to begin, bids us to settle into our seats, stop chatting with fellow moviegoers, and drift into its daydream.[9]

However, from table 5.2, the "Main Titles" music only returns four more times, and not until the second half of the film. While the opening music denotes horror, that horror is not present, or at least, does not manifest itself in the way that the audience would expect throughout much of the film. The physical horror of the aliens is shown much earlier than the horror of losing one's faith. One of the ways that the genre of horror is classified in the "Main Titles" for *Signs* is that a tonal context is largely absent. In place of functional tonality, only a motive is present. A typical common-practice harmonic progression is not used, nor can a tonic pitch be easily identified. Neil Lerner writes,

> It may be regarded as a commonplace of twentieth-century music history that film music absorbed some of the practices of aesthetic modernism from the concert hall, and that in particular the genre of the horror film turned to unresolved dissonance, atonality, and timbral experimentation as part of its characteristic stylistic qualities. Frightening images and ideas can be made even more intense when accompanied with frightening musical sounds.[10]

Lerner clearly illustrates that horror music commonly avoids tonality and functional harmony, as atonality untethers the audience's ears from familiar sounds. Perhaps the first note of the TNM is tonic, but only because of its continued return and its prominence on the beat, rather than on a weaker part of the beat. *Signs* is not really a horror film, either in the sense of the old "monster" movies, or in terms of the horror/slasher films since the 1970s, but the "Main Titles" lead the audience to believe that some shocking event will ultimately occur, and that moment finally happens when the Brazilian video is shown, the first place where the "Main Titles" TNM returns. The music sounds horrific, gaining comparisons with Herrmann's music in *Psycho*. Since the film does not conclude with the same version of the TNM as it began, the horror has been defeated, and life can resume.

Significance of the Absence of Music

Shyamalan is on record as stating that he attempts to make films without musical scores.[11] Howard has also mentioned Shyamalan's approach stating, "He never wants music."[12] Howard states that he feels as though contemporary films are overscored, and that "I have tried to start off from the following: only put the least music in the movie that is possible. And always add more. Because that's always going to happen."[13] Howard's view is that director and composer should be collaborators, that the music should only accent the narrative in order to elevate it. Howard says,

In the case of Night, *Signs* was the best example. Originally *Signs* was not going to have any music in it until the last ten minutes. And then we screened it. So let's just see if I can create—thinking about *The Birds* (1963)—a piece that would just be so bursting with tension that you didn't need anything. Of course, then we screened it, and it was ZZZ [*snoring sounds*]. It obviously needed more music than that, so . . .[14]

By putting into practice his method of using the least amount of music, Howard was able to isolate points in the film where music could enhance the scene, while still knowing when and where to back off from composing music.

Allowing the dialogue to attract 100 percent of the viewer's attention is something that Howard has been aware of since his early scoring days. In *The Prince of Tides*, Howard did not score the scene where Tom (Nick Nolte) reveals to Dr. Lowenstein (Barbra Streisand) that, as a child, escaped convicts broke into his house and raped him, his sister, and his mother. The power of the scene is entirely on the actors. In *The Sixth Sense*, Howard did not score the scene where Cole reveals that he sees ghosts to his mother. As part of that scene, Cole acts as a medium for his mother and her dead mother. Again, the power of the scene comes from the interaction of the two actors, and underscore would diminish the scene. Howard is quoted as saying that he doesn't like to compose too much music because he doesn't want to tell the audience exactly what to think.[15] These are just two examples, but they speak to the consistency over Howard's career that he consciously tries not to overspot films.

The parallel interaction to *The Prince of Tides* and *The Sixth Sense* is the scene where Merrill asks for comfort, and the cue ends as Graham asks, "What kind of a person are you?" After Graham concludes that "there is no one watching out for us, Merrill. We are all on our own," he slips into a flashback, and music is absent for the scene overlap, police sirens fulfilling music's function. Through the absence of music Howard is not just conservatively spotting the music, he is also commenting on Graham's absence of faith. This is not to say that the presence of music should be equated with Graham's belief in God, but as Graham describes his wife's death, which corresponds to his lack of belief in God, music is absent.

A second important scene in *Signs* has no music. This is the interaction that Graham has with Ray Reddy, followed by Graham's encounter with the alien locked inside Ray's pantry. During this interaction Ray does the talking, stating that the accident had to happen at just the right moment, apologizing for what he had done, and leaving to be near water, as none of the crop circles were near water. Much of the groundwork for the "twist" at the end is laid in Ray's dialogue. When Graham enters Ray's house, he sees the shadow of something moving inside the pantry, and pretends to be a police officer. He then tries to look under the door, and when that doesn't work, he grabs a kitchen knife to try to get a reflection of what is inside the pantry.

Further supporting the theory that the lack of music is representative of Graham's absence of faith is that the bulk of the music is used in the second half of the film, when Graham begins to find his way back to his faith. The lack of music in the first half of the film corresponds to Graham's absence of faith and lack of belief in the impending alien invasion. Once Graham accepts that aliens are present, after he sees the leg of one in the cornfield, music is used more often. Once he accepts that God is real, cursing at Him from the basement when Morgan has an asthma attack, music is almost nonstop. After this point in the film, musical silence only occurs while Graham is asleep and having a flashback, and when they check the baby monitor for the "all clear" to leave the basement and head back upstairs; the added tension from checking the monitor demonstrates that the scene doesn't actually need any underscoring, typical of Howard's work.

The absence of music in *Signs* is significant, as approximately half of the film has no musical score. In several cases, Graham is speaking directly to someone, and the dialogue is clearly emphasized. At the start of the film, the first music heard after the "Main Titles" is right after Morgan says to Graham, "I think God did it," approximately three minutes after the "Main Titles" end. Howard's music emphasizes the mysteriousness and wonder of the crop circles. Before that, everyday ambient sounds that would be typically heard in and around a farm are heard. The sounds are not extraordinary, but they serve to make the audience aware of the music's return.

Sketches of *Signs*

The cue list provided earlier in the chapter contains information about where in the film the cue exists. For example, the cue "Main Titles" is 1m1 v4. This information indicates that it is on Reel 1, is the first cue on Reel 1, and is the fourth version of the cue. The next cue, "First Crop Circles," 1m2 v6, is on Reel 1, is the second cue on Reel 1, and is the sixth version of the cue. Because the final version of the cue is usually the only one fully orchestrated and recorded, multiple versions of "finished" cues rarely exist. As discussed in chapter 2, Howard does his composing at the keyboard, and makes MIDI mockups of cues that sound relatively close to complete. Until 1995, Howard was able to essentially orchestrate his cues on his own, taking his MIDI versions and fleshing them out. Even now, Howard's MIDI sketches are significantly more than how a "sketch" is typically defined. While MIDI sketches exist for every cue in the film, the majority of them are the final incarnation of the cue, before it went to the orchestrator. However, in some cases, multiple sketches exist, offering special insight into the evolution of the music.

The role of the three orchestrators, Pete Anthony, Jeff Atmajian, and Brad Dechter, is to try to sound similar, while working for Howard and helping to realize his vision and sound of the sketches. Additionally, the orchestrators have to try to ensure that the style is consistent with the chronology of the film, as they are not working in chronological order. The orchestrators also have to share significant musical elements, as Anthony orchestrated the "Main Titles," but Atmajian orchestrated "Brazilian Video" and "The Hand of Fate, Part 1." Similarly, Dechter orchestrated "First Crop Circles" and "Death of Houdini," while Atmajian orchestrated "The Hand of Fate, Part 2."

All three orchestrators had worked together prior to *Signs*. Three orchestrators were necessary due to time restraints, which is common in present-day Hollywood. The sketches are grouped by the orchestrator, and then chronologically within the film. Only the most significant changes from sketch to score are discussed.

The Orchestrations of Pete Anthony

1m1 v2 "Main Titles" (Sketch) to 1m1 v2 "Main Titles" to 1m1 v4 "Main Titles"

The MIDI sketch only contains the initially stacked TNM in the violin, while the orchestrated version adds sustained harmonics in the viola and cello, for additional tension and eeriness. Once the TNM begins in earnest, the sketch strongly resembles the orchestrated 1m1 v2, with only a couple of alterations. The sketch contains occasional quintuplets in the "Winds Stacc," or woodwinds playing staccato part. These quintuplets are removed in the fully orchestrated version. Examples 5.2a and 5.2b show these rhythmic differences.

Example 5.2a – 1m1 v2 "Main Titles," Sketch, mm. 13-14

Example 5.2b – 1m1 v2 "Main Titles," mm. 13-14

Examples 5.2a and 5.2b also show how a relatively complete MIDI sketch is orchestrated. In this instance, Anthony orchestrated the part with specific woodwind families, allowing each family to perform soloistically, rather than having the passage played by a single instrument over and over. Anthony used the phrase "stark contrasts, pure colors."[16] The effect of having the gesture played by multiple instruments is that the music seems to be propelled forward rather than sitting statically.

At the end of this section of the cue, the sketch has a boy choir singing the pitches C#, E, and F, on the syllable "ah." In the orchestrated version, the choir is replaced with ocarinas and four violas. Examples 5.3a and 5.3b show these differences.

Example 5.3a – 1m1 v2 "Main Titles," Sketch, mm. 21-25

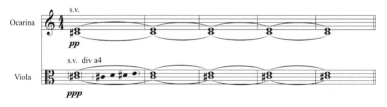

Example 5.3b – 1m1v2 "Main Titles," mm. 21-25

The final significant difference from sketch to orchestration is the addition of harp sextuplets near the end of the cue in the orchestrated version. These are very audible in the recording, both in the film and on CD. This adds yet another musical layer that drives the music toward its conclusion in the cue.

The changes from 1m1 v2 to 1m1 v4 are relatively small, and have little to do with orchestration. The most noticeable change is in the initial measures. The tempo in v4 is increased to ♩=97 from ♩=95, and the meters are changed. In v2, there are thirty-one beats before the TNM enters. In v4, there are thirty-nine beats. This was likely done in order to get better sync points for the visuals of the title sequence. Once the TNM enters, the tempo in v4 becomes ♩=95, agreeing with the tempo in v2. The other significant difference between v2 and v4 is that two measures of mm. 17-20 from v2 are cut in v4. Again, this was likely done in order to get the best sync points with the title sequence visuals. A couple of minor changes in sustained notes occur between v2 and v4, but they do not change the cue in a significant way.

1m4 v3 "Roof Intruder" (Sketch) to 1m4 v3 "Roof Intruder"

Very few changes occur between the rest of the sketch and the orchestrated cue. The initial attacks between the sketch and the orchestrated cue are markedly different. The sketch has a string note and a piano harmony in an extremely high register. The orchestrated cue contains much more than the sketch, including an articulation on the downbeat in measure 2. Examples 5.4a and 5.4b show the differences between the opening measures in the sketch and orchestration.

2m1A v2 "Recruiting Office" (Sketch) to 2m1A v2 "Recruiting Office"

This cue is an example where Howard's MIDI sketch and the finished orchestration are almost the exact same thing. Anthony had to make very few changes to the sketch to complete the cue. The sketch is so complete that unlike other sketches that simply say "woodwinds," the parts and musical lines are assigned to specific instruments.

3m2 v5 "Interesting Developments" (Sketch) to 3m2 v5 "Interesting Developments"

Like many of Howard's sketches, wordless choir is used. When Anthony orchestrated the cue, he did not attempt to move the choir part to another instrument. Instead he deleted that music from the final orchestration. Aside from the deletion of the choir part, the first thirteen measures of the cue, from sketch to score, are basically the same.

One of the more extraordinary events occurs in the sketch at m. 14. In addition to a tempo change to ♩=86.75, the sketch features nothing but blank staves in mm. 14-16. In mm. 17-21, a single sustained pitch, D, is notated in the "OrFx (ligeti)" part. The "OrFx (ligeti)" patch on MIDI is designed to be a string effect in the style of composer György Ligeti, involving sound mass, or tone clusters. However, the MIDI notation is imprecise. Due to this fact, the entire orchestrated score in mm. 14-21 is handwritten by Anthony to ensure clarity. The violin and viola parts of mm. 17-20 appear as example 5.5.

Example 5.4a – 1m4 v3 "Roof Intruder," Sketch, mm. 1-2₁

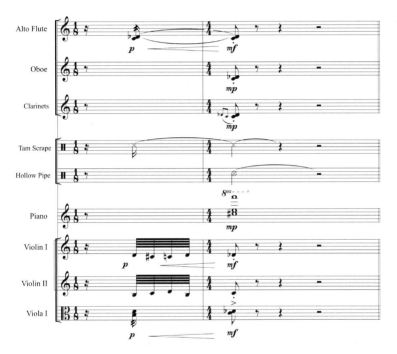

Example 5.4b – 1m4 v3 "Roof Intruder," mm. 1-2₁

Example 5.5 – 3m2 v5 "Interesting Developments," mm. 17-20

In mm. 19-21, the second violins add to the violas with their own tone cluster, with every pitch from C4 to F#5 sounding. In this passage, musical effect, and not melody, is what is most important.

Summary

As an orchestrator, Pete Anthony's contributions involve taking single lines of MIDI parts and assigning them to multiple instruments in such a way that the music, while repetitive, never feels static. The orchestration is done so that each part, even though it may only last a single beat, is featured, extracted from the texture like a soloist. Anthony also had the task of realizing sound mass clusters from the MIDI sketch, and had to assign the notes of the clusters to various instruments, sometimes placing four to six notes within one string part. He had perhaps the most important task, orchestrating the "Main Titles" cue, which would lay the groundwork for the complete film, and necessitating that whenever the initial three-note gesture, A-D-E♭, was heard in the film, that it needed to be clearly reminiscent of that cue.

The Orchestrations of Brad Dechter

1m2 v6 "First Crop Circles" (Sketch) to 1m2 v6 "First Crop Circles"

The changes from sketch to score in "First Crop Circles" are small. The fully orchestrated cue, shown in example 5.6, adds counterpoint in the woodwinds not present in the sketch, both as prerecorded sounds and as live instruments. Measures 37-39 only contained sustain pitches in the sketch.

Example 5.6 – 1m2 v6 "First Crop Circles," mm. 37-39

1m3 v10 "Death of Houdini" (Sketch) to 1m3 v10 "Death of Houdini"

This cue is very similar to the previous cue, "First Crop Circles," both in its musical content and in its orchestration. Dechter again added counterpoint in the woodwinds in the orchestrated cue, as it did not appear in the sketch. This newly composed music is nearly identical to how it appeared in "First Crop Circles," clearly showing a connection between the two cues.

2m1 v10 "Crop Circles in India" (Sketch) to 2m1 v12 (Sketch) to 2m1 v14 (Sketch)

"Crop Circles in India" is the cue for which the most versions of the sketch exist. Because of that a better idea as to how the cue developed is gained through the sketches. The sketches for the cue "Crop Circles in India" demonstrate a large difference from version 10 to version 12 to the final incarnation, version 14. While version 12 much more closely resembles version 14 than version 10, there are significant differences between 12 and 14. But first, the differences between versions 10 and 12 will be discussed.

When the tempo changes from $\b=49.5$ to $\b=91$ in m. 10 of v12, the differences in the music are drastic. In v10, the TNM from "First Crop Circles" and "Death of Houdini" is present. However, in v12, both the contour and pitch content are different. Additionally, v10 contains a sustained open fifth in the strings; this is absent in v12. A comparison between these two examples show that Howard had, quite significantly, changed his approach from version 10 to version 12.

A tempo change to $\b=91$ occurs in both versions. This change doesn't occur in the same measure in each version, but m. 41 of v10 is parallel to m. 47 in v12. Once again, the music is drastically different in these parallel places. The TNM from "First Crop Circles" is present in both versions, but it begins on E in v10 and B in v12.

Near the end of the sketch, v10 contains a single measure of ⅜, m. 60, and that measure contains an eighth note triplet. Neither the rhythmic contents of the measure, nor the meter change appear in v12. While the title and mood of the cue are the same between versions 10 and 12, the musical content noticeably differs, from small changes in harmony to larger content changes, indicating a significant rewrite between these two sketches.

The differences in sketches between versions 12 and 14 are less extreme, but they are still noticeable. On the first page of v14, a new instrument, the kantele, is present. The instrument isn't used until much later in the cue, but the use of the instrument in the sketch indicates that Howard wanted to use this particular instrument due to its highly specific sound. The other significant difference between versions 12 and

14 is when the TNM moves from B to B♭ in mm. 56-57 in v12. This shift does not occur in v14, as the TNM moves directly from B to F#. When this change happens in v14, the kantele enters, adding a new timbre to the longer, sustained string parts. Examples 5.7a and 5.7b compare the two sketches.

Example 5.7a – 2m1 v10 "Crop Circles in India," Sketch, mm. 9-11

Example 5.7b – 2m1 v12 "Crop Circles in India," Sketch, mm. 9-11

Based only on the changes made by Howard in his sketches for "Crop Circles in India" from version 10 to 12 to 14, insight is gained into the composer's thoughts on harmony and timbre. The changes made in tempo, in metric notation, in thematic content, and in harmony shows a cue that continued to evolve until the final orchestrated version of the cue. We can also see that Howard initially used the TNM much earlier in the cue, directly tying it to the previous cue that accompanied crop circles by sounding the TNM at the same pitch level.

2m1 v12 "Crop Circles in India" to 2m1 v14 "Crop Circles in India"

Two versions of the cue were orchestrated and recorded, versions 12 and 14. Unsurprisingly, v14 was recorded on the last day of the session, giving Howard and Dechter no more than seventy-two hours to revise the cue, first as a sketch, then fully orchestrated. The orchestrated v12 has a slightly different beginning than the sketch. The sketch's tempo is marked at ♩=49.5, while the orchestration's tempo is marked at ♩=50.

The final version of the cue, version 14, is closely aligned with its sketch. The counterpoint that Dechter added in v12 is still present in v14. The shift from B to B♭ that was present in v12 is actually present in v14, but is crossed out. This is surprising given that the shift didn't appear in the sketch for v14. But it is not surprising because v12 was likely used as a template for v14, due to the compressed time, and changes were made directly into the file, rather than creating an entirely new version from scratch.

2m2 v2 "Pizza Parlour" (Sketch) to 2m2 v3 "Pizza Parlour" (Sketch) to 2m2 v3 "Pizza Parlour"

The changes between the two versions of the sketches are quite obvious. In version 3, the opening measure is ⅜, rather than the ¼ of version 2. Near the end of v2, the music mm. 18-20 is cut from v3. Other changes occur between the two sketches. As has been common in other cues in this film, the meter change and abbreviated ending were likely due to timing issues at the start and end of the cue. Like "Recruiting Office," "Pizza Parlour" is a cue where the MIDI sketch is largely complete, and very few revisions or additions were necessary to complete the orchestration.

2m3 v2 "Baby Monitor" (Sketch) to 2m3 v2 "Baby Monitor"

No structural changes occur between the sketch and the final orchestrated version of this cue. Aside from the addition of harp and xylophone to add different timbres to the already-composed music, Dechter removed the wordless choir part from the sketch and added vibraphone.

3m3 v1 "Through the Telescope" (Sketch) to 3m3 v1 "Through the Telescope"

This cue is particularly fascinating, as it is the first and only version of the cue. It did not go through multiple iterations or revisions, and therefore would likely have been one of the last cues composed. Like the

previous chronological cue, "Interesting Developments," which was
assigned to Pete Anthony, this sketch contains nothing but notated effects in passages.

Unlike Anthony's orchestration, Dechter's orchestration for this
cue contains no handwritten music—everything is notated convention-
ally. Even though the "OrFx (ligeti)" part is notated in the sketch in
exactly the same fashion as in "Interesting Development," the two cues
differ in how the orchestrators completed their respective work. In
"Telescope" the cluster is not realized chromatically within each part,
but as a series of whole tones—C and D in the cellos, Db-Eb-F-G-A in
the violas and E-F#-G#-A# in the second violins. These eleven pitches
nearly account for the chromatic aggregate, but the approach that
Dechter employs is different from Anthony's.

Dechter adds a countermelody to the TNM beginning in m. 37 of
the cue. The three clarinet parts play the rhythm of the TNM, but beginning in various metric locations, and without the pitch content of the
TNM. Example 5.8 shows the three parts in the orchestrated score.

Example 5.8 – 3m3 v1 "Through the Telescope," mm. 37-39

This is the same idea that Anthony employed when breaking a single
melodic line into multiple instruments, allowing soloistic writing. This
example also looks extremely similar to the passage that Dechter added
to "First Crop Circles," shown in example 5.6.

Summary

Of Howard's three orchestrators on this film, Brad Dechter is the orchestrator who has worked with Howard the longest, and is most familiar with his music. Dechter is the one who consistently added
contrapuntal lines to the score from Howard's sketches, as well as doublings with melodic percussion to accentuate the orchestral colors chosen by Howard. In an interview, Dechter said,

Orchestration consists of many elements. And, of course, James
[Newton Howard] and John [Williams] contribute most of the orches-

tration ideas. I am taking what they are doing and, number one, cleaning it up, and, as I said before, adding my five percent. . . . I will certainly add my own voicing or counterpoint if it's appropriate. . . . I guess all of this is really a collaborative effort, and it's really hard to pick out a very specific thing that's an orchestrator's input. It does happen, but I'm working to try to make the composer's music on which he's worked so hard to be dramatically correct. I'm trying to make it even better than his demo is. That's really what it comes down to. I think it's my job to work in the whole style and approach that the composer is using in a film. I really feel like I'm more of a chameleon than a creative voice when I'm doing film orchestration.[17]

Dechter's word choices of "collaborative" and "chameleon" should not be overlooked, as those words were used to describe Howard in chapter 2. These words reinforce the idea that everyone in the musical process is working to serve the picture to its fullest ability. By adding contrapuntal lines to the texture, Dechter's contributions emphasize the independent lines of music of Howard's writing.

The Orchestrations of Jeff Atmajian

3m1 v7 "In the Corn Field" (Sketch) to 3m1 v7 "In the Corn Field" to 3m1 v8 "In the Corn Field" (Sketch) to 3m1 v8 Alt Insert

Nearly all of Jeff Atmajian's orchestrations, aside from the prerecorded parts, are handwritten. The sketch actually has the specific string parts notated, rather than just "strings." Again, the sketch makes use of a wordless boy choir, and Atmajian replaces it with a solo violin. Nearly 100 percent of the remainder of the cue is just transferred from sketch to orchestration. However, two main elements stand out. An ocarina is used in mm. 99-100 of the cue, playing the notes C4 and D♭5. The ocarinas are doubling the violins at that point. More interesting are Atmajian's instructions in the score in mm. 76-78. The sketches do not contain dynamics or performance instructions, so the performance instructions, written in Atmajian's handwriting, are particularly interesting. Example 5.9 shows the score excerpt in question. The full string section, which is not shown, is given an instruction of *con calore*, meaning "with warmth." In contrast, the solo oboist, also not shown in example 5.9, is instructed to play "not sweet!"[18] The piano part, which has been heard multiple times already in the film, is now instructed to play "ethereal/espr.[essivo]" and "with soft pedal."[19] But the most interesting direction is given to the two solo violins and the solo viola, who are told "to sound as Viols." A viol, also referred to as

Example 5.9 – 3m1 v7 "In the Corn Field," mm. 76-78

a viola da gamba, was popular in the sixteenth and seventeenth centuries. In contrast to modern violins and violas,which are placed on the shoulder, all sizes of viols were played between the legs, in a similar fashion to a modern cello. Atmajian's instructions continue: "If poss.[ible] hold bow and instr.[ument] like a viol (in lap) and bow between L.H. [left hand] and pegs. (otherwise play s.p.n.v.)" The abbreviation "s.p.n.v." stands for "sul ponticello non-vibrato." The direction "sul ponticello" means to play or bow on the bridge of the instrument, achieving a thinner, and sometimes more metallic sound. The expressiveness of Atmajian's instructions shows that these directions are permanent, and not just a last-minute change made during the recording sessions.

The differences between the sketches of v7 and v8 are striking. In the opening section of the cue, mm. 1-30, Howard uses a kantele, a new addition to v8. But the biggest and most notable change is that the music in mm. 27-62 of version 8 is basically a newly composed section of the cue. This new portion of the cue uses the TNM, but at a new pitch level from the start of the cue. However, once m. 53 is reached in v8, the music starts to return to the music of v7, and m. 65 of v8 is identical to m. 70 of v7. The music in the two versions is parallel from this point to the end of the respective sketches.

The orchestration of v8 only applies to mm. 27-61, as the music before and after those measures is identical to v7. This version of the score doesn't contain any instructions quite as detailed as mm. 76-78, but he does write in m. 45 that the vibraphone player should use "soft sticks" and play "w/ slow motor." The v8 orchestration contains a tempo change at m. 53, where Atmajian has written "Faster ♩=90 (91?)." While a difference of one beat per minute may not seem significant, it could potentially make a large difference if Howard had composed the cue to hit specific sync points and the music was incorrectly aligned with the image.

The portion of v7 of "In the Corn Field" that was replaced by the alternate v8 had been heard earlier in the film in the cues "First Crop

Circles" and "Crop Circles in India." As Graham is in the cornfield when he has his alien encounter, making reference to music that applied to crop circles may have initially been a strong choice. However, Howard made a better choice by revising this section of the cue, as the magic and mystery imbued in the crop circle music is stylistically inappropriate for the action in the scene.

4m2A v5 "Brazilian Video" (Sketch) to 4m2A v5 "Brazilian Video"

Most changes to this cue are minimal. On the downbeat of m. 19, the MIDI sketch indicates both orchestral hits and "calmo hits" on the downbeat. Atmajian realizes the hits through snap pizzicatos in the strings, and adds xylophone, timbale, and a second bass drum hit to the bass drum, the only notated percussion in the sketch. He also adds attacks in the piano part. Measure 19 is also the location where the TNM appears in the cue. The remainder of the sketch is essentially worked out in the cue, with little for Atmajian to add or change.

4m5 v7 "Throwing a Stone" (Sketch) to 4m5 v9 "Throwing a Stone" (Sketch) to 4m5 v9 "Throwing a Stone"

The cue "Throwing a Stone" is one of the few in the film that is over one hundred measures in length. On the top of the sketch for v9, a note is typed above the score that reads, "Jeff, Bars 60-61 are new inserted bars. They are a repeat of 59-60." From Howard's message, it appears that two extra measures were added, even though one of the measures overlaps in his description.

The first fifty-nine measures of the two sketches, including the first four that are blank, are absolutely identical between v7 and v9. In mm. 60-61 of v9, a typed note is added above the score that reads "New inserted bars (repeat of 58-59)." This corrects the note at the top of the first page of the sketch of v9. Following this two-measure insertion, the music between the sketches is totally identical. If the only change from v7 to v9 was the insertion of two measures, repeating the previous two, then what was different about version 8? Since v8 is not part of the collection, the reasons for its absence are only speculative. Perhaps v8 attempted a more radical departure from both the existing music and from the repetition of music. Perhaps it added beats and changed meters, but the time added was not enough, or even too much. Whatever the reason, the final solution of fixing v7 was simply to repeat two measures in the middle of the cue in order to meet both time and style requirements, as v9 is the version that was ultimately orchestrated.

Like Atmajian's other cues, most of the music in the score is handwritten, and the cue is largely a realization of the sketch. Atmajian adds performance instructions into the score in m. 30, where an instruction is written above the piano part that reads, "Let harp predominate." In that same measure, in the solo string parts, the directions say, "Like Viols." Likewise, in the vibraphone part beginning in m. 48, specific mallets are indicated, "Med. rubber sticks" and "no pedal." The type of mallet, rubber versus yarn, and the hardness of the mallet, soft, medium, or hard, makes a difference in the way the bars on the vibraphone resonate. Without the pedal, no sustain will occur. However, it will sound different from the xylophone and marimba, since those instruments are both made of wood, and the vibraphone's bars are metal.

The last place where Atmajian's efforts go well beyond Howard's sketch is in mm. 77-84. Several directions are written into the score, including one where Atmajian has written the word "Look!" in the margin before the instrument names. The percussion part has been written over and the ocarina is used. The alto flutes and clarinets enter in m. 82 and are instructed to play with a "Hollow Tone." Measure 83 features a bowed cymbal, a suspended cymbal played with a bow against the edge, rather than struck with a stick or rolled with two mallets. In this cue, Atmajian's biggest contribution is in score directions, including dynamics and performance instructions.

5m1 v10 "Boarding Up the House" (Sketch) to 5m1 v10 "Boarding Up the House"

In anticipation of potential problems, Howard has left a typed note on the top of the sketch that states, "Possible tempo problems: bar 31, beat 3; bar 92, beat 3." As has happened so many times in the sketches, Howard uses a solo boy voice, which is ignored in the final orchestration. Atmajian takes the line in the sketch marked "Winds Stacc" and breaks it up between the oboe and piccolo. Examples 5.10a and 5.10b show the opening measure of both the sketch and the score. The process of breaking up the single line of music from the sketch was something that Anthony and Dechter did. In contrast to what Anthony's work, Atmajian's example only uses two instruments, rather than passing around the full gesture from instrument to instrument.

In mm. 13-15 of the sketch, sustained pitches only appear in the strings and horns. However, Atmajian places these sustained pitches, with bends, glissandi, and multiple doublings, throughout the orchestra. As a result, his handwritten score has the typical instruments in score order crossed out, and the desired instruments in their places, making the score somewhat difficult to read.

Example 5.10a – 5m1 v10 "Boarding Up the House," Sketch, mm. 1-3

Example 5.10b – 5m1 v10 "Boarding Up the House," mm. 1-3

After an extended length of time where no significant alterations were made between sketch and score, the ending of the cue differs between sketch and score. Measures 121-128 of the score are extremely busy, with most of the score filled out, but the sketch only uses flute, harp, piano, strings, and Fx for harmonics and "ligeti." In these measures, it appears as though Atmajian is using nearly all of the one hundred musicians, but the music never is louder than *mezzo-forte*.

5m2 v14 "Into the Basement" (Sketch) to 5m2 v14 "Into the Basement"

Unlike Atmajian's previous orchestrations, which feature a large amount of handwritten notation in the score, "Into the Basement" is completely handwritten, with no printed notation in the score.

Beginning in m. 25, and occurring every other measure through m. 31, Atmajian adds an extremely soft bass drum hit to accentuate downbeats. This is an addition that was not in the sketch, but aids in keeping the tempo clear. Atmajian also adds the brass section to the cue, starting in m. 40. The end of the section, designated by the tempo change at m. 46, concludes with horn "rips" that he added, emphasizing the fear of the family. Beginning in m. 67, he adds clarinets and horns, doubling the sustained pitches in the strings, in order to add a different timbre to the music.

5m3 v9 "Asthma Attack" (Sketch) to 5m3 v9 "Asthma Attack" (prerecord) to 5m3 v10 "Asthma Attack"

This sketch may be the most detailed sketch that Howard made for the film. Within the opening eighteen measures, several meter discrepancies exist between the sketch of v9 and the prerecorded score of v9. Despite the different meters, both sketch and score contain the same number of beats, and correspond to each other again at the tempo change in m. 19.

The biggest difference between the sketch of v9 and the score of v9 is located in the final measures. The sketch contains a tempo change to ♩=58 in m. 61, and has sustained pitches through the end of m. 66, the end of the cue. In the score, no tempo change occurs, and the sustained pitches are not held nearly as long.

Although the score of v9 has a stamp on it that indicates "prerecord," it appears to be the full score, with prerecorded parts notated in that score. Because it is a complete score, it is much easier to compare versions 9 and 10, in order to see how the final adjustments were made. The differences between v9 and v10 are not large, but they are noticeable. The first change is in m. 39 of v10. The final version contains additional doublings in the clarinets and bassoons that were not present in either the sketch or score for v9. Version 10 also contains an increase in tempo in m. 55, from ♩=63 to ♩=70. The music between versions 9 and 10 remains the same, but less time elapses in v10, likely because the cue needed to end earlier than was written in v9.

6m1 v37 (w/o efx) (Sketch) to 6m1 v37 (Jeff's meters) (Sketch) to 6m1 v41 "The Hand of Fate" (Sketch) to 6m1 v43 "The Hand of Fate" (Sketch)

This is the cue that underwent, by far, the most revisions for the film. Two others, "Crop Circles in India" and "Into the Basement" both had fourteen versions. This cue had nearly thirty more revisions. It should come as no surprise that this was the second cue that Howard composed for the film, following "Main Titles," and the number of revisions seems appropriate considering the timing elements, the number of different moods and emotions projected, and the fact that much of the earlier music was generated from this cue.

When comparing 6m1 v37 (w/o efx) to 6m1 v37 (Jeff's meters), there is only one difference between the two, other than the addition of MIDI effects in the second one. The sketch without the effects ends with m. 121 while the sketch with effects concludes with m. 188. One of two options potentially happened. Either the "w/o efx" sketch was abruptly ended, because there were no differences between the two, or those pages were not included in the archive. Of the two choices, the latter is much more likely. The inclusion of the phrase "Jeff's meters" indicates that Jeff Atmajian had some influence over the music before it appeared in its final version. It is likely that somewhere in versions 34-36, Atmajian had an opportunity to hear and see the sketches, and made recommendations to Howard on more effective meters, which were then updated and used in v37. The effects used in v37 are more wide-ranging than in any other cue, as many of the same effects are present, but elements like the kantele and hurdy-gurdy are also used.

The next point of comparison is between versions 37 and 41 of the sketches. Immediately, the most notable element is that v37 contains 188 measures while v41 only contains 113, 75 fewer measures. Clearly a great deal of music was cut from v37. What appears to be the case is that 6m1 v37 contains the music for the final versions of 6m1 and 6m2, and that somewhere between v37 and v41 of the sketches of 6m1, the decision was made to split the cue into two separate cues.

While v41 doesn't sound like an entirely new cue, parts of it are significantly different. The tempos at the start of the two versions are different, with ♩=58 in v37, and ♩=58.10 in v41. While this change may seem negligible, it was done in order to make the tempo just a shade faster than in v37, but not a full, or even a half beat per minute. Howard composed a new line in the contrabass clarinet, replacing the single note that appeared in m. 1. The music between the two versions stays similar until the tempo change in m. 14.

At that tempo change, from ♩=58(.1) to ♩=91, the music in v41 drastically differs from that in v37. The meters between the two are different, an entire measure present in v37 is eliminated in v41, and the solo violin part has been completely changed. Additionally, a new line in the "Winds Stacc" part has been added by Howard.

A new section begins at m. 26 in v41. This is indicated through a tempo change from ♩=91 to ♩=56.40. The parallel location in v37 is in m. 24, with a tempo of ♩=57, but this entire section has been recomposed by Howard. In v37, the section is in mm. 24-34. In v41, this section is now mm. 26-42, substantially longer. Almost none of the music in this section from v37 remains. The conclusion to this cue is completely different, owing to the fact that in v37, the cue continued into what became 6m2.

In comparing v43 to v41, much of the cue remains identical. The sketch for v43 is only eight pages long, as opposed to v41, which is twenty-eight pages long. This is because three passages are abbreviated in the sketch of v43. In all three cases, these abbreviations indicate to use the music present in v41. These measures are 1-6, 19-78, and 81-100, meaning that the new music in v43 is in mm. 7-18, 79-80, and 101-113.

The changes in mm. 7-18 are minimal and might not even be noticed by most people. Measures 79-80 contain the same number of beats, but are metrically notated differently between the two versions. However, mm. 101-113, the end of the cue, drastically differs between v41 and v43. Version 41 almost exclusively consists of sustained pitches in the strings and occasional melodic half notes in the horns. In version 43, continuous sixteenth notes and the TNM rhythm dominate the texture. As the cue comes to its conclusion, it slowly unwinds, with the texture becoming less dense.

6m1 v43 "The Hand of Fate" (Sketch) to 6m1 v43 "The Hand of Fate, Part 1"

The sketch is almost a fully realized version of the cue. In this cue, the TNM is printed whenever it is present, but the rest of the score is handwritten. In the sketch, m. 53 has six beats, but in the score, it is changed to $\frac{5}{4}$. Measure 54 in the sketch is in $\frac{4}{4}$, but in the score, it is changed to $\frac{5}{4}$. While both examples contain ten beats, the metric accent falls in different places. In the final score, the accents are evenly placed, unlike in the sketch. Also, in m. 54, the solo violin has written instructions, "Getting more and more frantic," representing the agony of the characters' situation.

In moving from sketch to score, "The Hand of Fate, Part 1" needed very little adjustment. Atmajian took Howard's sketch and assigned specific parts, in some cases, breaking up a line marked "solo" in the sketch into two, and sometimes, three instruments. After more than forty versions of the sketch, the musical and orchestral ideas were finalized.

6m2 v3 (Sketch) to 6m2 v4 (Sketch) to 6m2 v3-4

This is the final cue in the film, and is untitled in both sketches and both orchestrated scores. This is because the cue originally belonged to the 6m1 cue, later titled "The Hand of Fate" in sketches, and in its final orchestrated version, "The Hand of Fate, Part 1." Because of how the music is titled on the audio soundtrack release, and because a "Part 1" necessitates a second part, this cue will be referred to as "The Hand of Fate, Part 2." Before comparing versions 3 and 4 of the sketch, a comparison of 6m1 v37 must be made to 6m2 v3, since the music was in the previous cue before becoming its own cue.

When the two sketches, 6m1 v37 and 6m2 v3, correspond to each other, only slight differences are present in the sketches. But when the two sketches are different, they are very different, indicating a great deal of rethinking and revising in those places. Sometimes the thematic material between the sketches is similar, but different harmonies are used. Other times, the content is completely different. Because of the extreme differences, comparing these two sketches does not provide significant insight.

Very little music between 6m2 v3 and 6m2 v4 was changed. In fact, like versions 41 and 43 of "Hand of Fate, Part 1," version 4 of 6m2 contains statements where the music is indicated to be the same as version 3. In the sketch for v4, the score reads, "1-48 6m2 v3" and "55-end 6m2 v3," leaving only mm. 49-54 as those where any changes are present. The biggest difference is the change in harmonies. The six-measure passage is shown in examples 5.11a and 5.11b.

Version 3 contains a pedal C major triad for the first three measures, then A minor, back to C major, and an open fifth D-A-E. In version 4 pedal chords alternate between C major and D major for the first four measures before dropping out. The harmonies above the pedal chords are also different. In version 3, Howard uses an E minor triad followed by D major in mm. 49-54. Version 4 doubles the harmonies present in the pedal chords, but uses suspensions rather than completely different chords as the source of dissonance.

The differences between versions 3 and 4 of the sketches are small, but not insignificant. Only six measures were changed, but the change must have been late in the recording. Unsurprisingly, v3 of the score corresponds to the sketch of v3, while v4 of the score corresponds directly to its sketch. The score of v4 is not a synthesis of the two; it is a replacement of those six measures from the sketch, mm. 49-54. Following these inserted measures, the cue continues being a realization of the sketch, from mm. 55-84, the end of the cue.

Summary

Of the three orchestrators on *Signs*, Jeff Atmajian orchestrated the most music, including the entire second half of the film. Atmajian's orchestrations go well beyond the notes on the page, as he provides specific performance instructions. He also had the opportunity to use the full force of the orchestra with the cues at the end of the film, which gave him the ability to make choices regarding doublings in different octaves and timbres, while not overwhelming the texture. Regarding the process of sketch to score, he said,

> My greatest goal is to represent in the orchestra what they [composers] are hearing and portraying in their demos and transcriptions. Sometimes it is a matter of doing a bit of final crafting; other times it is making sure what comes through on synths also comes through clearly in the orchestra. . . . It may also be the case that, in addition to what's been written for the orchestra, there are big hits or dissonant clusters that are represented by a little dot or a triangle on the sketch. For those, we need to recreate the sound that the composer gets with

a single sample. Another difference is that we don't get dynamics or phrasings. They come via demos.[20]

Example 5.11a – 6m2 v3 "The Hand of Fate, Part 2," Sketch, mm. 49-54

Example 5.11b – 6m2 v4 "The Hand of Fate, Part 2," Sketch, mm. 49-54

Atmajian's tasks for *Signs* ran the gamut of his descriptions—final crafting, adding dynamics and phrasings, and representing clusters—and his orchestrations, particularly those with the complete orchestra, are extremely elegant.

Signs End Fix (Sketch) to Signs End Fix

The final element of music composed for the film has no reel indication, and is referred to as "End Fix," likely in place of an "End Credits." This is certainly curious, as Howard is on record as stating the importance of the End Credits to him. The "End Fix" is only twenty-two measures long. The music, while composed for the film, does not actually appear in the film. The music used during the End Credits, after "The Hand of Fate, Part 2" concludes, takes elements from cues already heard, and essentially cuts and pastes previously heard music from the film. The "End Fix" may have originally been intended to take the place of what ultimately occurred, but with only long suspended harmonies and no presence of the TNM, it seems to have missed its mark.

The sketch for the "End Fix" uses only strings, and no values shorter than a half note. In several cases, notes and chords are tied across multiple measures. The sketch and the score are almost exactly the same. Atmajian assigns parts to the various string instruments, as the sketch uses only four string parts. There appears to be no recording of this music, which makes sense because it was not used in the film.

Signs Trailer 15 (Sketch) to Signs Trailer 15

One of the more fascinating elements of the music for *Signs* is that Howard composed music for the teaser trailer. This is an extremely uncommon practice in Hollywood, as the first trailer almost always uses pre-existing music, and rarely is that music featured in the film at all. This is because the trailer is made well before the composer begins scoring the film. However, in the case of Howard's films with Shyamalan, he writes the Main Title music before shooting commences, and therefore, has the opportunity to use some of that material in the trailer.

Pete Anthony, the orchestrator of the "Main Titles," also orchestrated the score for the trailer. Anthony fills in the texture of the sketch, which uses only upper woodwinds, harp, piano, and strings, with bassoons doubling a string line and horns playing syncopated staccato accents in mm. 15-19. The process of filling out the texture with doublings continues through m. 27, where a note appears in the sketch that reads, "Cue only – Do not orchestrate." This final harmony is intended to be held as long as necessary, with nothing else sounds.

The trailer music only uses the first part of the Main Titles, which is unsurprising, as Howard would likely not want to give away the complete emotional impact of his opening music in the trailer. But the music used, including the TNM, is certainly enough that the audience's interest would be piqued by the aural and visual elements in the trailer.

Conclusion

The sketches that James Newton Howard made for *Signs* are sketches only in name. The music is nearly fully composed, but not to the point where orchestrators are superfluous. The job of the orchestrators was to take the sectional music, in the woodwinds and strings, and to orchestrate it appropriately for each instrument within the respective section. The clearest example of this is Pete Anthony's work on the "Main Titles," taking the part for Winds (staccato), and moving each beat around the section, keeping the music moving from player to player, and allowing the instruments to have one beat of a solo. The effect is that different orchestral colors pop out, rather than having a *tutti* section playing the same gesture over and over again.

With three orchestrators simultaneously working on the music, they must not only sound like Howard, but they must also sound like each other. All three orchestrators on the film had worked with each other before *Signs*, and all had worked with Howard as well. Anthony, who conducted the recording sessions for *Signs*, had conducted previous scores of Howard's as well. All three orchestrators were interviewed by Christian DesJardins for his book *Inside Film Music*, and all were asked about unifying style. Anthony replied, "You do hear differences in style, but teams of people who work together usually work out the details so that you don't hear large contrasts when going from one orchestrator to the next. The orchestrator is responsible for being well-rounded."[21] Jeff Atmajian addressed issues of blending styles with multiple orchestrators as well, stating, "It has never really been an issue, because we are all working for the same composer with the same intention. The thing that is amazing is seeing how often we do similar things, even though we work separately. . . . We all seem to have our own unique ways of getting certain sounds from the orchestra, but things always coalesce."[22] Finally, Brad Dechter commented, "I don't really believe that my style as an orchestrator is as important as the job I do as an orchestrator to support the composer. That's what I want to be clear on. I don't sit down and say, 'I'm Brad Dechter trying to figure out how to make a Brad Dechter sound in this film score.'"[23] Through the quotes of the three orchestrators, all interviewed independently, it becomes clear that the job of the orchestrating team is to realize the composer's vision. And like Howard, all three are clearly willing to be subservient to the process, less apt to exert power over of the music, and are humble enough to know that they are working to improve the film. Howard has found an orchestrating team that is like him, fluent in multiple musical genres, hard-working, and precise to get just the right sounds.

In order to create a unified whole, certain aspects of the music had to be emphasized. One of these aspects is the fact that multiple independent lines were composed by Howard. Sometimes, an orchestrator would add another contrapuntal line to the texture. Other times, a line would be doubled by a different orchestral instrument, providing a new color and timbre. The compositional technique of layering, or stratification, is a trait associated with Igor Stravinsky, and in chapter 6, we will see just how much influence Stravinsky exerted on Howard's score.

All three orchestrators have praise for Howard, with Dechter saying, "James, to me, is as good of a film composer as there has ever been."[24] Atmajian stated, "I feel that I am always driven to expand myself and push that much harder because of his material. May I also add that he is a truly gifted and kind person, and that also inspires me."[25] Anthony has commented that Howard is an extremely intelligent person and said, "James is never content to rest on his laurels. . . . he is creatively restless, always looking for new challenges. I have worked with many great composers, but James stands out as one who consistently and intentionally challenges his own comfort zone at every opportunity."[26] When asked by DesJardins about his favorite projects, Anthony's first response was, "I had a great time working on *Signs* by James Newton Howard."[27] Howard's orchestrators clearly respect him, both personally and professionally, and when working with someone of that caliber, the likelihood of creating outstanding music is extremely high.

Through the changes made from sketches of the same cue, to changes made from sketch to score, insight can be acquired regarding the editing process regarding tempo, adding or deleting beats to hit a specific synchronization point, and choices in orchestration. The orchestrator's role is to help facilitate the composer's vision of the music. The composer's role is to help facilitate the vision of the director. On all accounts, both the orchestrators and composer worked to create a successful musical vision, one that served the film appropriately and meritously.

6

Analysis of the Score

The final chapter of this book presents the analysis of James Newton Howard's music for *Signs*. Since nearly all of the music in the film is derived from the opening three-note motive, discussion of the use of that gesture will dominate the analysis. Unlike most film music, which is grounded in some sort of tonal center, the three-note motive does its best to avoid any sort of tonal grounding, so the tools available through set theory, which was developed to help understand atonal music, are the best analytical tools for the music in *Signs*. Despite the prominence of the three-note motive, not every moment of music in *Signs* is without a tonal center.

Chapter 6 begins with an explanation of the tools that are commonly used to analyze atonal music, and that will be employed, along with harmonic function, Roman numerals, and key areas, which are commonly used in melodic and harmonic analysis of tonal music. Following these definitions, the cues will be grouped in various ways to show the various relationships between them.

The majority of this final chapter is dedicated to a close reading of each cue, which will demonstrate how each cue functions individually and within the greater narrative of the film. Unlike chapter 5, the cues in the analytical section will be discussed chronologically. The three-note motive, referred to throughout the rest of the chapter as the TNM, goes through multiple variations, developing and transforming over the course of the film. While it is nearly impossible to try to impose a single style on Howard's music, the analysis will show that Howard's music for *Signs* is strongly influenced by the music of Igor Stravinsky, and notably his work *The Rite of Spring*.

Atonal Theory Background and Terminology

Before presenting the analysis, a number of terms must be defined in order to make sense of the analysis. These terms and analytical tools are widely used to discuss music that does not operate within the typical common-practice tonal framework to which music from 1700 to 1890 generally adhered. Arnold Schoenberg, Alban Berg, and Anton Webern are the most famous composers to have their music analyzed through these tools, as their music, particularly after 1909, did not have a tonal center. These composers are commonly referred to as comprising the Second Viennese School, a compositional school of thought where tonality was eschewed in favor of music that did not contain a single clearly identifiable tonal center, usually referred to as "atonal."[1] Schoenberg rejected the term "atonal," as he felt the word did not properly serve the music. In his *Theory of Harmony*, Schoenberg wrote, "I have to dissociate myself from that, however, for I am a musician and have nothing to do with things atonal. The word 'atonal' could only signify something entirely inconsistent with the nature of tone."[2] While Schoenberg, Berg, and Webern may be the most familiar atonal composers, the tools of atonal analysis can be applied to music that is less clearly tonally defined, such as the music of Igor Stravinsky, Béla Bartók, Dmitri Shostakovich, and Leonard Bernstein, among many others. Many film composers use sections of cues or even complete cues that lack a clearly defined tonal center, or a tonal center at all. The following terms will be used in this chapter:

Pitch: The specific note and octave in which it appears. The note that appears just below the staff in the treble clef is "Middle C;" this note's pitch is C4. One octave above is C5; one octave below is C3.

Pitch-Class: All octaves are equivalent, meaning that regardless of the octave in which a note appears, all octaves are the same. Additionally, enharmonic pitches are equivalent, meaning that a note can be spelled as either F# or G♭, and it is the same pitch. This is rarely true in common-practice tonal music, where specific spelling is intentional.

Integer Notation: The application of numbers to pitch-classes. The easiest way to conceptualize this idea is to place the twelve chromatic pitch-classes on a clock face. The pitch-class that appears at the top of the clock is C, but it does not have an integer of 12. Instead, its integer notation is 0. Each of the other pitches are then placed, in ascending order, around the clock. Therefore, C = 0, C# = 1, D = 2, ... F = 5, F# =

6, ... A = 9, A# = T, and B = E. The letters "T" and "E" are used in place of "10" and "11" in order to avoid confusion.

Ordered Pitch Intervals (OPI): The absolute distance between pitches, as measured in half-steps. A "+" or "-" sign indicates the direction of the interval, with "+" indicating ascending and "-" indicating descending. The distance from F#3 up to A3 is +3, while the distance from A4 down to F#3 is -15.

Ordered Pitch-Class Intervals (OPCI): The distance from one pitch-class to the next, always moving in a clockwise fashion. The distance from F# to A is 3, while the distance from A to F# is 9.

Unordered Pitch-Class Intervals (UPCI): The distance from one pitch-class to the next, always covering the shortest distance possible. The distances from both F# to A and A to F# are 3.

Pitch-Class Set: An unordered collection of pitch-classes, most commonly given in order of appearance in the music.

Normal Order: A representation of a pitch-class set that presents the set in its most compact form. The integers in normal order always move clockwise.

Prime Form: An abstract representation of normal order that allows easy comparison between sets.

Grouping the Cues

The film's cues can be grouped in multiple ways. The initial statement of the TNM occurs in the opening music of the film, the cue "Main Titles." This version of the TNM will be referred to as the "Alien TNM," because of its menacing sound, and its association throughout the film with the aliens. The TNM occurs in the second cue in the film, "First Crop Circles," where Graham finds the crop circle in his cornfield. This version of the TNM will be referred to as the "Belief TNM," because Morgan says to his father, "I think God did it," when the cue begins, and because of its continued association with faith and belief throughout the film.

The only cue that contains both the Alien and Belief TNMs is "The Hand of Fate, Part 1," which makes sense as that cue accompanies the climax of the film, the big reveal, shown in table 6.1.

Cues containing the Alien TNM	Cues containing the Belief TNM
Main Titles	First Crop Circles
Roof Intruder	Death of Houdini
Interesting Developments	Crop Circles in India
Brazilian Video	Baby Monitor
Boarding Up the House	In the Cornfield
Into the Basement	Through the Telescope
The Hand of Fate, Part 1	Throwing a Stone
	The Hand of Fate, Part 1

Table 6.1 – Cues Containing Either the Alien TNM or Belief TNM

In terms of the three-act structure of the film, the cues fall into the following acts:

Act I	Main Titles, First Crop Circles, Death of Houdini, Roof Intruder, Crop Circles in India, Recruiting Office, Pizza Parlour, Baby Monitor
Act II	In the Cornfield, Interesting Developments, Through the Telescope, Brazilian Video, Throwing a Stone
Act III	Boarding Up the House, Into the Basement, Asthma Attack, The Hand of Fate, Part 1, The Hand of Fate, Part 2

Table 6.2 – The Three-Act Structure of *Signs*

Act I presents the primary impetus of the film—aliens or not—for both the audience and the characters to solve. Act II begins when Graham, now a skeptic of everything, firmly believes that aliens are present after seeing one in his cornfield. Act III features the actual attack on the home and subsequent resolution. While Act I has the greatest number of cues, many of them are shorter than two minutes in length. Acts II and III have the same number of cues, five, but the cues in Act III are longer in duration, extending the music throughout the entire act. Once the assault on the house begins, the music is constant.

Because of the changes and variations to the TNM that occur throughout the film, and the fact that two specific versions, the Alien TNM and the Belief TNM, regularly recur, the cues will be presented chronologically. Through close examination of each cue, specific style traits of Howard's will become clear. While Howard's style is not one that can be adequately summarized, due to his ability to compose in all styles and genres, the style traits that will be highlighted are those that are similar to concert composer Igor Stravinsky, namely rhythm and stratification, or multiple independent layers occurring simultaneously.

Act I

Main Titles 1m1 v4 (0:00:29-0:02:09)

In his book *Music and Levels of Narration in Film*, Guido Heldt writes, "The transitional nature of title sequences is not just an introduction into a narrative, but also into a frame of mind."[3] *Signs* opens in silence and darkness.[4] Two credits are provided before the Main Title sequence begins. First, the Touchstone Pictures logo is shown followed by the Blinding Edge Pictures logo, each displayed for approximately fifteen seconds. The cue, which has several sections, as shown below in table 6.3, begins at 0:00:29 in the film.

Section	1	2a	2b	3a	3b
Measures	1-12	13-21	21-25	26-29	30-42
Time	0:29-0:52	0:53-1:13	1:13-1:26	1:26-1:36	1:36-2:09

Table 6.3 – Sections in "Main Titles"

The first sounds heard are those of two violins playing a tritone, the notes A and E-flat over a sustained D; these notes create the span of a minor ninth, shown in example 6.1a.

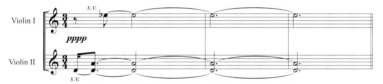

Example 6.1a – "Main Titles," mm. 1-3

The normal order of these three notes is (923), and its prime form is (016). As each iteration of the tritone is sounded, a new credit fades in and out on the screen, presenting the four main credits of the film. At 0:00:29, the film's distributer, "Touchstone Pictures Presents," is shown, followed by "A Blinding Edge Pictures/Kennedy/Marshall Production" at 0:00:34. Blinding Edge is Shyamalan's production company, and Kathleen Kennedy and Frank Marshall are the two executive producers of the film. Next, the two main stars of the film, Mel Gibson, at 0:00:41, and Joaquin Phoenix, at 0:00:46, are credited. Following Phoenix's credit, the screen fully fades to black, so that when the film's title, "Signs," is displayed, it does so with a flash of light. These four titles end the opening segment of the "Main Titles," mm. 1-12 of the cue, which serve as a musical introduction.

The second section of the "Main Titles" begins with the first statement of the Alien TNM, shown in example 6.1b, from which the majority of this film's music is derived. The TNM is synchronized to sound as the film's title appears on screen, which occurs at 0:00:53.

Example 6.1b – "Main Titles," mm. 13-14

In this second section of the cue, mm. 13-21, from 0:00:53 to 0:01:13, there is no further synchronization between audio and visual elements. The only credit other than actors in this section is the casting director. Once the TNM is first sounded, it appears on every beat in every measure in this section, and then stops very suddenly.

A brief interlude and respite from the intensity of the TNM, which functions as a transition at the end of the second section, lasts for ten seconds, 0:01:13-0:01:26, mm. 21-25 of the cue. In this section, the two harps play a repeated pattern over sustained harmonies in the strings. After the casting director's credit has faded, James Newton Howard's credit appears before the screen once again fully fades to black.

The start of the third section begins at 0:01:26. The credits no longer fade on screen; now they immediately appear, or "pop." These "pops" are synchronized with the horns, which play sixteenth notes, shown in example 6.1c. The prime form of these notes is (012), a very dissonant pitch-class collection. The "pops" occur twice, once for the credits for the visual effects, and once for the costume designer. This portion of the cue is mm. 26-29. The "pops" occur on the downbeats of m. 26 and m. 28. Measure 26 in the piano lacks the accented downbeat chord, but that chord is present on the downbeats of mm. 27-29.

Example 6.1c – "Main Titles," mm. 26-27

The cue continues to grow in intensity, and the final part of the cue, which is also the longest, begins at 0:01:36. To visually accompany the growing intensity of the music, the titles no longer pop, but appear to "fly" at the screen from some unseen location behind the viewer's head. As the credits "land" on screen, they are synchronized with the orchestral accents. The TNM is no longer present, but a variation is used in this section. Instead of beginning on the beat, the three notes here begin in the middle of the beat, shown in example 6.1d.

Example 6.1d – "Main Titles," String parts in mm. 33-34

Throughout this section, the dynamics grow, the texture grows, and the overall energy grows until the final moment of the cue, which is only scored for bass drum and taiko drum, suddenly ending the cue. With this final attack, it is almost like a door being slammed shut, as the screen moves immediately to black. After two additional seconds of black screen, the film begins.

Multiple three-note gestures are used in the "Main Titles," including the alien version of the TNM. Table 6.4 provides a list of those elements in the cue.

Instrument	Violin	Piano/Harp	Horns	Piano/WW
Section	1	2a	3a	3b
Measures	1-12	13-20	26-29	32-33
Pitch-classes	D-A-E♭	A-D-E♭	E-F-E♭	G-B-A#
OPI	<+7, +6>	<+5, +1>	<+1, -2>	<+4, -1>
NO	(923)	(923)	(345)	(7TE)
Prime Form	(016)	(016)	(012)	(014)

Table 6.4 – Use of TNM in "Main Titles"

From the table, it can be seen that all four instances contain a half step, as shown in their prime forms. In the case of the violin, the half step is displaced by an octave. In three of the four uses, the half step is used very directly, as shown in the OPI. And only once is that half step descending. Even in the case of the violin, the half step is ascending over an octave.

The transition in Section 2 of the cue uses a four-note gesture in the harps, which has an OPI of <+1, +5, -1>, a normal order of (45TE), and a prime form of (0167). This passage is shown in example 6.2.

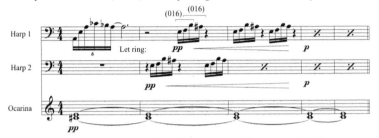

Example 6.2 – "Main Titles," Transition, mm. 21-25

While the TNM is not present here, many attributes of it are, such as the distance from the first to last note spanning a tritone (E-A#), the ascending leap of a perfect fourth, and the embedding of (016) twice in the collection. Underneath the harps' notes, the violas are sustaining the pitches C#-D-D#-E, (1234) in normal order and (0123) in prime form. This dissonant collection foreshadows the (012) motive in the horns that appears in mm. 26-29 of the cue, and the dissonance adds extra suspense and anticipation to the music, as well as the visual element of the titles.

The Alien TNM, specifically the notes A-D-E♭, (016), is not just representative of the aliens. It is also representative of Graham's absence of faith and feelings of loss, represented and manifested in the tritone. Regarding this music, Howard said, in an interview,

> The main-title sequence, which has attracted a fair bit of attention, is one of those unusual situations in that that was a piece of music that was written after Night storyboarded the movie for me. He hadn't shot the movie yet, and I wrote that piece, and at the time he responded to it very positively, but his concern and mine based on the storyboarding was that there didn't seem to be an obvious place for that level of intensity in the movie. But we kept it in the back of our minds hoping that somewhere later in the process we'd find a home for it. It was really his idea to use it as the main title and cue the titles to the music.[5]

Howard has previously mentioned that not every musical idea that ends up in the film is what he would have chosen, or even that he would pursue. Directors often hear something they like and ask him to alter or expand upon an idea. The "Main Titles" is one such case, as Howard gives the credit to Shyamalan for hearing how the music could ultimately be used in the film, and, rather than asking Howard to change it, cut the credits to match it, keeping the power and intensity of the music.

In addition to declaring what will be seen and heard over the course of the film, the "Main Titles" also provides a template for how the music will be constructed. In this way, the first hints of Stravinsky can be heard. These influences include both the repeating gesture of the TNM and the orchestration technique of stratification. The term stratification refers to multiple independent layers of music sounding simultaneously. This is different from polyphony, as the musical lines in polyphony are all related to each other, whereas in stratification, those lines are truly independent and unrelated. Like Stravinsky's music in *The Rite of Spring*, lengthy melodies are rarely heard, instead favoring short gestures. The music in *Signs* certainly favors this model, as the TNM is nearly as short a gesture as can exist, and the music favors the TNM over melodic content. A final point of comparison can be made between the "Main Titles" and the famous "Dances of the Young Girls" portion of *The Rite of Spring*. The dance begins with a chord sounded thirty-two times in a row, but with accents that do not regularly occur, thus preventing the music from becoming dull and boring. But because this music occurs for so long, the term harmonic stasis applies, as the harmony does not change during these thirty-two iterations. In "Main Titles," the Alien TNM is sounded thirty-two times in a row, with no change in the underlying harmony. Instead of using accents, Pete Anthony orchestrated the TNM to move around the woodwind section, allowing the different colors and timbres to pop. The fact that the number of occurrences, thirty-two, is the same between the two works is largely coincidental, as each passage in question consists of eight measures, with four statements of the respective gesture in each measure, a fully common musical idea. The music in "Main Titles" bears a striking resemblance to approaches that Stravinsky took in his own music.

First Crop Circles 1m2 v6 (0:05:00-0:06:50)

As it is used in the film, the cue begins in m. 32. For the first half of the cue, the God's-Eye View is shown, giving the audience the view of how the cornfield looks from the sky. Then, the screen briefly goes black, and time and place are established through titles on the screen. The image then cuts back to Graham on the phone. The music remains consistent throughout the cue, as the piano is the musical focus:

Example 6.3 – "First Crop Circles," mm. 39-48
(String harmonies are indicated under the piano part.)

The strings harmonize the piano with C major and C minor triads, in alternation. The perceived slow tempo, along with the emphasis on the piano, imbues the cue with wonder and mystery. These elements are reinforced when the God's-Eye View of the cornfield is presented, and the crop circles are shown to be perfect. Because of the consistency of the music, even when Graham is on the phone, looking for a rational explanation, the audience knows that his search will be in vain, as nothing terrestrial could have made those circles so perfectly.

Death of Houdini 1m3 v10 (0:11:36-0:12:05)

The cue is very short, both in terms of time and in terms of measures, just twelve, and contains the first appearance of the Belief TNM. The opening six measures are shown in example 6.4. The strings fluctuate between C major and C minor twice, ending on the C minor triad, as the dynamics fade to nothing. The loudest dynamic of the entire cue is *piano*, as the music is intended to be mysterious and unexplained. This cue functions as a scene overlap, showing that time passes between when Houdini, the dog, is killed, and when Bo interrupts Graham's sleep that evening.

Example 6.4 – "Death of Houdini," mm. 1-6

Roof Intruder 1m4 v3 (0:13:26-0:15:39)

The cue "Roof Intruder" begins shortly after the famous clip from the film's trailer where Bo says to her father, "There's a monster outside my room. Can I have a glass of water?" Graham has a short conversation with her about prayer and "talking to mommy," and both admit that she doesn't answer them. Graham's eyes then turn to the window, and he sees a figure on the roof, which is when the cue begins. Table 6.5 shows the sections in the cue.

Section	1	2a	2b	3
Measures	1-5	6-29	30-44	45-62
Tempo	♩=58.85	♩=127	♩=127	♩=89.25
Time	13:26-13:39	13:40-14:24	14:25-14:52	14:53-15:39

Table 6.5 – Sections in "Roof Intruder"

The startling attack, a quick turn of four notes, D-C#-C-D, is accentuated with the use of a triangle beater scraping on a tam-tam.[6] This collection, (012) in prime form, recalls the horns in Section 4 of the "Main Titles" cue, with its extreme dissonance. The bassoons and cellos then descend and arpeggiate through a C#°[7] chord, which contains two pairs of tritones, to continue the sense of dread.

Graham then runs downstairs and grabs Merrill to let him know that "Lionel Pritchard and the Wolfington Brothers are back." Because Graham and Merrill believe it to be "these goofballs," the music reflects this, and turns from menacing to innocuous. As Merrill and Graham plan their "attack" inside the doorway of the house, the music is essentially static for approximately forty seconds, from 0:13:40 to 0:14:25, mm. 6-29 in the cue. This music serves as unfrightening accompaniment, but also stays out of the way of the dialogue between the characters. Only flute, piccolo, and piano are used in this passage, and even though the TNM is not present, a variation on it is. Example 6.5 shows these three instruments in mm. 14-17.

Example 6.5 – "Roof Intruder," mm. 14-17

What keeps the music from actually becoming static is the changing pattern in the flutes, adding the pitch G, and beginning patterns in different locations than the piccolo. In this way, the stasis is similar to "The Dances of the Young Girls" in the early part of Stravinsky's *The Rite of Spring*, which sounds the exact same harmony in the exact same instruments thirty-two times in a row. What prevents that music from becoming fully static is the uncertainty and seemingly random accent pattern. The notes and timbres in this cue are analogous to Stravinsky's accents. Metric displacement of the piccolo G, a technique used in Stravinsky's "Introduction to Part I" with the opening bassoon melody, also occurs in "Roof Intruder."

Once the motion detector light triggers, Graham and Merrill run outside the house to corner Lionel and the Wolfingtons. This third section of the cue begins at 14:25, and is marked by a change in pitch from what was just heard. To continue the humorous chase, a marimba enters, and while the range of the orchestra is no longer limited to the very upper reaches, there continues to be no bass register. But when Graham and Merrill meet on the other side of the house, without either seeing the mysterious figure(s), the music slows and loses its repetitive nature, with Merrill asking, "How did *he* get up *there*?" This is the point where the fourth part of the cue begins.

The orchestra no longer resides in just the upper or upper and middle registers; instead, this part of the cue begins in the extreme low register, with a bass drum roll to enhance the low rumble of ominousness. The cellos play an extremely soft version of the opening gesture of the film two octaves lower—D2-A2-E♭3—followed by the violins playing the same gesture at the original pitch.

The TNM returns in the harps and flutes near the end of the cue. We view Merrill, as we would see him from the vantage point on the roof; Merrill looks up in stunned amazement as the TNM sounds, and asks Graham, "Are you sure it's just Lionel Pritchard?" The presence of the TNM tells the audience that it certainly is not just Lionel, that something much more ominous was at the house that night.

Crop Circles in India (0:20:35-0:24:14)

This cue contains four separate sections, shown in table 6.6, and begins when an expert on crop circles is discussing all of their global appearances. The opening of the cue contains a low rumble from the basses, harps, piano, and bass drum. The brass enter seventeen seconds into the cue, with slow-moving harmonies, reminiscent of the piano part in "First Crop Circles." When the expert provides the two possibilities, the cue enters its second section, with a tempo and gesture similar to the TNM. This is shown in example 6.6.

Section	1	2	3	4
Measures	1-9	10-16	17-46	47-67
Time	20:35-21:18 (0:43)	21:19-21:33 (0:14)	21:34-23:21 (1:47)	23:22-24:14 (0:52)
Tempo	♩=50	♩=91	♩=63	♩=91

Table 6.6 – Sections in "Crop Circles in India"

Example 6.6 – "Crop Circles in India," mm. 5-10

Very quickly, the action moves from inside to outside the house, and a tempo change, from ♩=91 to ♩=63, occurs in m. 17, initiating the third section of the cue. This section, which accompanies Office Paski's "research report" to Graham, is by far the longest section of the cue. This section is basically a four-measure pattern that is repeated, with layers added or subtracted on each repetition. Example 6.7 provides a reduction of mm. 17-20.

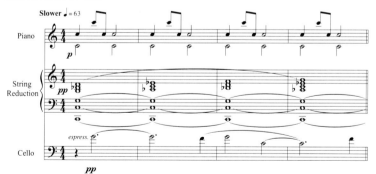

Example 6.7 – "Crop Circles in India," mm. 17-20

The moderately static nature of this section allows the audience to focus on the dialogue while still allowing the music to grow in intensity, due to its repetitive nature. The repetition creates anticipation for what will occur when the cue changes.

The family gets into the car and heads into town. As they are close to arrival, the fourth and final section of the cue begins. This part of the cue uses the God version of the TNM, beginning in m. 47, at 0:23:22. As the car enters town, we are shown the God's-Eye View of the town. For the first time, the God's-Eye View is accompanied by the Belief TNM, connecting the musical and visual elements. Unlike the initial use of the Belief TNM, this version begins on the note B, and is harmonized with both B major and B minor. While it may sound exactly like the original version, which begins on the note C, it is just different enough that the audience might notice a slight difference.

Recruiting Office (0:26:05-0:28:19)

This cue is divided into two parts, and the start of the second part is not marked by a tempo change. While an actual tempo change does not occur, the tempo is certainly perceived to have slowed down.

The cue begins while Merrill is in the Army recruiting office in town. The recruiter, identified by his nameplate as SFC Cunningham, begins talking to Merrill, describing to Merrill what has been happening, that no one has been hurt, and "that's the giveaway." As he says "No one's been hurt," the music heard during the cue "Roof Intruder" begins. When the music was heard in "Roof Intruder," it did not feel ominous. That same music sounds here, even though what Cunningham describes, probing, is quite frightening, evaluating the danger level, "for the rest of them." Merrill attempts to deflect the distress of Cunningham's statement by chuckling and asking for a pamphlet, and the second part of the cue begins.

This second part is initiated by Cunningham recognizing Merrill as a former minor league baseball player who held home run records. As he recognizes Merrill, at 0:26:45, the music seems to slow down, as long durations and tied notes appear throughout the remainder of the cue. As Cunningham asks Merrill about his minor league baseball career, the music moves in a similar fashion to the piano at the start of "First Crop Circles."

This motion ceases once Lionel Pritchard interjects himself into the conversation, mentioning that Merrill also has strikeout records, notably that he has more strikeouts than any two players combined. The music in the strings and harp is a polychord, using both an E major triad and a B♭ major triad simultaneously. The distance between the two chord roots is a tritone. The negativity of the tritone is still present, but instead of being motivated by the aliens, it is motivated by Lionel.

Stravinsky, as well as many other composers throughout the twentieth century, used polychords in their compositions. However, Stravinsky's use of polychords in his ballets *Petrushka* and *The Rite of Spring* may be the most famous use. He used two triads, CM and F#M, to signify the "Petrushka Chord." In *The Rite of Spring*, the chord at the beginning of the "Dance of the Young Girls" is an F♭M triad and an E♭Mm^7 chord. The "Petrushka Chord" has roots that are a tritone apart, like the EM and B♭M polychord in "Recruiting Office." The use of this specific polychord is another indication of the influence of Stravinsky on this score.

As Lionel continues his diatribe against Merrill, Cunningham disappointedly asks, "You really got the strikeout record?" Merrill stands in silence, as he thinks of a response to Cunningham's question. Of particular significance is the motion between the last two chords, B♭ major and C# major. The two chord roots are an enharmonic minor third apart, and the triadic quality between both is the same. This creates a relationship between the two chords known as a chromatic mediant relationship. This relationship does not naturally exist within a key, and therefore, has special importance within tonal music. Chromatic mediants rarely occur in this film, with the other occurrences at the end, in both parts of "The Hand of Fate." In its use at the end of "Recruiting Office," it foreshadows the revelation that everything happens for a reason. Merrill says, "It felt wrong not to swing." In the film's climactic moment, Merrill has to "Swing away" in order to save the family, and the use of the chromatic mediant in this cue, particularly because of the dialogue, very subtly and retrospectively, connects the conclusion of the film to this moment.

Pizza Parlour 2m2 v3 (0:29:35-0:30:54)

"Pizza Parlour" is a relatively short cue, lasting approximately eighty seconds. Unlike most cues, "Pizza Parlour" does not have separate sections within the cue, and the music remains at the same tempo, ♩=58, throughout the cue. This cue accompanies a scene where the Hess family is eating pizza, and Graham sees a man outside. When that man makes eye contact with Graham, he quickly gets into his car and speeds away. The moment he drives away, the gesture in the piccolos changes, but the style remains the same.

Very little dialogue occurs while the Hess family is eating. Morgan asks, "Is that him?" Merrill, after a long pause, responds, "Yeah." After another long pause, Bo asks, "Who is he?" The fact that the music changes very little during the scene helps make the scene more intense. The mystery of the man's identity, coupled with nearly a minute of the same gesture in the piccolos, gives the cue a sense of questioning.

The gesture played in the piccolos at the outset of the cue is a variation of the TNM, shown in example 6.8.

Example 6.8 – "Pizza Parlour," mm. 1-2

This variation, the Reddy TNM, shows similarities to the Alien and Belief versions of the TNM. However, the differences are more substantial. The Reddy TNM has a normal order of (E16) and a prime form of (027), with an OPI of <+2, +5>. The most noticeable difference between this variation and the Alien and Belief TNMs is that this variation lacks a half step. Additionally, the Reddy TNM has its largest leap between the second and third notes, rather than between the first and second, like the alien and God versions of the TNM. Finally, the prime form of the Reddy TNM's is symmetrical, unlike the others.

Because of the absence of the half step in the Reddy TNM, it lacks the danger of the Alien TNM, and the added dissonance of the Belief TNM. As Reddy's car peels away, the Reddy TNM immediately ends, as his on-screen presence immediately ends. In its place is a different three-note gesture, played by the piccolos. The rhythm of the TNM is gone, as is the fully ascending contour of the gesture. This idea has a normal order of (126), a prime form of (015), and an OPI of <-5, +1>. The ascending half step is reinstated, and the prime form of the gesture is exactly the same as the prime form of the Belief TNM. The large difference is that this gesture is not fully ascending, as the first note of the group is higher than the last.

Despite having a clearly defined tonic pitch of F#, the final melodic pitch is dissonant, a D, over the C#-F#-C# in the strings, removing the clarity of the tonic note. Taking those three notes, their normal order is (126), just like the gesture in the piccolos, and the same prime form as the Belief TNM. The idea being conveyed through the music is that the death of Graham's wife was part of God's plan, and Ray Reddy was simply the instrument through which that plan was realized. This explains why the Reddy TNM has a prime form of (027), but the three-note gesture after he leaves the scene is (015).

The symmetry present in the prime form of the Reddy TNM implies perfection, which in turn implies God. Later in the film, Reddy will tell Graham that the accident had to happen at "that right moment," implying a level of divine intervention, and that he was the instrument of God, in this case. The Reddy TNM is rare, never appearing for more than two consecutive measures after this cue. It returns in "Throwing a Stone," in two nonconsecutive measures, "Asthma Attack," at its original pitch level, and in "The Hand of Fate, Part 2," in two nonconsecutive measures, transposed to begin on the note C, and solving the B-C problem that was also present in "Crop Circles in India."

Baby Monitor 2m3 v2 (0:33:25-0:34:28)

Like "Pizza Parlour," "Baby Monitor" is relatively short, lasting just over a minute. Also like "Pizza Parlour" "Baby Monitor" operates in the same style for the duration of the cue. The only tempo change is at the very end of the cue, which is marked with a *ritardando*, and not a new tempo.

The cue occurs after the Hess family returns from their outing, as Morgan picks up sounds on the baby monitor. Graham and Merrill dismiss the sounds as "just noise," with Merrill ranting about nerds being behind the crop circles and the noises. Graham takes the monitor from Morgan, but Merrill begins to hear voices within the noise on the baby monitor. As Graham says he's putting the monitor down, Morgan, Bo, and Merrill implore him not to do it. Merrill says, "You'll lose the signal," and the cue begins.

The opening measures set the tone of the cue, with the Belief TNM presented in m. 1. The TNM changes in m. 2, and then again in m. 3. These changes are shown in Example 6.9. Measures 1-4 are essentially the same as mm. 5-8 and mm. 9-12. Example 6.9, which shows mm. 5-8, provides the fullest version of the harmonic accompaniment in the strings. Table 6.7 provides a comparison of the TNMs in the first three measures of each repetition.

The size of the largest ascending leap grows from 7 to 8 to 10. The smaller leap also grows, from 1 to 3 to 4. While the Belief TNM is used in the first measure of each four-measure statement, it does not quite sound like the Belief TNM because of the surrounding accompaniment. The harmonization, the beginning pitch, and the rapid changes in the intervals prevent the TNM from sounding too much like the original statement of the Belief TNM. The clicks and taps of the conversation sound distinctly nonhuman.

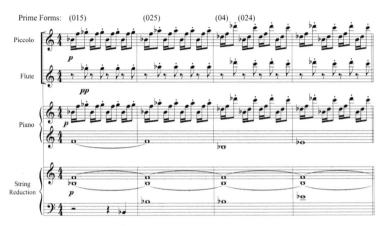

Example 6.9 – "Baby Monitor," mm. 5-8

Measure	1	2	3a	3b
Pitches	B♭-F-G♭	B♭-F-A♭	D♭-F-D♭	B♭-D-C
OPI	<+7, +1>	<+7, +3>	<+4, +8>	<+4, +10>
NO	(56T)	(58T)	(15)	(T02)
PF	(015)	(025)	(04)	(024)

Table 6.7 – Use of TNM in mm. 1-3 of "Baby Monitor"

A new pattern begins in m. 13, at 0:33:57, as the family's hands all connect, using the car as a sort of receiver. The pattern is stated three times, like the first pattern, but this one is twice as short, with mm. 13-14 equating to 15-16 and 17-18. Example 6.10 shows a reduction of mm. 13-14. The example shows the last note of the TNM rising in these two measures, from A to B to C#, which is also done, in parallel motion, in the first violins, which move from D♭ to E♭ to F. Enharmonically, these are parallel sixths, a standard contrapuntal technique used since the fifteenth century. The accompaniment sounds like the "Hollywood cadence," a specific gesture in music that, in functional harmony, can be represented in Roman numerals as IV-ii$^{ø6}_5$-I. In the key of C major, the chords would be FM-D$^{ø6}_5$-CM; the melody would be C-D-E (Do-Re-Mi) while the bass line would be F-D-C (Fa-Re-Do). In "Baby Monitor," the harmonies are G♭m and D♭M$^6_4$, iv-I$^6_4$ in D♭ major, but the melody in the first violins is still "Do-Re-Mi," and the progression still moves from a borrowed predominant harmony to the tonic. Instead of indicating the end of the scene, the accompaniment signals the wonder of the family's hands connecting and the improved clarity of the conversation on the monitor. Table 6.8 shows the TNM in mm. 13-14.

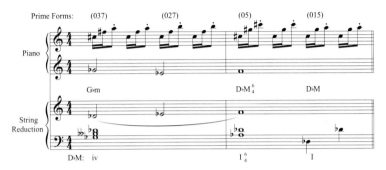

Example 6.10 – "Baby Monitor," mm. 13-14

Measure	13a	13b	14a	14b
Pitches	C#-F#-A	C#-F#-B	C#-G#-C#	C#-G#-A
OPI	<+5, +3>	<+5, +5>	<+7, +5>	<+7, +1>
NO	(691)	(E16)	(81)	(891)
PF	(037)	(027)	(05)	(015)

Table 6.8 – Use of TNM in mm. 13-14 of "Baby Monitor"

Like earlier in the cue, the largest ascending leap in each of the four statements expands, from 5 to 7. Earlier, the group began with (015). Here, the group ends with (015).

The TNM no longer changes at the end of the cue, remaining on (015) from the end of the previous pairs of measures. Measures 19-20 are repeated in mm. 21-22; measures 23-25 consist solely of a sustained dyad of E and A. The conversation on the monitor ends, goes to static, and the cue dies away.

While the prime form of (015) plays a significant role, and it is an exact transposition of the Belief TNM, its use in this cue is not the same, largely because God is in no way invoked in this scene, but also because the accompaniment is completely different. Additionally, the TNM changes from measure to measure, something that does not occur when the Belief TNM is used. "Baby Monitor" projects the mystery and wonder of who, or what, is on the other end of the transmission. It doesn't sound hostile, like the music does during the Main Titles, yet it doesn't sound benevolent. It's somewhere in between the two, much like Graham, trying to decide if the aliens are real or not, even though he saw one on the roof of his house. The fact that four versions of the TNM are used may be representative of each of the four family members. By the time the cue begins, Graham is the only member of the family who does not believe that aliens are present. This will change during his encounter in the cornfield later that night.

Summary of Act I

Act I of the film contains both the Alien TNM and the Belief TNM, as well as several other variations of the TNM. The "probing" variation of the TNM occurs twice in Act I, and does not appear in the rest of the film, as the aliens no longer are probing. The Reddy TNM, which eliminates the half step from the Alien and Belief TNMs, is first used in the "Pizza Parlour" cue, when the audience is introduced to him. The Alien TNM is only used once in Act I after the Main Titles, and that is in "Roof Intruder," when Merrill and Graham question how "he" got "up there." But the dominant TNM in Act I is the Belief TNM, imbuing wonder and belief in something larger than humanity, whether it is in God, benevolent alien travelers, or something else. The Belief TNM appears in three cues in Act I, and musically focuses the audience's attention on the positive elements that could come from alien visitors.

Act II

In the Cornfield 3m1 v7-8 (0:38:14-0:43:49)

Act II of the film is initiated once Graham believes that aliens are actually invading Earth. After the baby monitor incident, Graham goes outside and into the cornfield with a flashlight. Graham begins heading back toward the house and pauses, again hearing the alien's clicks. Scared, he drops the flashlight, picks it up, slaps it until the light comes back on, shines it out into the corn, and sees the leg of a being. Terrified, Graham runs back through the corn to the house. The cue begins as Graham sees the leg.

"In the Cornfield" contains three large sections. The first is when Graham runs back to the house, and then is inside with the rest of the family, finally acknowledging the need to turn on the television. The second takes place as the whole family watches television. The third is a conversation between Graham and Merrill as the kids are asleep; Merrill asks for comfort. Table 6.9 provides a breakdown of the cue.

Section	1	2	3
Measures	1-30	31-53	54-122
Time	38:14-39:35 (1:21)	39:35-41:11 (1:36)	41:11-43:49 (2:38)
Tempo	♩=91	♩=49.5	♩=91

Table 6.9 – Sections in "In the Cornfield"

The music in Section 1 of the cue is quite familiar, as parts of it have been heard in the cues "Death of Houdini" and in the final part of "Crop Circles in India." This portion of "In the Cornfield" contains the Belief TNM, at its original pitch level, C-G-A♭, with the proper accompaniment, and at the appropriate tempo. This is the first time in the film that the entire harmonic progression has been heard. The full progression is shown in example 6.11. What is surprising about the first section of this cue is the presence of the Belief TNM. But when the Belief TNM has been used in the film, it is used to express the beliefs of a particular character. In this instance, Graham, the last holdout in the family, finally believes that aliens are here.

The second part of this cue is also familiar. This portion of the cue is the Alternate Insert, version 8, replacing the music composed in version 7. The familiar element used is the music from the cue "Baby Monitor." In its use here, it is transposed and almost twice as slow, changing from ♩=91 to ♩=49.5. The music from "Baby Monitor" begins at 39:49, in m. 35. It is used to underscore the family's reaction to what they see and hear on the television, and also to underscore the commentator's statements. The music in Section 2 even follows a structure similar to that of "Baby Monitor"—a four-measure pattern stated twice, a two-measure pattern stated once, and a two-measure pattern stated three times.

Because this music has been heard before, it carries associations from the earlier cue, in that the music is not necessarily hostile, but full of mystery and wonder. The Hess family sees the lights from the spaceship broadcast on the television set, wondering if they are here to help or harm. The news broadcast is not decisive, nor is the music.

The third section of the cue begins with an English horn solo over a sustained A♭ major chord. Merrill is worried and gets mad at Graham for not immediately providing comforting words to him. At 41:36, Merrill asks Graham to pretend to be like he used to be, and just provide comfort. The music sounds similar to the piano music first heard in "First Crop Circles." Finally, at 41:50, m. 76, the piano texture returns, and Graham responds with his analysis of people falling into two groups—those who see signs and miracles, and those who think people just get lucky. The piano is instructed by Atmajian to be "ethere-

al/*espressivo*" while the strings are marked *con calore*, "with warmth."
Merrill is asking for comfort, and it comes from the music.

Example 6.11 – "In the Cornfield," mm. 1-20,
Belief TNM and Accompanying Harmonies

When Graham begins discussing the group who is on their own,
the comforting piano texture ends, and a new gesture begins with the
flutes in m. 90—a simple neighbor gesture, from C to D♭ and back to
C. It is a three-note gesture, clearly derived from the TNM. The harmonies in this section project dissonance, musically depicting the group
who is on their own.

Graham comes back to the group that sees signs and miracles, and
the music returns to the piano texture in m. 106, at 43:08. He comments
that the group is filled with hope, much as the music is. Graham asks
what kind of a person, meaning which group, Merrill is, and then
quickly rephrases the question asking, "Is it possible there are no coincidences?" As the piano texture ends, all that is left sounding is a trichord in the strings of C-D♭-E♭, a prime form of (013). The dissonant

harmony at the end of the cue is intended to build suspense for Merrill's answer and for the reason of the presence of the aliens.

Very little "new" music is used in the cue, as the Belief TNM, the music from "Baby Monitor," and the piano texture from "First Crop Circles" are all reused. Instead of breaking new musical ground, Howard is asking the audience to connect the musical material from earlier cues in order to create meaning in this cue. The presence of the Belief TNM demonstrates that Graham now believes that aliens are here. The music from "Baby Monitor" inspires wonderment at the possibilities that have been created. These possibilities do not musically sound negative. And the piano texture recalls not just that "God [possibly] did it," but the God's-Eye View from the camera, demonstrating that someone is watching from above. Graham questions if it is God or not, and the cue ends dissonantly, not choosing. After the music ends, Merrill declares he sees signs and miracles, while Graham is insistent that there is no one watching out for us. They fall asleep, and once Graham wakes up, it leads to the next cue.

Interesting Developments 3m2 v5 (0:47:04-0:48:53)

Graham wakes up on the couch the following morning, having briefly dreamt of the night his wife died, but no one is around. He finds Merrill in a utility closet watching television, having sent the kids off to play, and tells Graham of some "interesting developments" regarding the alien crafts, which are camouflaged in the daylight. After Graham exits, Merrill continues on about a theory regarding the crop circles, that they could be used to "navigate, coordinate . . . makes sense."

This cue is divided into two parts, mm. 1-13, 47:04-47:54, and mm. 14-35, 47:55-48:53. In the first part of the cue, Graham awakens, gets his bearings, and follows the power cord of the television into the closet. For the first nine measures of the cue, the violins move back and forth between three chords, shown in example 6.12.

Example 6.12 – "Interesting Developments," mm. 1-9

The three chords, F minor, E major, and A major, do not occur together in any key. Because it both initiates the harmonies, and because the other two chords return to F minor, it can be considered as tonic. If this is the case, extraordinary relationships are being used.

Tchaikovsky's *Symphony No. 4 in F minor*, op. 36, begins with a fanfare on the note F, but the first actual chord to be played is an E major chord, a chord that has no function in the key of F minor. Finding nonfunctional harmonies in tonal-functional music is not easy. In Tchaikovsky's case, he uses the E major triad as the first of three "fate" chords. In a letter to his patroness Nadezhda von Meck in 1878, Tchaikovsky wrote, "This is Fate, the force of destiny, which ever prevents our pursuit of happiness from reaching its goal, which jealously stands watch lest our peace and well-being be full and cloudless. . . . It is invincible, inescapable."[7] Tchaikovsky's view of fate is certainly much more grim than what Shyamalan projects in *Signs*. Howard, knowingly or not, uses Tchaikovsky's musical representation of Fate just after Graham dreams about his wife's death.

The start of the second part of the cue begins with a tempo change from ♩=57.5 to ♩=86.75. As Merrill explains that the schools are closed, and what has happened with the alien ships, chromatic clusters are used in the violas, then the second violins, so that all chromatic pitches between C4 and F#5 are sounded. The boundaries are significant because the distance from bottom to top is an octave plus a tritone.

When Merrill says, "They're still here" at 48:18, the alien TNM, at its original pitch level of A-D-E♭, enters, along with the chromatic cluster in the strings, and additional doublings in the woodwinds and brass. This is the first time since the end of "Roof Intruder" that the Alien TNM has been sounded, now indicating that the intentions of the aliens are likely hostile, rather than benevolent. The TNM ends, leaving only strings sustaining the chromatic clusters and other pitches, until the only instruments left playing are the first violins in a high register. As the music fades out, Merrill gives his theory on the crop circles to Graham, who has already left.

Graham appears to be doing his best to resist the idea that the aliens are even here. The odd harmonies in the first part of the cue can be attributed to Graham's grogginess and confusion from waking up on the couch, but also speak to the fact that events are fated to happen, via Tchaikovsky's harmonies. The element of harmonic stasis, both to prevent forward motion, and to keep attention focused on the dialogue, is used in this cue.

Through the Telescope 3m3 v1 (0:51:42-0:53:11)

This is the only cue that Howard composed for *Signs* that made it to orchestration as version 1. Interestingly, the complete cue is not used in the film, as it begins in m. 16, and is faded out in m. 47, rather than reaching the end of the cue in m. 51. Graham gets a phone call from Ray Reddy, and leaves the house. Morgan looks through a telescope in his room, in search of some bit of evidence of aliens, while Bo has a bad feeling about the upcoming events.

Much of this cue has already been heard. In fact, mm. 21-47 of "Through the Telescope" are essentially identical to mm. 1-27 of "In the Cornfield." The Belief TNM is present, the number of repetitions and the harmonies are the same between the two cues; this cue is clearly designed to recall the music from "In the Cornfield."

Graham believes that Ray Reddy called him, so he heads to Ray's house to check on him. Immediately before the cue begins, Graham again tries to deny to his children that aliens are present, but to no avail. They certainly believe that something is happening. Bo believes that something bad is going to happen to her brother, telling him, "I don't want you to die." Merrill will see the video evidence soon enough.

Brazilian Video 4m2A v5 (0:57:15-0:59:03)

The cue is divided into two parts—before and after the alien is shown in the video. The first part of the cue, mm. 1-18, 57:15-58:24, consists mainly of a pedal fifth, E and B, in the low strings, with a melodic line in the viola and clarinet, and a statement of the Belief TNM in the harp and flutes. This music lasts until m. 14, when the horns and upper strings enter, with directions to bend their pitches. The cellos have a chromatic cluster, spanning a minor sixth, from E4 to C5. This added dissonance increases the tension as the person filming the video moves from room to room, trying to get a better shot of the thing outside. As the child shouts out, "It's behind," the music reaches its loudest volume, and the second part begins with a loud percussion attack as the alien becomes visible from behind a hedge.

The presence of the Belief TNM seems, at first, quite unusual since the video is showing an alien in urban Brazil. The explanation comes from something that the broadcaster says, which is that the news media believes the video to be genuine. It is the belief in the authenticity of the video that allows the Belief TNM to be used here. The expected accompaniment for the Belief TNM is absent, lessening the significance of God's influence, but allowing for belief to be present.

The cue is another example of Howard using the idea of harmonic stasis to heighten the tension in the scene. By having the "melody" last so long, it increases the tension and anxiety of the scene, enhanced by the television broadcaster saying, "What you are about to see may disturb you." Our anxiety grows, but the melody doesn't change, and the payoff works.

At the moment of the big reveal, the downbeat of m. 19, at 58:25, nine of the possible twelve chromatic notes are articulated. Accompanying these notes are accented *sfz* hits in the percussion, and snap pizzicatos in the string basses. After the impact, musical and visual, the Alien TNM begins in the harp, eventually joined by several other instruments. The Alien TNM begins on the note B rather than the original note of A. An explanation for this is that the Belief TNM, heard earlier in this cue, also began on B, so the starting pitch remains consistent throughout the cue.

As Merrill recoils in fear from the television set, then moves closer to watch the clip again, instruments are added to the Alien TNM until the orchestra reaches a *fortissimo* dynamic. As the video, upon replay, is paused at the moment the alien is revealed, the TNM ends, leaving only sustained pitches in the strings that quickly decrescendo, and the cue ends. Even though the alien performs no hostile actions, it is clear what the audience is supposed to think of the aliens by this point.

Throwing a Stone 4m5 v9 (1:06:32-1:10:54)

The title of the cue comes from the action that Merrill takes, throwing a stone into the cornfield. This moment is an homage to a moment in Spielberg's *E.T.*, where Elliott, the boy, throws a ball into the shed, and E.T., unseen, throws it back to him. As we see Merrill throw this stone, we are unsure of what we want to happen, or even what we expect to happen. Do we want an alien to throw it back? Would that make it more friendly? If the stone isn't thrown back, does that mean the aliens aren't in the cornfield?

In its use in the film, nearly all of the first twenty-one measures of the cue are missing. Through editing, a very short lead-in, containing music found in mm. 5-6, initiates the cue, and at 1:06:41, m. 22 to the end of the cue is used. The cue, over four minutes in length, is an anomaly in that it doesn't clearly separate into sections based on tempo or style. The tempo is consistent, the style is consistent, but the versions of the TNM are different.

The Belief TNM appears in m. 22, at 1:06:41, with its expected accompaniment. However, instead of the alternation between the C major and C minor triads every two measures, the harmony remains on C minor after leaving C major. While the Belief TNM is sounding, Merrill walks into the house, and a television broadcaster is heard discussing the number and location of alien crafts around the world. At 1:07:02, m. 30, he begins naming cities with crafts hovering above them, and the TNM changes, reminiscent of the use in the cue "Baby Monitor." Measures 30-31 are shown in example 6.13.

Example 6.13 – "Throwing a Stone," mm. 30-31

The gesture in m. 30 has a normal order of (701), a prime form of (016), and an OPI of <+7, +6>. The prime form is the same as the alien TNM, and the OPI is like the initial violin part in "Main Titles." In m. 31, the gesture expands to a normal order of (803), a prime form of (037), and an OPI of <+8, +7>, as both leaps are enlarged by a half step. Additionally, this is the first time in the film where the TNM in any version is used exclusively in the lower register. The direct hostility first portrayed in the Main Titles is not present, but the underlying danger in the immediate future is what the music projects. Morgan and Merrill realize the horror of the situation—that the crop circles were for navigation—and that the aliens are hostile. Throughout all of this, the music remains fairly static, simply continuing its two-measure pattern. Occasionally, a four-measure idea is added to prevent the music from total stasis, but the music is intentionally designed to stay out of the way of the dialogue.

During this passage, the broadcaster announces that people everywhere are fleeing to their places of worship, hoping to find refuge and solace there, followed by, "God be with us all." As he speaks these words, the camera does a close-up on Graham's face, and we wait for some sort of reaction or response from him. The music at this point, mm. 50-61, consists of a four-measure pattern, mm. 50-53, repeated twice, in mm. 54-57 and mm. 58-61. The static nature of these measures, with no new musical elements, causes anxiety and raises the intensity level, waiting for Graham to either side with or against God. Graham finally says, "I'm going to get back to the windows." By taking some action, the music changes in m. 62, at 1:08:27, sounding more hopeful, and with a change to the TNM, an OPI of <+8, +7>.

In m. 70, at 1:08:48, the TNM moves out of the lower register and begins climbing above C4. The TNM in the harp and piano also adds a note, turning the rhythm into four sixteenth notes. Example 6.14 shows mm. 70-76. The strangeness of a fourth note as part of the motive is not the only unusual element in the example. Throughout this entire cue, the music has operated in four-measure groups. This has largely been true throughout the entire film. However, mm. 74-76 subvert this, changing the four-measure pattern to a three-measure pattern. This strangeness can be attributed to the fact that Morgan tells Merrill that he wishes Merrill was his father. Merrill responds angrily to Morgan, and the three-measure pattern is used. The climax of the cue, m. 77, at 1:09:06, is the most texturally dense part, as Graham looks out a window before nailing a board over it, locking himself and his family inside.

The music slowly begins to unwind as each member of the family declares what he or she will have for their "last supper." The TNM is gone, replaced by a four-note descending arpeggiating gesture in the piano. After all of the food choices have been made, the music stops, as Howard has left the meal unscored, emphasizing the dialogue and relationships between the family members.

Multiple versions of the TNM are used in the cue, beginning with the Belief TNM, which represents the now unwavering belief in the presence of the aliens. The prime form of the alien TNM, (016), is used, but with the OPI of the opening notes of the film. It still sounds menacing, but not quite as hostile as the original alien TNM. The family becomes more dependent upon each other, as the attack is imminent, and Act III of the film is about to begin.

Summary of Act II

The TNM appears in all five cues, with the Alien TNM in two of them and the Belief TNM in the other three. Additionally, the use of the two TNMs alternates during the five cues. While the narrative is certainly focusing on the negative elements of the aliens, the music keeps the potential available that they are friendly, ready to help humanity. In this way, the music represents Morgan's view, which is that he hopes they are friendly. Morgan continues to have faith. Graham's faith is gone, and he focuses on all the negative possibilities of the aliens.

Example 6.14 – "Throwing a Stone," mm. 70-76

Act III

Boarding Up the House 5m1 v10 (1:13:05-1:16:00)

The film's third and final act begins as noise is once again heard on the baby monitor, and all broadcast stations are plunged into their emergency signals. Graham says, "It's happening," as the cue begins. The cue can be broken into three parts, as shown Table 6.10.

Section	1	2	3
Measures	1-15	16-113	114-139
Time	1:13:05-1:13:43 (0:38)	1:13:44-1:15:08 (1:24)	1:15:09-1:16:00 (0:51)

Table 6.10 – Sections in "Boarding Up the House"

While Section 2 of the cue contains the most measures, by far, it is not the longest section of the cue by the same margin. This can be attributed to the fact that the meter in much of Section 2 is § with a tempo marking of ♪=357 (or ♩.=119) while sections 1 and 3 are in ¼, with much slower tempos, ♩=91 and ♩=89.25, respectively.

Section 1 of the cue accompanies Merrill and Graham nailing boards to door frames, in an attempt to stay safe inside the house. Graham looks out a window, and the crickets stop chirping, an eerie event. The TNM used in this section is the same as the one heard in the previous cue, with a prime form of (016) and an OPI of <+7, +6>, but it is broken between the oboe and piccolos. The first pitch in the group here is G#, as opposed to C in the previous cue. The rest of the orchestra has sustained dissonant clusters, emphasizing the horror of the situation.

Section 2 is much more hopeful and much faster. It begins with a six-note gesture played by the harp and piano, shown in example 6.15.

Example 6.15 – "Boarding Up the House," mm. 16-19,
Six-Note Gesture in Piano

This six-note gesture is not two TNMs back-to-back. The prime form of this gesture is (013478), and while (016) is an abstract subset once, (015) is an abstract subset twice, meaning that the six-note gesture is closer to the Belief TNM than the alien TNM. As Graham and Merrill board up the doorway together, Graham turns and sees Bo standing in the hallway, and tells her the story of when she was born. This story begins at 1:14:01, and the meter changes to ⅝.

While Howard has used ⅝ meter in *Signs*, it has almost always been for a single measure, often to extend that measure for the purposes of time. He has written quite a lot of music in ⅝ and ⅞ meters, particularly in the 1990s, as discussed in chapter 2. This is the only extended passage of music in *Signs* that is in ⅞ (or ⅝).

The texture in Section 2 for the story of Bo's Birth, in mm. 33-113, begins very sparsely, using only violins, flutes, harp, and piano. The five-note gesture heard in the harp and piano is shown in example 6.16. Even though five notes are present in the gesture, only four pitch-classes are used, which is why the prime form of that five-note gesture is (0148) and the OPI is <-7, -5, +9, +4>, leaving a net gain of <+1>, the interval that has dominated the TNM throughout the course of the film. As Graham tells Bo of her birth, additional instruments slowly sneak into the texture, with harmonies fluctuating every four measures between Emm[7] and FMM[7]. The five-note gesture changes pitch and contour when these harmonies change, as Graham mentions the nurses looking at Bo's eyes and gasping. When Graham quotes the nurses saying, "She's like an angel," an English horn enters. In mm. 83-113, the strings have a chord progression—Gm-B♭M-Dm-B♭M-Dm-CM-Dm—that instills some sort of hope for the family.

Example 6.16 – "Boarding Up the House," mm. 33-36,
Five-Note Gesture in Harp and Piano

The story that Graham tells to Bo is not just intended to assuage her fears, but the fears of the audience as well. In his story, Bo was referred to as "an angel," and she smiled, an action that newborns cannot voluntarily perform. His words tell us that she is something extraordinary. Howard's music supports this idea by using a meter than has not been substantially used in the film, by avoiding the TNM and using a radically different texture and style than the other sections of the cue, and to an extent, the rest of the film. The music helps the audience feel safe, even for just a minute, despite the current events.

The third and final section of the cue begins as the family heads back downstairs into the living room to wait for whatever is about to happen. The music immediately turns more dissonant, similar to Section 1 of the cue. The alto flutes play the Alien TNM at its original pitch level, while the dissonance in the orchestra grows. In m. 121, the violas are instructed to "start w/ cluster then every few beats (3-6), change to another pitch in the group and hold s.p.n.v. 3-6 beats before changing to the next chosen pitch." The six-note cluster will have arbitrarily chosen dissonance, as the players select the notes. The cluster ends as Isabel is heard whimpering in pain, and the family is left standing closely together, waiting for what is about to happen to them. The only thing sounding is a B5-D6 dyad in the violins, which ends when the wind chimes outside of the house resonate.

Into the Basement 5m2 v14 (1:17:12-1:22:24)

"Into the Basement" can be broken into four distinct parts, as seen in table 6.11. The beginning of each section is marked by a tempo change. The cue is just over five minutes in length, covering multiple narrative elements, which explains the various sections within the cue.

Section	1	2	3	4
Measures	1-16	17-45	46-76	77-142
Time	1:17:12- 1:18:15 (1:03)	1:18:16- 1:18:45 (0:29)	1:18:46- 1:19:32 (0:46)	1:19:33- 1:22:24 (2:51)
Tempo	♩=51	♩=178	♩=150 → 75.5	♩=89.25

Table 6.11 – Sections in "Into the Basement"

Section 1 of this cue tells the story of Morgan's birth. In the previous cue, "Boarding Up the House," Graham told the story of Bo's birth. Morgan's birth was much more difficult. Howard's music in this section is unlike anything else heard in this film, as it is in the style of a chorale, and one that is almost tonally functional. Unlike a chorale in the style of Bach, Howard's chorale has tonal centers that change quickly—F minor, A♭ major, D♭ major, and back to F minor—with key areas linked through stepwise motion or common-tone motion. Although it looks like the tonal centers would cause anxiety because of the rapid changes, much of the connections are through stepwise bass motion, or by connecting chords that share two common tones.

The music momentarily removes the audience from the terror occurring outside of the house. Even though the music is sounding, the aliens can be heard running around the house, banging on windows and doors, looking for a way inside. The goal of most parents is to ensure their children's safety. Graham is attempting to keep his children calm by telling them these stories. He is also not planning on surviving the attack, so he is giving them this information, like a prepared last statement. The chorale emphasizes Graham's calm demeanor.

In Section 2 of the cue, the family stands in the family room, waiting for the aliens to break in. However, Merrill notices the attic door not boarded. The music that accompanies this section was previously heard in Section 2 of "Boarding Up the House," the six-note gesture. The music, based on its usage in both cues, operates as a placeholder, meaning that it doesn't propel the action forward. The action that moves the family into the basement, which has only a single door in or out, is the presence of an alien hand reaching under the front door.

When this happens, the six-note gesture disappears, and the music changes. A few seconds later, the section ends quite dramatically, with two horn "rips," from D4 to E♭5.

Section 3 finds Graham descending the stairs, and through trying to prevent the aliens from getting in, finding the will to live, as he says, "I'm not ready." A version of the Belief TNM is present here, with a normal order of (TE4), and the standard OPI of <+7, +1>, but without the expected accompaniment. Instead, the accompaniment consists only of long tied harmonies in the strings, then with brass added to the chords. As Graham speaks the words, "I'm not ready," the chord, an E♭M^{add9} changes to C#m, motion of only a whole step, as D# and E♭ are enharmonically equivalent, but a significant change in the sound of the chord, one that makes Graham's admission more meaningful.

Section 4 begins in darkness and with a new tempo, and within three measures, the Alien TNM is presented in the cellos. But this version, while having a normal order of (5TE), has an OPI of <+1, +5>, reversing the order of the intervals from the previous uses of the TMN. The intervallic order is reversed to signify the family being in the basement, underground, figuratively in Hell.

After a brief flurry, representing the chaos of the darkness, the music stabilizes, as Graham and Merrill can assess the situation armed with flashlights and the knowledge of where both children are. Throughout this first unstable part of Section 4, the Alien TNM is sounded in multiple instruments. Merrill finds a radio, which only broadcasts static. This leads to a subsection of Section 4, which begins at 1:21:03.

A trumpet initiates this part of the cue, with a melody previously heard in the cue "Throwing a Stone," mm. 46-48, beginning at 1:07:45. In that cue, the melody was played by a solo horn. Here, it is more than an octave higher, and marked as "Solo–Distant," as Graham and Merrill try to figure out why the aliens are simply banging on the door, rather than trying to get in that way. They decide that the aliens are trying to solve this problem, and remember that there is a coal chute somewhere in the basement. This melody, then, articulates the strategic nature of these aliens in that they made navigational maps and can solve complex problems. As Graham and Merrill look for the coal chute, the music remains tense and repetitive. The TNM changes from the Alien version to the God version, with the brothers sure that they will find the coal chute and cover it. The music is soft, as Graham and Merrill work to find the chute, and it dies away as they find Morgan standing directly in front of the chute. Only two seconds pass before the next cue begins.

The cue "Into the Basement" supports a significant amount of action. It allows Graham to give his final words to his son, drives the family into Hell, and creates suspense, with only one way in or out of in the basement. The Alien TNM occurs frequently in this cue, as the aliens are attacking the house, in an attempt to "get" the family. The Alien TNM is replaced by the Belief TNM at the end of the cue, indicating that Graham believes that his family can stay safe, and wait out the attack in the basement, that living in Hell is better than dying.

Asthma Attack (1:22:27-1:26:08)

This cue occurs while Graham is trying to help Morgan breathe after Morgan has an asthma attack, triggered by being grabbed by the alien. The cue can be broken into three sections, as seen in table 6.12.

Section	1	2	3
Measures	1-8	8-19	19-62
Time	1:22:27- 1:22:53 (0:26)	1:22:54- 1:23:29 (0:35)	1:23:30- 1:26:08 (2:38)

Table 6.12 – Sections in "Asthma Attack"

The table shows the three sections within the cue: terror as Morgan is grabbed, the covering of the coal chute, and Graham holding Morgan, trying to slow and help his breathing. As the effort to keep his son from dying is clearly the most important element to this scene, it is logical that the majority of the music would reside in that section of the cue.

Section 1 consists only of clusters and aleatoric music. Example 6.17 reproduces the opening measures of the strings, which sound like shrieking and screaming to prevent being abducted. The struggle in the darkness, which is not actually shown, is presented musically.

After the situation is under control, and Graham has Morgan in his grasp, Merrill covers the coal chute with sacks of corn seed and anything else he can find in Section 2 of the cue. A single line, played in octaves by the contrabass clarinet, celesta, and harp, represents some level of calm, just by the dynamic. This line is shown in example 6.18.

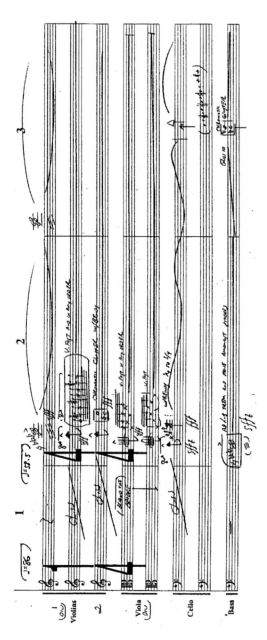

Example 6.17 – "Asthma Attack," mm. 1-3,
String Effects

Example 6.18 – "Asthma Attack," mm. 8-13,
Calming Harp Line

What the melodic line in example 6.18 does is demonstrate how horrible the situation actually is. This line is not particularly melodic at all, with those notes unable to fit into a scale. The rhythm of the first three notes also projects the horrible nature of the scene, beginning on an offbeat, and containing irregular rhythms at its start. The bassoons and cellos enter with their own line in m. 14 as the previous one ends, but this tonal center is no more clear than the previous one. This new melody serves as transition, as the characters refocus on the severity of Morgan's asthma attack, leading to the third section of the cue.

The third section has a tempo change from $\quarternote$=57.5 to $\quarternote$=65, and begins with a version of the Belief TNM in the piccolo, but its OPI is <+1, +4>, spanning the interval of only a P4 rather than a m6. Much like the inversion of the OPI for the alien TNM in the previous cue, so too is this cue's OPI altered, again due to the location of the family in the basement. Graham announces that Morgan's medicine is not with them, and begins speaking to Morgan, willing his son to breathe with him, to feel his chest, and to help him through the attack.

In mm. 19-23, 1:23:30-1:23:49, only an open fifth of F# and C# are sounded. In mm. 24-25, an E is added to those two notes. In mm. 26-27, the harmony is a quintal chord—B-F#-C#— before returning to the open fifth of F# and C# in mm. 27-29.

Beginning in m. 30, at 1:24:11, the music begins moving in the familiar four-measure pattern. The harmonies move stepwise—E♭m-D♭M-C♭M-D♭M—all over an E♭ pedal in the basses. Additional synthesizer parts are added to give the harmonies a wordless choir feel, as though something magical or mystical is about to happen. During the second statement of this four-measure pattern, Graham stops speaking to Morgan and directly addresses God, stating, "Don't do this to me again. Not again," and then, "I hate You. I hate You." This is a significant moment for Graham, as this is the first time in the film that he has acknowledged the presence of God. Up to this point, Graham has refused to believe in God, having lost his faith and given up his position as a minister. Now Graham believes again, but hates God for trying to take away his family, one member at a time.

A new four-measure pattern begins in m. 39, at 1:24:43, as Graham tells Morgan not to fear what is happening, and to believe that it will pass. The Belief TNM cannot be here as Graham's belief in God has manifested itself through hate. The chords in this new pattern—Bm-C#m-Bm⁶-C#m over F#—sound more hopeful because of the richer texture and the rising bass line.

A third and final four-measure pattern begins in m. 47, at 1:25:14. This pattern is like the first, only transposed up a step to begin on F rather than E♭. Graham continues to try to help Morgan, and on the second statement of this pattern, the pedal F in the bass is gone, leaving only root position triads Fm-E♭M-D♭M-E♭M as Graham says to Morgan, "We're the same." The absence of the pedal musically conveys or represents the sameness of Graham and Morgan. While Graham may hate God at this point, he believes in Him, a seismic shift in Graham's attitude. As Merrill suggests they turn off the flashlights, a brief solo horn motive is intoned, and the music fades on a unison F4.

The Hand of Fate, Part 1 (1:32:59-1:38:22)

This cue marks the film's climax, as it is the first of two parts that carry the film through its conclusion to the End Credits. To restate Jeff Bond of *Film Score Monthly*, "Howard's *Signs* starts off with a bang, spends the bulk of the movie subtly, insidiously chipping away at your psyche, then launches this magnificent piece of redemptive wonder that has it all—suspense, propulsive action, transforming awe, and an incredibly satisfying denouement."[8] The cue can be broken into three large sections—before Graham's flashback, the flashback, after Graham's flashback—and with smaller sections within the first and third sections. The table below highlights the divisions.

Section	1		2	3			
Subsection	a 1-13	b 14-25	none	a 41-56	b 57-80	c 81-100	d 101-113
Measures	1-25		25-41	41-113			
Time	1:32:59-1:34:21 (1:22)		1:34:22-1:35:28 (1:16)	1:35:28-1:38:22 (2:54)			

Table 6.13 – Sections in "The Hand of Fate, Part 1"

The final section of this cue contains the most action, as Merrill attacks the alien, swinging away, Graham gets Bo and Morgan outside, and Merrill kills the alien. The end of Section 2 leading into Section 3 is where the "Shyamalan Twist" occurs in the film, as Graham remembers asking the question, "Is it possible there are no coincidences?"

The first section of the cue coincides with the moment that Graham sees the alien in the reflection of·the television in their living room. In the *sforzando* attack, the pitches E, F, and B♭ are sounded, which have a prime form of (016), the Alien TNM. This attack recalls the final note of "Main Titles," with its percussion hit, but this opening note is scored for the full orchestra. While this chord is sustained, the piano and harp have a version of the Belief TNM, beginning on the pitch E as well. As this is the climactic showdown, it seems natural that the Alien and Belief TNMs would be fighting each other. The battle continues throughout Section 1a. When Section 1b begins, the tempo increases, and now only the Alien TNM is sounded in the harp and piano, beginning on the pitch E. In Section 1 of the cue, the alien TNM is stronger than the Belief TNM, as the alien holds Morgan hostage.

The flashback, the only one that shows the interaction between Graham and his wife during the film, comprises all of Section 2. The music is much more reflective and contemplative, with the absence of the TNM. It is similar to the opening chorale of "Into the Basement," in terms of its nature. This music appears to be in the mode of E Dorian, as the harmonies are modal and not tonally functional. The first four measures of this music are shown in example 6.19.

Example 6.19 – "The Hand of Fate, Part 1," mm. 26-29, Flashback

Like so many of the melodies in *Signs*, the tonal centers change quickly, and as the strings take over for the piano, the tonal center shifts to C in m. 32, and then D in m. 36. During the piano chords, Caroline says, "It was meant to be." When the tonal center is C, she talks about Morgan. When it is D, she talks about Bo, Graham's music changes from D major to D minor. Also helping to delineate the keys and characters are the presence of additional instruments. Morgan's music doesn't have any. Bo's music has an English horn solo, and Graham's has a cello solo, as she tells him "to see." And when she says, "And tell Merrill to swing away," the peaceful music ends, replaced with harmonies consisting of half and whole steps, leading into Section 3 of the cue.

As Graham recalls his conversation with Merrill, the Alien TNM resumes in m. 44, at 1:35:36, and Section 3a begins. Graham realizes that everything that has happened had to happen the way that it did. He surveys the room, and sees a baseball bat. Once he locks onto the bat, Section 3b begins, at 1:36:09.

The Alien TNM disappears, replaced by a four-note gesture, which was first heard in the "Main Titles," shown in example 6.20.

Example 6.20 – "The Hand of Fate, Part 1," mm. 57-58

The Alien TNM, with its prime form of (016), is embedded twice in that four-note gesture—the first three notes and the last three notes. The cello begins playing a version of the Alien TNM on beat 4 of the same measure, but with the OPI reversed, <+1, +5>. The harp, in m. 60, also has a variant of the Alien TNM, but with an OPI of <+5, +6>. During this passage, Graham tells Merrill to "swing away." The variations on the Alien TNM are because the alien is about to be defeated, now that Graham has recovered his faith. Even though the correct prime form is used, the OPI is wrong, indicating a lessening of the power of the alien.

At 1:36:26, in m. 65, Merrill looks up at the bat, and the two TNMs, God and alien, are once again used simultaneously, with the Belief TNM in the harp (F-C-Db) and the Alien TNM in the piano (C-F-Gb). The battle between faith and disbelief, which is manifested in this final altercation between Merrill and the alien, continues to rage.

At 1:36:49, in m. 74, Merrill hits the alien, who drops Morgan to the floor. The music heard here was heard only once before, all the way back in the Main Titles, in the third and most intense section of that cue. Retrospectively, the Main Titles foreshadow the ultimate defeat of the single alien. In the Main Titles, the cue simply ended, as it didn't need to resolve. At the parallel point in "The Hand of Fate, Part 1," m. 80, the music experiences a type of *Durchbruch*, a breakthrough, which leads to Section 3c.

The concept of *Durchbruch* is most closely associated with German musicologist and philosopher Theodor Adorno, in his writings on Gustav Mahler.[9] In summarizing Adorno's ideas, James Buhler writes,

> Breakthrough is a moment of structural reorientation, a deflection or 'turning-aside' (*Ablenkung*) from the expected formal course of a piece. . . . The opposite of tragic reversal or catastrophe, breakthrough is an unforeseen event, a sudden turn toward transcendence from an expected formal trajectory of tragedy. . . . In short, break-

through is an attempt to represent transcendence through immanent means.[10]

The corresponding moment in *Signs*, the water "burning" the skin of the alien, and seeing all of the water glasses available throughout the room, is the unforeseen event that Buhler describes. The turn toward transcendence is the reinstatement of Graham's faith, his belief in the goodness of God. While Graham's flashback may have helped him make the turn back to God, the *Durchbruch* solidifies the narrative move musically.

The texture is reduced at the start of Section 3c, at 1:37:04. A C#M chord is played and sustained by the strings and brass, while the flutes play the Belief TNM, beginning on C#. The *Durchbruch* is accomplished through the visual and narrative of the alien being hurt by water that pours onto its shoulder. The slowly changing harmonies in this passage are C#M, mm. 80-82, AM^6, mm. 83-84, and E♭Mm$^4_3$, mm. 85-87, and they support the realization that Bo has left water glasses all around the family room because her "tic" is meaningful.

Graham takes Morgan and runs out of the house, with Bo following behind. Merrill hits the glasses with the bat, spraying the alien with water. The TNM changes every two beats, and while the harmonies underneath are not part of a pattern, the chord roots do form an ascending line, providing hope and excitement that Merrill will be triumphant now that he knows exactly how to defeat the alien. Measures 88-93 are shown in a reduction in example 6.21.

The harmonies don't belong within any functional key, nor does the quartal chord that ends that passage. Additionally, a rising bass line such as this would rarely be harmonized, in functional tonality, with root position triads. But, like so many instances throughout this score, the most effective music is rarely harmonically functional.

The alien makes its proverbial last stand, literally and figuratively, visually and musically. The prime form of the alien TNM returns in m. 94, at 1:37:38, but with an OPI of <+7, +6>, lessening its power. Merrill takes a final swing, and knocks the alien into a desk, water spilling onto its face. With this action, the Alien TNM is not heard again during the film; only the Belief TNM remains.

The final portion of this cue, Section 3d, begins at 1:37:57, as the water cascades onto the alien, killing it. The TNM is not present, instead replaced with a gesture having the same rhythm in some parts, but a group of four sixteenth notes in the piano, shown in example 6.22.

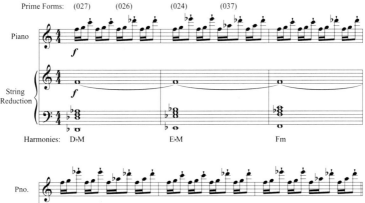

Example 6.21 – "The Hand of Fate, Part 1," mm. 88-93,
Attacking the Alien

Example 6.22 – "The Hand of Fate, Part 1," mm. 101-104,
Triumph/Water Pouring on the Alien

The harmonies in mm. 101-104 are all related by chromatic mediant—
CM-A♭M-FM-A♭M. The alien attack, which itself was unbelievable,
has been defeated, largely due to the recognition that events had to occur in order for the family to win this battle. The music slowly unwinds
and decrescendos from *fortissimo* at m. 101 to *piano* by the end of the
cue, moving directly into the final cue.

"The Hand of Fate, Part 1" is the cue to which the entire score has been building. It is the cue where the Alien TNM and the Belief TNM battle, and ultimately Graham's faith is restored. The cue also accompanies the twist in the film. The three parts of the cue are constructed in a ternary form, ABA', but instead of the Alien TNM winning the final section, the Belief TNM ultimately wins. The Belief TNM moves to having an OPI of <+7, +5>, emphasizing the first interval, a perfect fifth, and the interval from bottom to top, a perfect octave, the two consonant intervals that are both perfect, as only perfect consonance could prove to Graham that God had a plan for his life.

The Hand of Fate, Part 2 6m2 v3-4 (1:38:23-1:41:56)

Like "Throwing a Stone," this cue does not feature a tempo or style change. The cue begins *attacca* from the previous one and substantially spills over into the End Credits, and is the only one in which nearly every measure contains some use of the TNM. The TNM is used benevolently throughout the complete cue. If "Part 1" is the climax and the realization that events happen for a reason, then "Part 2" is the result of those effects, which is why the TNM sounds benevolent.

The beginning of the cue is one that has been heard multiple times in the film, most notably at the start of "In the Cornfield." The music presents the Belief TNM with its appropriate accompaniment, alternating CM and Cm. Once it reaches the GM chord, the TNM changes to (025) with an OPI of <+7, +2> and is exclusively harmonically supported by a GM harmony, the second *Durchbruch*.

These opening measures find Graham outside holding Morgan, repeating the words, "His lungs were closed. No poison got in." But the longer that Morgan fails to respond, the more likely it is that he has died. The *Durchbruch* in m. 16 indicates that things have now changed—Graham once again believes in God, regaining his faith through his epiphany only moments earlier. In m. 19, Morgan awakens, saying, "Dad . . . What happened?" in a questioning voice. The harmonies in mm. 21-22 are Bm and AM, respectively, implying a tonality of D major, with a harmonic progression of vi-V. The expectation is that the chord in m. 23 would be DM, but it is not. Instead, the harmony is CM, a chord related by chromatic mediant to AM. The use of the *Durchbruch* and the chromatic mediant indicates that things are changed because of some unseen, mystical element.

For much of the remainder of the cue, the music operates in four-measure units. In mm. 25-28, Morgan asks, "Did someone save me?" Graham responds, "Yeah, baby, I think someone did." That someone, whether it is God or Caroline, is not of the Earth, reinforcing that mystical element. Measure 29 initiates a new four-measure unit, with a camera shot from the upstairs bedroom looking down onto the swing set, the start of a time lapse from Fall to Winter.

The TNM remains consistently used throughout the passage of time, with harmonies changing every measure. Though they are not functional in the tonal sense, nearly every chord connection has at least one common tone, if not two. After the time lapse, Graham is shown exiting the bathroom in his ministerial collar, putting in his cuff links, with a slight smile on his face. As he exits his room, at 1:41:06, the only passage in the entire cue that does not have the TNM is used, shown in example 6.23.

Example 6.23 – "The Hand of Fate, Part 2," mm. 65-69,
Absence of the TNM

This moment in the cue when the TNM disappears is the end of the film; as Graham exits his room, the screen fades to black and the End Credits begin, displaying a single, unmoving credit: "An M. Night Shyamalan film." As the credits begin to roll, the cue continues with the resumption of the TNM. The fact that a cue from the narrative portion of the film spills into the End Credits is completely atypical for Howard's music, as Howard uses the End Credits to have the final word about a film. "Part 2" plays over nearly the first full minute of the End Credits, ending as shown in example 6.24.

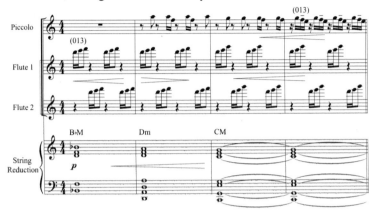

Example 6.24 – "The Hand of Fate, Part 2," mm. 77-80,
Final Harmonies of the Cue

The final harmonies, B♭M, Dm, and CM, imply a tonal center of C at the conclusion of this film. The melodic line in the strings, B♭-A-G, implies the use of the C Mixolydian mode, as those notes are common-ly harmonized as a ♭VII-IV-I progression in C Mixolydian. That is not the case, as the chord roots circle around the tonic C, a whole step be-low and a whole step above; this film and this music are both uncom-mon. The final use of the TNM has a prime form of (013), essentially unused up until the film's conclusion, indicating a complete change for the Hess family.

It is significant that the film ends on the CM harmony. The Belief TNM, throughout the film, begins on the note C, harmonized with CM and Cm chords, in alternation, but the pattern always begins on CM. The key of C major is often referred to as the "key of nature," one that is "pure."[11] Over the course of the film, Graham has fought his way back to the purity of C major, and the fact that the final cue ends with this chord as the tonic harmony shows that Graham has truly recovered his faith in God, and his life can continue after his crisis of faith.

End Credits (1:41:57-1:46:17)

Surprisingly, Howard did not write an "End Credits" cue. Instead, a pastiche of music, simply cut from other cues, is used in place of a proper cue. Four different musical cues are used during the End Credits. The music from 1:41:57 to 1:43:50 is the "Roof Intruder" cue, followed by the first seventy seconds of "Into the Basement," from 1:43:51 to 1:45:01. Next, "Baby Monitor" sounds, from 1:45:02 to 1:46:01, and a fifteen-second piano-only statement of the Belief TNM sounds from 1:46:02 to 1:46:17. Perhaps Howard did not find it necessary to compose an "End Credits" cue, as he very clearly expressed his feelings through the music, particularly at the end.

Conclusion

James Newton Howard's score for *Signs* is one of the most unified scores composed in the past thirty years. Nearly every cue contains some version of the three-note motive, and even though not every cue contains the Alien TNM or Belief TNM, the rhythm of the TNM permeates the score. The brief moments where the TNM is not used are stunning, not just because of the absence of the TNM, but because of the lush orchestral sounds, or the sparseness of the solo piano; the textures when the TNM is absent stand apart from the TNM textures.

The number 3 plays a prominent role in both the film and its music. As Graham is a former minister, the number 3 would represent the Holy Trinity. Graham has three people in his life: his two children and his brother. Prior to that, it was his two children and his wife. Many cues in the film contain three parts, including the "Main Titles" and "The Hand of Fate, Part 1," the two most important cues in the film. The vast majority of the music is derived from a single three-note motive, which becomes so ubiquitous during the film that it is easily forgotten that it contains just three notes, no more and no less.

The music has a clear trajectory in the film, beginning with the Alien TNM and beginning the final cue with the Belief TNM. The Alien TNM contains nothing but dissonant intervals: a perfect fourth, a minor second, and a tritone for the outer boundaries. The tritone is historically representative of the devil. In *Signs*, the devil can be both Graham's absence of faith, on a spiritual level, and the presence of aliens, on a physical level. The tritone in the Alien TNM is spelled as a diminished fifth. The significance of the spelling is because a diminished fifth will typically resolve into a major third. The Belief TNM contains mostly consonant intervals: a perfect fifth, a minor second, and an outer boundary of a minor sixth. Only the minor second is dissonant in the Belief TNM, but its presence is necessary to connect it to the Alien TNM. The interval of the minor sixth is important to the resolution of the Alien TNM. Because of the expansion of the Alien TNM, the Belief

TNM presents a consonant possibility, and the specific type of sixth, the minor as opposed to the major, is significant because the inversion of a minor sixth is a major third, the interval to which the diminished fifth should resolve. While unseen and unheard on the surface, the musical dissonance presented and personified by Graham's absence of faith is appropriately resolved when Graham's faith is restored at the end of the film.

By focusing on one element of Howard's style, the influence of Igor Stravinsky on his work, a great deal can be learned from and seen in the music. Using Stravinsky's *The Rite of Spring* as the point of departure, Howard uses many of the compositional techniques from the ballet, such as stratification, syncopation and asymmetrical meters, polychords, and a distinct lack of memorable melodic motion, instead favoring small gestures. Beyond Stravinsky's music, the sound mass composers of the 1960s, particularly György Ligeti, are imitated in order to create a string texture of dissonance and density. Howard's interest in Ligeti's music goes back to 1990 and his work on *Flatliners*. The chorale at the beginning of the cue "Into the Basement" recalls the chorales of Johann Sebastian Bach and, later, Johannes Brahms, composers with whom Howard would be very familiar, as he likely played several compositions of theirs in his youth. Despite Howard's adeptness at composing long melodies and themes, as he did in *Unbreakable*, he shies away from that side of his compositional abilities in *Signs*, instead favoring a dedication to the three-note motive. Through that adherence to a minimum of compositional means, Howard created a film score that can be described as an example of minimalism, a term typically associated with composers such as Philip Glass and Steve Reich. In *Signs*, Howard's music doesn't slowly change over time, nor are the process and the final product the same thing,[12] but the three-note motive from the beginning develops and transforms into something wonderful. In German, the word would be *verklaren*, to transfigure. The Alien TNM is transfigured into the Belief TNM, Graham regains his faith, and his family is made whole.

Epilogue

Even though Shyamalan's films contain a clear ending point, they often leave the story open enough that questions persist concerning the characters. In *The Sixth Sense*, we want to know if Malcolm's wife moves on with her life and if Cole's gift of communing with the dead is as positive an experience as it was with Malcolm. In *Unbreakable*, we want to know if David continues as a "superhero," if his relationship with his wife recovers, and if other supervillains are out there for David to defeat. In *Signs*, we want to know how the community feels about Graham's return to ministry, and now that his life is somewhat stable, is Merrill still living with them? Of that group, *Signs* is the film that is the most finished, the most resolved. Curiously, it is the only one of the four films that does not contain a separate cue for the End Credits, perhaps implying that everything that needed to be stated during the film was actually stated.

After composing music for *Signs*, Howard composed the music for five more films directed by Shyamalan, and dozens of other Hollywood movies. Howard has become one of the most successful composers in Hollywood, but in some ways he is still anonymous. He is not as popular as Hans Zimmer, nor an Oscar winner like Alexandre Desplat. He is not the elder statesman like John Williams, not the hot new thing like Steven Price, nor is his music as easily recognizable as Danny Elfman's. Howard just keeps writing highly effective music in all styles, for all film genres, and is highly respected among peers and fans. His work rate continues to be high, and he is always looking for the next challenge, the next film on which he can work his magic.

It is clear that Howard is proud of his music for *Signs*. In Jon Burlingame's 2006 piece, Howard said about *Signs*, "Probably the best score I ever wrote for a Night Shyamalan movie. It was (all based on) a three-note device. I was very happy with its evolution from being something so wildly threatening to something that could be so beneficent and gentle."[1] In his interview with Christopher Reynolds and Mark Brill in 2010, Howard said,

I felt that *Signs* should have been nominated [for an Academy Award], because that was an accomplished score, and I thought it really did a lot in the movie. But it was the kind of movie they didn't want to do. They finally gave me a nomination for *The Village*. But I think *The Village*, and *Signs*, and somewhat *Unbreakable* (2000)— those [scores] served the picture really well; but there is a thematic discipline, there's a central idea in each one of those movies that came later, that I think is more distinctive [than the score for *The Sixth Sense*] and yet serves the film brilliantly, or very well.[2]

Film Score Monthly interviewed Howard for their "2002 in Review" issue. He spoke at length about his music for *Signs*, saying,

The most meaningful thing about the *Signs* score to me is twofold— one has to do with the discipline of the writing. I felt like I've come closer to succeeding in using a minimum of thematic or melodic, motiphonal [sic] resources and trying to make that feel like a singular work that has a life beyond the movie. The guy who did that more effectively than anyone on earth was John Williams with *Jaws*, and he did it with two notes and it became part of the iconography of the age. That kind of an achievement in film music is a spectacular thing and I don't think I've ever come even close to it, but this work was closer. The other thing is that the most meaningful music in it really didn't have anything to do with horror but with transformation through fear, of walking through fear and coming out the other side. It had to do with faith, but faith in a totally nonreligious sense, that somehow life was worth living and that hope springs eternal, and particularly in the age of anxiety we live in it was a good message. I was inspired by it.[3]

Howard's reference to John Williams and *Jaws* once again raises the influence of Igor Stravinsky and *The Rite of Spring*. The accents in the shark's music mirror the accents from the "Dance of the Young Girls" in Stravinsky's ballet. Williams has noticeably "stolen" music from Stravinsky, as his music for Tatooine in *Star Wars: A New Hope* sounds remarkably like the Introduction to Part II of *The Rite of Spring*. Howard also used the phrase "a life beyond the movie." This phrase is significant because *The Rite of Spring* was music that accompanied a ballet. The choreography of the ballet was not embraced by the public, but Stravinsky's music became a beloved concert work that celebrated its one-hundredth birthday in 2013. That music had "a life beyond the ballet." It is unlikely that any film score will have a life beyond the film (or ballet) like *The Rite of Spring*, but Howard's score for *Signs* is one of his most effective, most inspired works, and will continue to affect anyone who watches the film long after the credits stop rolling.

Notes

Introduction

1. Stravinsky is quoted in the documentary *The Search for Nijinsky's Rite of Spring*, Classical Video Rarities, 1989 [DVD 2004].

Chapter 1

1. Joslyn Layne, "James Newton Howard," http://www.billboard.com/artist/304123/james-newton-howard/biography (September 2, 2014).

2. Howard is quoted on a website that is no longer active, *James Newton Howard*. It can be accessed at: http://web.archive.org/web/20071116162131/http://www.james-newton-howard.com/main.html (September 8, 2014).

3. *James Newton Howard.*

4. *James Newton Howard.*

5. Bob Doerschuk, "Elton John's Multi-Keyboard Sideman James Newton Howard," *Contemporary Keyboard* (February 1981): 44.

6. *James Newton Howard.*

7. Doerschuk, 44.

8. Doerschuk, 44. Howard is quoted in the article.

9. Doerschuk, 56. Howard is quoted in the article.

10. Will Davis Shivers, "James Newton Howard (interview)," *Film Score Monthly*, no. 41-43 (Jan.-Mar. 1994): 18.

11. Howard is quoted, as well as other members of the band, discussing "Don't Go Breaking My Heart" at http://www.eltonjohn.com/discussing-dont-go-breaking/ (September 25, 2014).

12. Doerschuk, 58.

13. James Newton Howard, *James Newton Howard & Friends*, Santa Barbara, CA, Sheffield Lab, Inc., 1984, CD-23. The Performance Credits and Production Credits in the CD liner notes list those specific instruments and synthesizers on pages 3-4. The album's executive producer, Doug Sax, said, "It should be pointed out that every sound you hear on this album is being produced by the various synthesizers, with the exception of the percussion and drums" (quote from page 6 of liner notes). The Yamaha GS1 was their first fully polyphonic FM synthesizer. It had eighty-eight weighted keys and sixteen voices. The DX7 was a professional grade synthesizer, but also an affordable one. It had a number of realistic sounds, including piano, woodwinds, strings, and percussion—a perfect synthesizer for Howard's needs!

14. *James Newton Howard.*

15. The film is often given a release date of 1986, but it was released in December 1985 in Canada, then a week later, in January 1986, in the United States. http://www.imdb.com/title/tt0091183/releaseinfo?ref_=tt_ov_inf+ (accessed September 25, 2014).

16. Rosemary D. Reninger, "James Newton Howard: JAMs with Tri-M," *Teaching Music* 8, no. 3 (December 2000): 42.

17. *James Newton Howard.*

18. The *Los Angeles Times'* review of *Diggstown* is titled "'Diggstown' Bets on Powerhouse Actors." The review can be accessed at http://articles.latimes.com/1992-08-14/entertainment/ca-5160_1_diggstown (October 6, 2014).

19. Jon Burlingame, "The Man Who Gives Film Voice," *Daily Variety*, July 17, 2006, A6.

20. Sharon Knolle, "Pledges of Allegiance," *Daily Variety*, July 17, 2006, A2.

21. Knolle, "Pledges of Allegiance," A2.

22. Michael Schelle, *The Score: Interviews with Film Composers* (Los Angeles: Silman-James Press, 1999), 180.

23. Schelle, 185-187. A number of issues are discussed in the interview.

24. Daniel Schweiger, "James Newton Howard (interview)," *Film Score Monthly*, no. 46-47 (June-July 1994): 13. Schweiger's interview originally appeared in the July 1994 issue of *Venice*.

25. Schweiger, 13.

26. *Promised Land* has a rating of 73 percent fresh, but only with eleven reviews, and the user ratings are much lower. http://www.rottentomatoes.com/m/promised_land_1987/ (accessed September 22, 2014).

27. Knolle, A2.

28. Knolle, A2.

29. Knolle, A2.

30. In Knolle's interview, Hogan briefly mentions that the two battled, with each man standing up for his beliefs about the use of music.

31. Schweiger, 12.

32. Schweiger, 12.

33. Shivers, 19.

34. Knolle, A2.

35. Knolle, A2.

36. Knolle, A2.

37. Shivers, 19.

38. Christopher Reynolds and Mark Brill, "On the Art and Craft of Film Music: A Conversation with James Newton Howard," *The Hopkins Review*, vol. 3, no. 3 (Summer 2010): 329-330.

39. Jon Burlingame, "Shyamalan's Go-To Tunesmith Weaves Music of the Night," *Daily Variety*, July 17, 2006: A1.

40. The closest film in recent memory to have nearly no music is *No Country for Old Men* (2007, dir. Joel and Ethan Coen), which contains more music during the end credits than in the rest of the film combined. Instead, the soundtrack is filled with sound effects, which act in place of music.

41. Reynolds and Brill, 326.

42. Reynolds and Brill, 325.

43. Burlingame, "Shyamalan's Go-To Tunesmith Weaves Music of the Night," A1.

44. Burlingame, "Shyamalan's Go-To Tunesmith Weaves Music of the Night," A6.

45. Reynolds and Brill, 332.

46. Burlingame addresses these issues in both "The Man Who Gives Films Voices" and "Shyamalan's Go-To Tunesmith Weaves Music of the Night," A1 and A6.

47. Fred Karlin and Rayburn Wright, *On the Track*, revised 2nd edition (New York: Routledge, 2004), 35.

48. Howard is quoted in Burlingame's "The Man Who Gives Films Voices," A6.

49. While the score was not nominated for an Academy Award, those voters are members of the Academy of Motion Picture Arts and Sciences, and most have little to no musical background.

50. Shivers, 19.

Chapter 2

1. Jon Burlingame, "Howard's High Scores List," *Daily Variety*, July 17, 2006: A4.

2. Reninger, 42.

3. Interview with John Cunha. Howard very casually mentions Stravinsky along side Beethoven, Debussy, and Ravel; this moment occurs at 2:56-3:54. https://www.youtube.com/watch?v=x3-nfpz7tqQ (February 23, 2015).

4. Stephen Meyer writes, "It was through the thematic guides to Wagner's works that Hans von Wolzogen published in the last decades of the nineteenth century that the term 'leitmotif' entered the mainstream of musical discourse and acquired its Wagnerian associations." Stephen C. Meyer, "'Leitmotif': On the Application of a Word to Film Music," *Journal of Film Music*, vol. 5/1-2 (2012): 102.

5. Stan Link, "Leitmotif" in *Sound and Music in Film and Visual Media: An Overview*, ed. Graeme Harper (New York: Continuum, 2009), 181.

6. Kathryn Kalinak's book *Settling the Score: Music and the Classical Hollywood Film* (Madison: University of Wisconsin Press, 1992) is strongly based on the Leitmotivic and thematic tradition of film scoring, and covers multiple films including Steiner's score for *The Informer*.

7. Meyer, 102.

8. Link, 183.

9. Meyer, 102. Among the "others" who have made this assertion is Kate Daubney in her book on Steiner's music for *Now, Voyager*. Daubney is Scarecrow Press's Film Score Guide Series Editor.

10. Kate Daubney, *Max Steiner's* Now, Voyager (Westport, CT: Greenwood Press, 2000), 1.

11. Ben Winters, *Erich Wolfgang Korngold's* The Adventures of Robin Hood: *A Film Score Guide* (Lanham, MD: Scarecrow Press, 2007), 32.

12. Reynolds and Brill, 332-333. Howard gives specific film examples to go along with each composer.

13. In a sound mass composition, individual pitches are not perceived. Instead, a group of chromatic pitches are played simultaneously. "In sound-mass compositions, musical elements such as texture, density, register, dynamics, and instrumental color replace such musical parameters as rhythm, meter, lines, chords, and harmony." Miguel Roig-Francoli, *Understanding Post-Tonal Music* (Boston: McGraw-Hill, 2008), 281.

14. Schelle, 188-189.

15. Schelle, 189.

16. Howard is quoted in John Keogh's article "James Newton Howard: Master of MIDI Orchestration," *Keyboard* (December 2000): 36.

17. Howard is quoted in Keogh, 36.

18. Karlin and Wright, 101-102. The quotation is not cited.

19. Karlin and Wright, 104. The quotation is not cited.

20. Karlin and Wright, 103.

21. Karlin and Wright, 103.

22. Robert L. Doerschuk, "Top Guns," *Keyboard* 16 (March 1990): 50.

23. Schelle, 177.

24. Schweiger, 13.

25. Howard is quoted in Keogh, 36.

26. Howard is quoted in Keogh, 36.

27. Schweiger, 13.

28. Jeff Rona, *The Reel World: Scoring for Pictures*, revised 2nd edition (New York: Hal Leonard Books, 2009), 101.

29. Interview with Dan Goldwasser for Soundtrack.net, published August 2004. http://www.soundtrack.net/content/article/?id=128 (accessed October 7, 2014).

30. The recent exception to this is in the Marvel films, which have one, and often two short scenes during the End Credits.

31. Reynolds and Brill, 348.

32. Schweiger, 13.

33. Shivers, 19.

34. Schelle, 179.

35. Reynolds and Brill, 323.

36. Reynolds and Brill, 323-324.

37. Rona, 101.

38. Reynolds and Brill, 324-325.

39. Christian DesJardins, "Brad Dechter," in *Inside Film Music: Composers Speak* (Los Angeles: Silman-James Press, 2006), 312.

40. Schweiger, 12-13.

41. The number of cues is based on my viewing of the film, as the cue sheets are not available, nor is a film score, or even soundtrack.

42. Schweiger, 13.

43. Director's commentary on the *Everybody's All-American* DVD.

44. Schweiger, 13.

45. Burlingame, "Howard's High Scores List," A4. Howard also makes comments regarding his relationship with Streisand on the film in Schweiger's interview.

46. Schweiger, 13.

47. Karlin and Wright, 266.

48. The speech contains no underscore. The sound of the rain outside the building can be heard throughout the speech. Additionally, Mamet added the speech to the screenplay; it is not in the original play.

49. Burlingame, "Howard's High Scores List," A4.

50. Schweiger, 13.

51. Reitman is quoted by Sharon Knolle in her article "Pledges of Allegiance," *Variety*, July 17, 2006: A2.

52. Reynolds and Brill, 347.

53. Shivers, 19.

54. Schweiger, 13.

55. Burlingame, "Howard's High Scores List," A4.

56. Laurence E. MacDonald, *The Invisible Art of Film Music: A Comprehensive History*, revised 2nd edition (Lanham, MD: The Scarecrow Press, 2013), 381.

57. Director's commentary on *The Fugitive* DVD.

58. Examples of the "Kimball Theme" are shown in Karlin and Wright in examples 14.31 and 14.32 on pages 266 and 267.

59. Director's commentary on *The Fugitive* DVD.

60. Director's commentary on *The Fugitive* DVD.

61. Schweiger, 12.

62. Schweiger, 12.

63. Schweiger, 12.

64. Uncoincidentally, Elmer Bernstein, who composed the score for *The Magnificent Seven*, was a student of Copland's.

65. Schelle, 182.

66. This motive is also heard in the film's introduction, which occurs before the Main Title sequence. Howard refers to this as "Wyatt's Theme."

67. Schweiger, 12.

68. Burlingame, "Howard's High Scores List," A4.

69. Schelle, 178.

70. Schelle, 182.

71. Schelle, 190.

72. Burlingame, "Howard's High Scores List," A4.

73. Karlin writes, "The temp track was a combination of renowned Polish composer Krzysztof Penderecki's music and obscure music performed by the Kronos Quartet," 152.

74. Hicks is quoted as stating that Glass's music was a temp track for the film in an interview with Nick Dawson in *Filmmaker Magazine*. The entire article can be accessed at http://filmmakermagazine.com/1312-scott-hicks-glass-a-portrait-of-philip-in-twelve-parts/#.VB7hai5dXXE (October 9, 2014).

75. A review of the soundtrack states, "Howard's music—with a much-discussed and striking resemblance to Arvo Part [sic], used by Hicks throughout the temp-track. . . ." James Southall does not provide any further evidence for this claim. His review can be accessed at http://www.movie-wave.net/titles/snow_falling_cedars.html (accessed October 10, 2014).

76. In the key of A minor, this is the solfège Me-Re-Fa-Me. It is significant because several of Arvo Pärt's compositions are in the key of A minor (really A Aeolian), and many compositions contain gestures such as this.

77. Director's commentary on the *Snow Falling on Cedars* DVD.

78. Howard is quoted in Keogh, 36.

79. Karlin and Wright quote Howard on p. 266.

80. Karlin and Wright, 266-267.

81. Jonathan Kaplan, "The Best Scores of 1999," *Film Score Daily*, March 27, 2000. http://filmscoremonthly.com/daily/article.cfm?articleID=3213

82. The review can be found at http://www.filmtracks.com/titles/snow_falling.html. Other reviews of the soundtrack can be found at http://www.movie-wave.net/titles/snow_falling_ cedars.html (five out of five), http://www.maintitles.net/reviews/snow-falling-on-cedars/ (four out of five), http://www.soundtrack.net/album/snow-falling-on-cedars/ (four out of five), and http://www.tracksounds.com/reviews/snowcedars.htm (eight out of ten) (all accessed October 10, 2014).

83. Reynolds and Brill, 347.

84. Burlingame, "Howard's High Scores List," A4.

85. Director's commentary on the *Snow Falling on Cedars* DVD.

Chapter 3

1. Shyamalan specifically mentions these three films and their reasons in a featurette entitled "Looking for *Signs*" on the *Signs* DVD.

2. Sidney Perkowitz, *Hollywood Science* (New York: Columbia University Press, 2007), 5.

3. Please see sources such as Vivian Sobchack, *Screening Space*, revised 2nd edition (New Brunswick, NJ: Rutgers University Press, 2004) and "The Alien," in *Icons of Horror and the Supernatural*, vol. 1, ed. S. T. Joshi (Westport, CT: Greenwood Press, 2007). Randall Larson's *Musique Fantastique* (Metuchen, NJ: Scarecrow Press, 1985) and Bill Warren's *Keep Watching the Skies!*, revised 2nd edition (Jefferson, NC: McFarland & Co., 2010) specifically address music in these films.

4. For a detailed examination of 1950s alien invasion films, please see Patrick Lucanio's *Them or Us* (Bloomington: Indiana University Press, 1987).

5. Sobchack, 21.

6. Sobchack, 21.

7. The title *When Worlds Collide* could indicate a cosmic war. Instead, the film is about a star on a collision course with Earth. The film is based on the novel of the same name, written by Edwin Balmer and Philip Gordon Wylie.

8. Perkowitz, 9.

9. Perkowitz, 9.

10. Perkowitz, 20.

11. Klaatu's final speech can be read at http://www.imdb.com/title/tt0043456/quotes and can be viewed at https://www.youtube.com/watch?v=_seKyGYlTHY (accessed October 26, 2014).

12. Lucanio devotes twenty pages of *Them or Us* (pp. 111-130) to specifically discuss and analyze the film.

13. Between *Close Encounters* and *E.T.*, Spielberg also directed *1941* (1979) and *Raiders of the Lost Ark* (1981). He also played the Cook County Assessor's Office Clerk in 1980's *The Blues Brothers*.

14. The film *Edge of Tomorrow* was released on DVD and Blu-Ray as *Live. Die. Repeat.*

15. Greg Garrett, *The Gospel according to Hollywood* (Louisville: Westminster John Knox Press, 2007). The *Signs* portion of the opening chapter appears in pages 17-23.

16. Garrett, 17-18.

17. Garrett, 18.

18. Garrett, 19.

19. Garrett, 23.

20. Robert K. Johnston, *Useless Beauty* (Grand Rapids, MI: Baker Academic, 2004), and J. Cheryl Exum, "Do You Feel Comforted? M. Night Shyamalan's *Signs* and the Book of Job" in *Foster Biblical Scholarship*, eds. Frank Ritchel Ames and Charles William Miller (Atlanta: Society of Biblical Literature, 2010).

21. Johnston, 129.

22. Johnston, 139.

23. Exum, 256.

24. Exum, 262.

25. Exum, 263.

26. Exum, 264.

27. Ann Donahue, "Indiana Jones and the Curse of Development Hell," *Premiere*. The two-page article on Premiere's website is no longer valid. The article can be accessed at: http://web.archive.org/web/20070106211130/http://www.premiere.com/movienews/3372/indiana-jones-and-the-curse-of-development-hell.html and http://web.archive.org/web/20070113103211/http://www.premiere.com/movienews/3372/indiana-jones-and-the-curse-of-development-hell-page2.html (accessed January 14, 2015).

28. Cornelia Klecker, "Mind-Tricking Narratives: Between Classical and Art-Cinema Narration," *Poetics Today* 34, nos. 1-2 (Spring-Summer 2013): 120.

29. Klecker, 120.

30. Michael Fleming, "Shyamalan 'Signs' Disney Megapact," *Daily Variety* 271, no. 40 (April 25, 2001): 1.

31. *Unbreakable* has a 68 percent fresh rating at Rotten Tomatoes: http://www.rottentomatoes.com/m/unbreakable/ (accessed July 18, 2014). The film grossed over $95 million domestically, and almost $250 million globally: http://www.imdb.com/title/tt0217869/business?ref_=tt_dt_bus (accessed July 18, 2014).

32. Fleming, 1.

33. The teaser trailer can be viewed here: http://youtu.be/G4f3X1TGSXY (accessed November 16, 2014).

34. Jeff Giles, "Out of This World," *Newsweek* 140, no. 6 (August 5, 2002): 48.

35. Giles, 49.

36. Giles, 51.

37. Austin Bramwell, "Children of Night," *National Review* 54, no. 16 (September 16, 2002): 55.

38. Bramwell, 55.

39. Author Unknown, "Ominous Signs," *Film Journal International*, 105, no. 8 (August 2002): 14.

40. Daniel Fierman, "Night of the Living Dread," *Entertainment Weekly*, 666 (August 9, 2002): 32.

41. Fierman, 32.

42. Fierman, 32.

43. This entire process is discussed in great detail in Michael Bamberger's *The Man Who Heard Voices* (New York: Gotham Books, 2006).

44. The "fresh" percentages for *The Village*, *Lady in the Water*, and *The Happening* are 43%, 23%, and 17%, respectively. www.rottentomatoes.com (accessed July 21, 2014).

45. Kim Owczarski, "Reshaping the Director as Star," in *Critical Approaches to the Films of M. Night Shyamalan*, ed. Jeffrey Andrew Weinstock, (New York: Palgrave Macmillan, 2010), 119-135.

46. Owczarski, 120.

47. Owczarski, 126-128. The films listed are those that Shyamalan stated have made a significant cultural impact. Owczarski adds *The Sixth Sense* to that list.

48. Owczarski, 129.

49. Owczarski, 130.

50. The posters for *After Earth* feature the names and images of Will Smith and his son Jaden Smith. Part of the lack of attribution is due to the fact that Shyamalan was only given a co-writer credit for the screenplay, but part of it is because his success had greatly diminished over the previous three films.

51. The screenplay can be found in some academic libraries in the United States and carries a stamp on the first page that reads "For educational purposes only." A cleaner and newly typeset version of the screenplay can be found at http://www.mnightfans.com/wp-content/uploads/2013/06/signs.pdf (accessed September 27, 2014).

52. M. Night Shyamalan, *Signs* screenplay, 2002.

53. The two birth stories are based on the stories of the births of Shyamalan's two children.

54. Shyamalan, 39.

55. This is different from Alfred Hitchcock having a cameo in the films he directed, Stephen King having very small roles in some film adaptations of his novels, or Stan Lee appearing in nearly every Marvel Comics film adaptation.

56. M. Night Shyamalan, quoted in the featurette "Making *Signs*: A Commentary by M. Night Shyamalan" on the *Signs* DVD release.

57. Shyamalan, 45.

58. Shyamalan, 74-75.

59. Shyamalan, 75.

60. http://www.rottentomatoes.com/m/signs (accessed September 9, 2014).

61. Roger Ebert, "Signs (film)," www.rogerebert.com/reviews/signs-2002 (accessed February 3, 2014).

62. Ebert.

63. Ebert.

64. A. O. Scott, "Finding Faith, or Something, in a Cornfield," *The New York Times*, August 2, 2002.

65. Scott.

66. Scott.

67. Todd McCarthy, "*Signs* Plants Scares but It's Familiar Turf," *Variety* 387, no. 10 (July 29, 2002): 23.

68. McCarthy, 23.

69. McCarthy, 23.

70. Owen Gleiberman, "Field of Screams," *Entertainment Weekly* 666 (August 9, 2002): 43.

71. Gleiberman, 43.

72. Gleiberman, 43.

73. Peter Travers, "Here's the Twist: Mel Gibson Sees Not-So-Dead People," *Rolling Stone* 903 (August 22, 2002): 91.

74. Travers, 91.

75. Anthony Lane, "Field Trip," *The New Yorker* 78, Issue 23 (August 12, 2002): 82-83; Peter Rainer, "Beyond Belief," *New York* 35, Issue 27 (August 12, 2002): 55-56; Stephen Holden, "Mysticism, Miracles and Mush," *The New York Times*, August 25, 2002.

76. Kim Newman, "Signs (review)," *Sight & Sound* 12, no. 10 (2002): 50.

77. According to Box Office Mojo, *The Sixth Sense* ranks #72 in all-time box office gross, with only seven films made in 1999 or earlier ahead of it. http://boxofficemojo.com/alltime/world/ (accessed July 22, 2014).

78. Lucius Shepard, "Signing Off," *Fantasy & Science Fiction* 104, no. 2 (February 2003): 98.

79. Shepard, 98.

80. Scott Brown, "Twist and Doubt," *Entertainment Weekly* 690 (January 10, 2003): 57.

81. Josef Krebs, "Signs (review)," *Sound & Vision* 68, no. 2 (February/March 2003): 114. In the rating system, "**movie** refers to the original film.

DVD refers to the film's presentation on disc, including picture and sound quality as well as extras."

82. Krebs, 115.

83. Krebs, 114.

84. Michael Sofair, "Signs (review)" *Film Quarterly* 57, no. 3 (Spring 2004): 57.

85. Sofair, 63.

86. The two middle chapters, which comprise the second part, deal with Shyamalan himself.

Chapter 4

1. Vivian Sobchack, *Screening Space: The American Science Fiction Film*, 2nd edition (New Brunswick: Rutgers University Press, 2004), 207.

2. Sobchack, 207-208.

3. Cara Marisa Deleon, "A Familiar Sound in a New Place," in *Sounds of the Future: Essays on Music in Science Fiction Film*, ed. Matthew J. Bartkowiak (Jefferson, NC: McFarland & Company, Inc., 2010), 13-14.

4. Deleon, 15.

5. Sobchack, 209.

6. Sobchack, 210-212.

7. Deleon, 17.

8. Neil Lerner, "Preface: Listening to Fear/Listening with Fear," in *Music in the Horror Film: Listening to Fear*, ed. Neil Lerner (New York: Routledge, 2010), ix-x.

9. James Wierzbicki, *Louis and Bebe Barron's* Forbidden Planet: *A Film Score Guide* (Lanham, MD: Scarecrow Press, 2005), 25.

10. David Cooper wrote a Film Score Guide for Scarecrow's series on Herrmann's *The Ghost and Mrs. Muir* in 2005.

11. Two videos can demonstrate the sound of the theremin better than I can describe it. The first is the instrument's creator, Leon Theremin: https://www.youtube.com/watch?v=w5qf9O6c20o; and the second is theremin virtuoso, Clara Rockmore: https://www.youtube.com/watch?v=pSzTPGlNa5U (both accessed January 14, 2015).

12. Rebecca Leydon, "Hooked on Aetherophonics: *The Day the Earth Stood Still*," in *Off the Planet: Music, Sound, and Science Fiction Cinema*, ed. Philip Hayward (Bloomington: Indiana University Press, 2004), 31.

13. Leydon, 34.

14. Prime form will be explained in chapter 6.

15. Leydon, 37-38.

16. Leydon, 40.

17. Deleon, 17.

18. MacDonald, 137.

19. On page 95 of *Musique Fantastique*, Larson writes, "While Kraushaar has spoken frequently about his composition of the score, there are a number of reliable sources contemporary to the film which have revealed that Kraushaar

was in reality only the music director on the picture, and that the actual score was ghostwritten for him by Mort Glickman."

20. Sobchack, 218.

21. Philip Hayward, "Sci Fidelity," in *Off the Planet*, 10.

22. This was the *Journal of Film Music* 1, no. 4 (2006).

23. William H. Rosar, "Music for Martians: Two Tonics and Harmony of Fourths in Leith Stevens' Score for *War of the Worlds* (1953)," *The Journal of Film Music*, vol. 1, no. 4 (2006): 411.

24. Rosar, 426.

25. Rosar, 427.

26. Wierzbicki, 21.

27. Rebecca Leydon, "*Forbidden Planet*: Effects and Affects in the Electro Avant-garde," in *Off the Planet*, 61.

28. Leydon, 63.

29. Lisa M. Schmidt, "A Popular Avant-Garde: The Paradoxical Tradition of Electronic and Atonal Sounds in Sci-Fi Music Scoring" in *Sounds of the Future*, 32-33.

30. Scott Murphy, "The Major Tritone Progression in Recent Hollywood Science Fiction Films," *Music Theory Online*, vol. 12, no. 2, 2006. http://www.mtosmt.org/issues/mto.06.12.2/mto.06.12.2.murphy.html

31. Neil Lerner, "Nostalgia, Masculinist Discourse and Authoritarianism" in *Off the Planet*, 102.

32. Lerner, "Nostalgia," 104-105.

33. Howard addresses the question of favorite film scores composed by other people in the interview with Cunha. His response regarding John Williams can be heard at 24:15-24:40. The interview is posted on YouTube at https://www.youtube.com/watch?v=x3-nfpz7tqQ (accessed February 23, 2015).

34. I am not aware of a major film where the aliens invade earth and defeat humanity, either eradicating them, or enslaving them. The closest thing is the television series *Falling Skies*, which, at the time of writing, has aired since 2011, and will be airing its fifth and final season in Summer 2015. Only small pockets of people survived the initial attack, and they have served as the "resistance" over the course of the series.

35. The president's inspiring speech from *Independence Day* can be seen on YouTube at: https://www.youtube.com/watch?v=oj16vfbsM9A (accessed February 8, 2015).

36. Murphy. The film that receives the most attention in the article is *Treasure Planet* (2002), which is scored by James Newton Howard.

37. The destruction of the Washington Monument from *Earth vs. the Flying Saucers* is taken to an absurd level as the Martian saucer in *Mars Attacks!* not only knocks it over, but then plays with it back and forth, trying to see how long it can keep the teetering object upright.

38. Philip Hayward, "Inter-planetary Soundclash: Music, Technology and Territorialisation in *Mars Attacks!*" in *Off the Planet*, 177.

39. Hayward, 177.

40. Hayward, 178.

41. Reynolds and Brill, 330.

42. Karlin and Wright, 497. Discussion of how the term applies to specific film music examples can be found on pages 290-295.

43. It appears at this pitch level when it is fully realized, after David has his flashback to the night of the car accident. He has super strength, no injuries, and saves Audrey from the burning car.

44. Thomas Glorieux, "Signs," www.maintitles.net/reviews/signs. His profile on the website, which does not provide any credentials, can be viewed at www.maintitles.net/profile/25 (accessed October 14, 2014).

45. Glorieux.

46. Andrew Granade, "Signs," www.soundtrack.net/albums/signs (accessed October 14, 2014).

47. Granade.

48. Granade.

49. Christian Clemmensen, "Signs," www.filmtracks.com/titles/signs.html (accessed October 14, 2014). The review was revised on February 17, 2009. Clemmensen is not a trained musician. His biography can be found at www.filmtracks.com/about/#editor.

50. Clemmensen.

51. Clemmensen.

52. Doug Adams, "Howard's SIGNS of Greatness," *Film Score Monthly* 7, no. 7 (September 2002): 35. On the cover of the issue, a teaser photo appears with the caption "SIGNS of greatness." Adams is a known expert on Howard Shore's music for *The Lord of the Rings* trilogy, having written an exhaustive book on the topic.

53. Adams, 35.

54. Adams, 35.

55. Adams, 35.

56. Adams, 35. One of the most important phrases in the film is "swing away," which is likely why Adams used it in his review.

57. Adams, 35.

58. Jon and Al Kaplan, "The Best (& the Worst) of 2002," *Film Score Monthly* 8, no. 1 (January 2003): 14.

59. Jeff Bond, "Not Too Far from Heaven," *Film Score Monthly* 8, no. 1 (January 2003): 19.

60. Bond, 19.

61. Wierzbicki, 25.

62. Interview with John Cunha; this moment occurs at 19:51-21:13. https://www.youtube.com/watch?v=x3-nfpz7tqQ (accessed February 23, 2015).

Chapter 5

1. Karlin and Wright, 60.

2. I am grateful for the assistance that I received from the librarians at USC, in particular Dace Taube and John Brockman.

3. Thank you to Eric Swanson of JoAnn Kane Music for providing the cue list and instrumentation information.

4. The recordings were made on May 28-31, 2002. The year is omitted from the table, since it seems superfluous.

5. The location of the superball is m. 77 in "Into the Basement." The instructions are written into the score.

6. This is on page 6 of the cue, m. 30.

7. Phone conversation with Pete Anthony, January 29, 2015.

8. Interview from the featurette "Last Voices: The Music of *Signs*" on the *Signs* DVD.

9. Claudia Gorbman, *Unheard Melodies: Narrative Film Music* (Bloomington: Indiana University Press, 1987), 82.

10. Neil Lerner, "Preface: Listening to Fear/Listening with Fear," in *Music in the Horror Film: Listening to Fear*, ed. Neil Lerner (New York: Routledge, 2010), ix.

11. "Last Voices: The Music of *Signs*," on the *Signs* DVD.

12. Reynolds and Brill, 325.

13. Reynolds and Brill, 325-326.

14. Reynolds and Brill, 326.

15. This reference appears earlier in the book on p. 48 in chapter 2.

16. Phone interview with Pete Anthony, January 29, 2015.

17. Christian DesJardins, "Interview with Brad Dechter," in *Inside Film Music: Composers Speak* (Los Angeles: Silman-James Press, 2006), 316-317.

18. I don't know why the Italian is inconsistent, as "senza dolce" would be easily translated by any musician. The exclamation point is part of Atmajian's instructions.

19. The abbreviation "espr." is short for *espressivo*.

20. DesJardins, "Interview with Jeff Atmajian," 306-307.

21. DesJardins, "Interview with Pete Anthony," 301.

22. DesJardins, "Interview with Jeff Atmajian," 307.

23. DesJardins, "Interview with Brad Dechter," 319.

24. DesJardins, "Interview with Brad Dechter," 312.

25. DesJardins, "Interview with Jeff Atmajian," 306.

26. Phone interview with Pete Anthony, January 29, 2015.

27. Desjardins, "Interview with Pete Anthony," 304.

Chapter 6

1. The first footnote in an article by Ethan Haimo states, "The term 'atonal' is now universally applied to this repertoire. Although the term is not particularly illuminating (and was rejected by Schoenberg), it has come to be so widely accepted that it would be futile to try to substitute a more apt term." Ethan Haimo, "Atonality, Analysis, and the Intentional Fallacy," *Music Theory Spectrum* 18, no. 2 (Autumn 1996): 167.

2. Arnold Schoenberg, *Theory of Harmony*, trans. Roy E. Carter (Berkeley: University of California Press, 1978), 432.

3. Guido Heldt, *Music and Levels of Narration in Film: Steps across the Border* (Chicago: Intellect, Ltd., 2013), 25.

4. Genesis 1:1-2 reads, "In the beginning God created the heavens and the earth. Now the earth was formless and empty, darkness was over the surface of the deep" (NIV). According to the Bible, the world began in silence and darkness.

5. James Newton Howard, "James Newton Howard on *Signs*," *Film Score Monthly* 8, no. 1 (January 2003): 19.

6. See example 5.4b for the musical excerpt.

7. The complete letter from Tchaikovsky to Nadezha von Meck appears on pp. 205-209 in Catherine Drinker Bowen and Barbara von Meck, *"Beloved Friend:" The Story of Tchaikovsky and Nadejda von Meck* (New York: Random House, 1937).

8. Bond, 19. He names "The Hand of Fate" as his Cue of the Year. Presumably this includes both parts of the cue.

9. Theodor W. Adorno, *Mahler: A Musical Physiognomy*, trans. Edmund Jephcott (Chicago: University of Chicago Press, 1992). Adorno begins addressing the concept of *Durchbruch* on p. 41 of the book.

10. James Buhler, "'Breakthrough' as Critique of Form: The Finale of Mahler's First Symphony," *19th Century Music* 20, no. 2, Special Mahler Issue (Autumn 1996): 129.

11. In her book *A History of Key Characteristics in the Eighteenth and Nineteenth Centuries*, revised 2nd edition (Rochester, NY: University of Rochester Press, 2002), Rita Steblin collects writings from dozens of European music theorists. The word that is most commonly associated with the key of C major, especially in the eighteenth century, is the word "pure." Numerous portions of the book address this, including page 91, the table on page 128, and Appendix A, which addresses all writings concerning C major on pages 226-230.

12. Roig-Francoli paraphrases Steve Reich on p. 323, writing, "Reich explained that in his early minimalist pieces, the compositional process and the sounding musical product were identical."

Epilogue

1. Jon Burlingame, "Howard's High Scores List," A4.

2. Reynolds and Brill, 331-332.

3. James Newton Howard, "James Newton Howard on *Signs*," 19.

Selected Bibliography

Adams, Doug. "Howard's SIGNS of Greatness." *Film Score Monthly* 7, no. 7 (September 2002): 35.

Adorno, Theodor W. *Mahler: A Musical Physiognomy*. Translated by Edmund Jephcott. Chicago: University of Chicago Press, 1992.

Ames, Frank Ritchel, and Charles William Miller, eds. *Foster Biblical Scholarship: Essays in Honor of Kent Harold Richards*. Atlanta: Society of Biblical Literature, 2010.

Anker, Roy. *Of Pilgrims and Fire: When God Shows Up at the Movies*. Grand Rapids, MI: William B. Eerdmans Publishing Company, 2010.

Bamberger, Michael. *The Man Who Heard Voices*. New York: Gotham Books, 2006.

Barron, Neil, ed. *Anatomy of Wonder: A Critical Guide to Science Fiction*. 5th edition. Westport, CT: Libraries Unlimited, 2004.

Barsotti, Catherine M., and Robert K. Johnston. *Finding God in the Movies: 33 Films of Reel Faith*. Grand Rapids, MI: Baker Academic, 2004.

Bartkowiak, Mathew J., ed. *Sounds of the Future: Essays on Music in Science Fiction Film*. Jefferson, NC: McFarland & Company, Inc., 2010.

Bond, Jeff. "Not Too Far from Heaven." *Film Score Monthly* 8, no. 1 (January 2003): 18-21.

Buhler, James. "'Breakthrough' as Critique of Form: The Finale of Mahler's First Symphony." *19th Century Music* 20, no. 2, Special Mahler Issue (Autumn 1996): 125-143.

Clareson, Thomas D. *Understanding Contemporary American Science Fiction: The Formative Period (1926-1970)*. Columbia: University of South Carolina Press, 1990.

Cooke, Mervyn, ed. *The Hollywood Film Reader*. New York: Oxford University Press, 2010.

Cooper, David. *Bernard Herrmann's* The Ghost and Mrs. Muir*: A Film Score Guide*. Lanham, MD: Scarecrow Press, 2005.

Cunha, John. "James Newton Howard Interview." *Youtube.com*. May 3, 2014. https://www.youtube.com/watch?v=x3-nfpz7tqQ (April 3, 2015).

Daubney, Kate. *Max Steiner's* Now Voyager. Westport, CT: Greenwood Press, 2000.

DesJardins, Christian. *Inside Film Music: Composers Speak*. Los Angeles: Silman-James Press, 2006.

Detweiler, Craig, and Barry Taylor. *A Matrix of Meanings: Finding God in Pop Culture*. Grand Rapids, MI: Baker Academic, 2003.

Doershuck, Bob. "Elton John's Multi-Keyboard Sideman James Newton Howard." *Contemporary Keyboard* (February 1981): 44, 56-58.

———. "Top Guns." *Keyboard* 16 (March 1990): 42-48.

Everybody's All-American. Dir. Taylor Hackford. Warner Home Video. 1988 [DVD 2004].

Flesher, Paul V. M., and Robert Torry. *Film & Religion: An Introduction*. Nashville: Abingdon Press, 2007.

The Fugitive: Special Edition. Dir. Andrew Davis. Warner Brothers. 1993 [DVD 2001].

Garrett, Greg. *The Gospel according to Hollywood*. Louisville: Westminster John Knox Press, 2007.

Goldwasser, Dan. "James Newton Howard Interview." *Soundtrack.net*. August 2004. www.soundtrack.net/content/article/?id=128 (October 7, 2014).

Gorbman, Claudia. *Unheard Melodies: Narrative Film Music*. Bloomington: Indiana University Press, 1987.

Grant, Barry Keith, ed. *Film Genre Reader IV*. Austin: University of Texas Press, 2012.

———. *100 Science Fiction Films: BFI Screen Guides*. New York: Palgrave Macmillan, 2013.

Haimo, Ethan. "Atonality, Analysis, and the Intentional Fallacy." *Music Theory Spectrum* 18, no. 2 (Autumn 1996): 167-199.

Halfyard, Janet. *Danny Elfman's* Batman*: A Film Score Guide*. Lanham, MD: Scarecrow Press, 2004.

Harper, Graeme, ed. *Sound and Music in Film and Visual Media: An Overview*. New York: Continuum, 2009.

Hayward, Philip, ed. *Off the Planet: Music, Sound, and Science Fiction Cinema*. Bloomington: Indiana University Press, 2004.

Heldt, Guido. *Music and Levels of Narration in Film: Steps across the Border*. Chicago: Intellect, Ltd. 2013.

Howard, James Newton. *James Newton Howard & Friends*. Santa Barbara, CA. Sheffield Lab, Inc. 1984 [CD].

Joe, Jeongwon, and Sander L. Gilman, eds. *Wagner and Cinema*. Bloomington: Indiana University Press, 2010.

Johnston, Robert K. *Useless Beauty: Ecclesiastes through the Lens of Contemporary Film*. Grand Rapids, MI: Baker Academic, 2004.

Joshi, S. T., ed. *Icons of Horror and the Supernatural*, vol. 1. New Brunswick, NJ: Rutgers University Press, 2004.

Kalinak, Kathryn. *Settling the Score: Music and the Classical Hollywood Film*. Madison: University of Wisconsin Press, 1992.

Kaplan, Jonathan. "The Best Scores of 1999." *Film Score Daily*, March 27, 2000. http://www.filmscoremonthly.com/daily/article.cfm/articleID/3213/The-Best-Scores-of-1999/

Kaplan, Jonathan, and Al. "The Best (& the Worst) of 2002." *Film Score Monthly* 8, no. 1 (January 2003): 14-17.

Karlin, Fred, and Rayburn Wright. *On the Track: A Guide to Contemporary Film Scoring*. Revised 2nd edition. New York: Routledge, 2004.

Keogh, John. "James Newton Howard: Master of MIDI Orchestration." *Keyboard* (December 2000): 34-36.

Klecker, Cornelia. "Mind-Tricking Narratives: Between Classical and Art-Cinema Narration." *Poetics Today* 34 (Spring-Summer 2013): 119-145. doi:10.1215/03335372-1894469

Krebs, Josef. "Signs (review)." *Sound & Vision* 68 (February/March 2003): 114-115.

Kuhn, Annette, ed. *Alien Zone: Cultural Theory and Contemporary Science Fiction Cinema*. New York: Verso, 1990.

Larson, Randall D. *Musique Fantastique: A Survey of Film Music in the Fantastic Cinema*. Metuchen, NJ: Scarecrow Press, 1985.

Lehman, Frank. "Music Theory through the Lens of Film." *Journal of Film Music* 5.1-2 (2012): 179-198. doi:10.1558/jfm.v5i1-2.179

Leinberger, Charles. *Ennio Morricone's The Good, the Bad, and the Ugly: A Film Score Guide*. Lanham, MD: Scarecrow Press, 2004.

Lerner, Neil, ed. *Music in the Horror Film: Listening to Fear*. New York: Routledge, 2010.

Lovell, Alan. *Don Siegel: American Cinema*. London: British Film Institute, 1975.

Lucanio, Patrick. *Them or Us: Archetypal Interpretations of Fifties Alien Invasion Films*. Bloomington: Indiana University Press, 1987.

MacDonald, Laurence E. *The Invisible Art of Film Music: A Comprehensive History*. Revised 2nd edition. Lanham, MD: Scarecrow Press, 2013.

Matthews, Melvin E. Jr., *Hostile Aliens, Hollywood and Today's News: 1950s Science Fiction Films and 9/11*. New York: Algora Publishing, 2007.

Meck, Barbara von, and Catherine Drinker Bowen. *"Beloved Friend:" The Story of Tchaikovsky and Nadejda von Meck*. New York: Random House, 1937.

Meyer, Stephen C. "Leitmotif: On the Application of a Word to Film Music." *Journal of Film Music* 5,1-2 (2012): 101-108. doi:10.1558/jfm.v5i1-2.101

Morgan, David. *Knowing the Score: Film Composers Talk about the Art, Craft, Blood, Sweat, and Tears of Writing for Cinema*. New York: Harper Collins Publishers, 2000.

Murphy, Scott. "The Major Tritone Progression in Recent Hollywood Science Fiction Films." *Music Theory Online* 12, no. 2 (2006). http://www.mtosmt.org/issues/mto.06.12.2/mto.06.12.2.murphy.html

Newman, Kim. "Signs (review)." *Sight & Sound* 12, no. 10 (2002): 50-51.

Parish, James Robert, and Michael R. Pitts. *The Great Science Fiction Pictures*. Metuchen, NJ: Scarecrow Press, 1977.

Perkowitz, Sidney. *Hollywood Science: Movies, Science, and the End of the World*. New York: Columbia University Press, 2007.

Poole, Jeannie Gayle, and H. Stephen Wright. *A Research Guide to Film and Television Music in the United States*. Lanham, MD: Scarecrow Press, 2011.

Prendergast, Roy M. *Film Music: A Neglected Art*. Revised 2nd edition. New York: W. W. Norton and Co., 1992.

Reninger, Rosemary D. "James Newton Howard: JAMs with Tri-M." *Teaching Music* 8, no. 3 (December 2000): 42-45.

Reynolds, Christopher, and Mark Brill. "On the Art and Craft of Film Music: A Conversation with James Newton Howard." *The Hopkins Review* 3, no. 3 (Summer 2010): 320-351. doi: 10.1353/thr.0.0193

Rickman, Gregg, ed. *The Science Fiction Film Reader*. New York: Limelight Editions, 2004.

Roberts, Adam. *Science Fiction*. New York: Routledge, 2000.

Roig-Francoli, Miguel. *Understanding Post-Tonal Music*. Boston: McGraw-Hill, 2008.

Rona, Jeff. *The Reel World: Scoring for Pictures*. Revised 2nd edition. New York: Hal Leonard Books, 2009.

Rosar, William. "Music for Martians: Two Tonics and Harmony of Fourths in Leith Stevens' Score for *War of the Worlds*." *The Journal of Film Music* 1, no. 4 (2006): 395-438.

Sanders, Steven M., ed. *The Philosophy of Science Fiction Film*. Lexington: University of Kentucky Press, 2009.

Sapiro, Ian. *Ilan Eshkeri's Stardust: A Film Score Guide*. Lanham, MD: Scarecrow Press, 2013.

Schelle, Michael. *The Score: Interviews with Film Composers*. Los Angeles: Silman-James Press, 1999.

Schoenberg, Arnold. *Theory of Harmony*. Translated by Roy E. Carter. Berkeley: University of California Press, 1978.

Schweiger, Daniel. "James Newton Howard (interview)." *Film Score Monthly*, no. 46-47 (June-July 1994): 12-13.

The Search for Nijinsky's Rite of Spring. Prod. Judy Kinberg and Thomas Grimm. Classical Video Rarities. 1989 [DVD 2004].

Sella, Marshall. "The 150-Second Sell, Take 34." *The New York Times Magazine*, July 28, 2002: 32-37.

Shepard, Lucius. "Signing Off." *Fantasy & Science Fiction* 104, no. 2 (February 2003): 98.

Sherk, Warren M., ed. *Film and Television Music: A Guide to Books, Articles, and Composer Interviews*. Lanham, MD: Scarecrow Press, 2011.

Shivers, Will Davis. "James Newton Howard (interview)." *Film Score Monthly*, no. 41-43 (January-March 1994): 18-19.

Shyamalan, M. Night. *Signs* (screenplay). 2002.

Signs. Dir. M. Night Shyamalan. Touchstone Pictures. 2002 [DVD 2003].

Snow Falling on Cedars. Dir. Scott Hicks. Universal Studios. 2000 [DVD].

Sobchack, Vivian. *Screening Space: The American Science Fiction Film*. Revised 2nd edition. New Brunswick, NJ: Rutgers University Press, 2004.

Sofair, Michael. "Signs (review)." *Film Quarterly* 57, no. 3 (Spring 2004): 56-63.

Steblin, Rita. *A History of Key Characteristics in the Eighteenth and Ninteenth Centuries*. Revised 2nd edition. Rochester, NY: University of Rochester Press, 2002.

Warren, Bill. *Keep Watching the Skies! American Science Fiction Movies of the Fifties*. The 21st Century Edition. Jefferson, NC: McFarland & Company, 2010.

Weinstock, Jeffrey Andrew, ed. *Critical Approaches to the Films of M. Night Shyamalan*. New York: Palgrave Macmillan, 2010.

Wierzbicki, James. *Louis and Bebe Barron's* Forbidden Planet: *A Film Score Guide*. Lanham, MD: Scarecrow Press, 2005.

Winters, Ben. *Erich Wolfgang Korngold's* The Adventures of Robin Hood: *A Film Score Guide*. Lanham, MD: Scarecrow Press, 2007.

Index

About the Author

Erik Heine is Professor of Music at the Wanda L. Bass School of Music at Oklahoma City University. His research interests include film music, Classical form and analysis, and music theory pedagogy. He is the author of multiple articles and book chapters on film music. When not teaching or researching, he is likely running.